Cognitive Automation and Organizational Psychology

Jobs that were once well-defined are now multifaceted. New business realities place a premium on employee attentional processing to fulfill increasingly complex occupational roles. But, human conscious capacity is limited, making it nearly impossible for employees to keep up with unprecedented changes in modern organizations without being susceptible to cognitive overload and its harmful psychological consequences. Stajković and Sergent refute the growing view that brain enhancement by technological automation will take care of employee suffering from alarmingly increasing stress, anxiety, and depression at work. Instead, the authors tackle the issue of skyrocketing employee cognitive overload more directly, by proposing cognitive automation via subconscious processing as an alternative. In particular, focusing this book on goals, the authors present a sampling of cutting-edge research showing that conscious guidance is not required for all goal pursuits; some goal-directed behavior in the contemporary workplace can be automated via priming of subconscious goals, saving on employees' attentional resources.

Building on research in social psychology and organizational behavior, Stajković and Sergent discuss four models of goal priming. These models conceptually explain how subconscious goals can be primed in organizations to automatically guide work behavior and to attain similar, if not the same, outcomes as would setting conscious goals:

- Auto-motive model: Practice with a goal makes cognitive automation possible.
- Goal contagion: Observing and inferring goals of others creates cognitive automation.
- Means-goal priming: Confidence in your goal pursuit enhances cognitive automation.
- A history of reinforcement: Money, feedback, and social recognition used to reinforce goal achievement become associated with the goal, resulting in cognitive automation.

The authors canvas a broad range of knowledge concerning the problem of employee cognitive overload in contemporary organizations and rely on multidisciplinary research to propose cognitive automation as a solution that could address it directly. This book is a deep well of valuable information for those interested in solving real work problems with application of science of organizational behavior (SOB).

Alexander D. Stajković is the M. Keith Weikel Distinguished Chair in Leadership and Professor of Organizational Behavior at the University of Wisconsin-Madison. Alexander earned both his Masters and Ph.D. in Organizational Behavior from the University of Nebraska-Lincoln.

Kayla Sergent is Assistant Professor of Management at Edgewood College. Kayla earned her Ph.D. in Organizational Behavior from the University of Wisconsin-Madison.

Routledge Studies in Leadership Research

For a full list of titles in this series, please visit www.routledge.com

Cognitive Automation and Organizational Psychology

Priming Goals as a New Source
of Competitive Advantage

Alexander D. Stajković
and Kayla Sergent

NEW YORK AND LONDON

First published 2019
by Routledge
605 Third Avenue, New York, NY 10017

and by Routledge
2 Park Square, Milton Park, Abingdon, Oxon, OX14 4RN

First issued in paperback 2021

Routledge is an imprint of the Taylor & Francis Group, an informa business

© 2019 Taylor & Francis

The right of Alexander D. Stajković and Kayla Sergent to be
identified as authors of this work has been asserted by them in
accordance with sections 77 and 78 of the Copyright, Designs
and Patents Act 1988.

Library of Congress Cataloging-in-Publication Data
Names: Stajkovic, Alexander. D., author. | Sergent, Kayla, author.
Title: Cognitive automation and organizational psychology :
    priming goals as a new source of competitive advantage /
    Alexander. D. Stajkovic and Kayla Sergent.
Description: New York, NY : Routledge, 2019. | Series: Routledge
    studies in leadership research | Includes index.
Identifiers: LCCN 2019010399 | ISBN 9780367272692 (hardback) |
    ISBN 9780429295881 (ebook)
Subjects: LCSH: Psychology, Industrial. | Organizational
    behavior. | Goal (Psychology)
Classification: LCC HF5548.8 .S7155 2019 | DDC 158.7—dc23
LC record available at https://lccn.loc.gov/2019010399

ISBN 13: 978-0-367-78599-4 (pbk)
ISBN 13: 978-0-367-27269-2 (hbk)

Typeset in Sabon
by Apex CoVantage, LLC

To our student J. D., RIP

Contents

Introduction

Our purpose in writing this book is to propose cognitive automation of some conscious processing as a new source of competitive advantage in organizations. We define cognitive automation as subconscious processing of information that replaces conscious, or attentional, processing of the same information and results in the same outcomes. Cognitive automation can have considerable functional value in organizations because it can free-up scarce attentional resources that can then be redirected to where they are irreplaceable. Thus, our main proposition is that more cognitive automation, not less, is the future of organizations. In essence, we contend that organizations will advance by extending the number of functions employees can perform well with less, not more, conscious deliberations. William James (1890, p. 122), widely considered the founding father of scientific psychology, has long called for this consideration: "We must make automatic and habitual, as early as possible, as many useful actions as we can."

Automation of some of the employee's conscious processing is akin, to an extent, to technological automation such as cruise control in automobiles and auto-pilot in planes. The purpose of these devices is to reduce human cognitive load by automating part of the attentional processing and behaviors. Attentional processing gauges, allocates, and reallocates sensory input for adaptive functioning at any moment (Wickens, 1980). Whereas long-term memory stores retrievable information for recurring needs (e.g., walking, driving, eating), attentional processing handles responses in the present when no heuristics exist. Examples include reacting to unexpected news, retorting a sarcastic remark, or responding to sudden changes in the traffic. The colloquial moniker *thinking on your feet* illustrates attentional processing in daily life.

Deliberately filtering out what is needed to adaptively function is hardly replaceable in the hustle-and-bustle of the modern world. However, this type of processing capacity, i.e., how much information one can consciously process in the now, is limited. This is because attentional processing developed during a time when acting adaptively in the moment meant nothing like it does today, not to mention that its capacity expands at an evolutionary snail's pace (Postle, 2015). Kierkegaard (1847) instructed us that "purity of heart is to will one thing." Those days are gone, for better or worse. Today's employees cannot afford to romanticize the sentiments of the past. Instead, they are facing pressing challenges caused by skyrocketing cognitive load.

In addition to traditional economic work dilemmas—e.g., to be a specialist or generalist, compete or cooperate, be efficient or creative—employees in contemporary organizations face a multitude of emerging psychological and social dualities. For example, new psychological perturbations of the modern-day workplace include choosing mindfulness (as if we preferred mindlessness before), pursuing self-interest while being emotionally intelligent about the needs of others, fostering a learning mindset while shunning a fixed learning style (even if it worked for us before), and being appraised of the latest research, such as knowing that telling others to "find their passion" is now "awful advice" (see O'Keefe, Dweck, & Walton, 2018). Socially, we should treat everyone equal while allowing for unequal distribution of rewards based on merit, simultaneously maintain work-life balance and be a top performer, and find the fine-line between being affable for mentoring but not socially imposing. Let us not forget the antediluvian favorites, i.e., do more with less, when in Rome do as Romans do, and get great results for the price of good.

These modern work dialectics fuel cognitive tension of employees. This reminds us of Voltaire, a French philosopher of the Enlightenment era, who had a premonition in *Candide*: Human life does not necessarily improve just because we move forward in time. Apropos, we question if organizational members can adapt to all the new contradictions in a timely manner and make optimal choices for any shifting priority to reduce cognitive tension. Simply put, how much can we take in at work these days before we blow a fuse? Inasmuch as the mounting gap between what organizational members face and what they can attentionally process creates an open-loop, self-regulation is no longer adaptive, and impairments to psychological functioning and mental health can unfold.

As evidence from clinical psychiatry points out, at a certain point, people get "maxed out, overloaded, and finally burned out" (Gustafson, 2005, p. 64). Failure to reconcile the "keep up and go into overload" challenge has costly psychological consequences such as anxiety, depression, and exhaustion (Gustafson, 2005; Swenson, 2003). For example, consider these titles in the recent business press: "The secret suffering of the middle manager" (Lam, 2015); "Maxed out doctors: The high cost of burnout" (Davis-Laack, 2014); "The psychological price of entrepreneurship" (Bruder, 2013); "Why are lawyers killing themselves?" (Flores & Arce, 2014); and "Why being a CEO should come with a health warning" (Tutton, 2010).

The open-loop created by dissonance between increasing cognitive load and limited attentional capacity will not be closed by reducing job demands; expecting such alteration in light of merciless business competition is probably unrealistic at this time (Cappelli, 2012). Nor are sustainable remedies found in simplifications of attentional processing, such as self-help seminars and techniques, or downloading software planners and calendar aids. Just as people buy a new computer with more random-access memory (RAM) instead of keeping a maxed-out old computer and using it less, new solutions are needed. In light of today's hypercompetitive business conditions, we posit that employee cognitive automation is more pertinent now than ever before. The question is how to meaningfully and affordably operationalize it in the workplace.

To foretell our conclusion, we first make a conceptual case that some of the deliberate guidance provided by conscious goals can be replaced by subconscious cognitive processing and automated behaviors triggered by primed subconscious goals. Then, we present a sampling of cutting-edge research that shows conscious guidance is not required for all goals. Instead, goal-directed behavior can be automated via priming of subconscious goals (Bargh, 1990; Bargh et al., 2001; Latham, Stajković, & Locke, 2010). Priming occurs when an environmental cue activates a mental representation of a goal. The primed goal then automatically triggers related behaviors without conscious control and awareness.

For some perspective, much of human behavior is organized and executed in service of a goal, where a goal is defined as a desired end state. Goal-directed tendencies depend on cognitive capacity to first create a mental representation of what one wants, i.e., have a goal, and then enact behaviors in that direction. The general notion of a goal as a predictor of human behavior has, arguably, survived the test of time. For example, St. Paul writes in his letter to the Philippians (12–13):

[B]ut one thing I do, I press on toward the goal for the prize of the upward call of God in Christ Jesus.

In the context of organizations, research has documented that goals positively affect a host of work-related outcomes (Locke & Latham, 2013). Conscious goals are top-ranked out of all organizational variables for their performance effectiveness (Miner, 2003). We argue that if organizations could garner similar effects caused by conscious goals by priming subconscious goals at little to no cost to attentional resources, then the competitive landscape would never be the same. We base this assertion on the following premise of goal priming research:

[N]ot only should conscious and nonconscious goals produce the same effects, but they should also produce the same effects in the same way.

(Chartrand & Bargh, 2002, p. 21)

How does priming subconscious goals work? Briefly, if a goal directs a behavior chronically in a given environment, then the goal and the behavior become associated in memory over time. This association becomes gradually automatic from repeated practice and then gets stored in the subconscious. When someone enters a social context in which a stored cue from the environment is present, the cue primes the goal. Once primed, the goal triggers its associated behaviors, which unfold automatically without conscious guidance. Priming subconscious goals creates considerable functional value because it saves attentional processing while positively affecting outcomes similar to conscious goals. Approximately two hundred studies support the effectiveness of primed goals (Bargh, 2017; Dijksterhuis, Chartrand, & Aarts, 2007; Weingarten et al., 2016).

On one hand, organizations are on the lookout perpetually for new sources of competitive advantage. On the other hand, findings on priming goals are burgeoning, and many of them potentially relate to organizations. So, what does it buy us to not consider the benefits of primed goals? One recurring reason where hear from our executive MBA students and leaders we consult with is that the subconscious is a chamber of unknown in the business world. But, by reversing the correlates, the subconscious becomes a gateway of possibilities that science can help open to the business world. We frame this book within this conceptual sandbox.

In particular, this work is intended to contribute primarily to the organizational quest for competitive advantage. The contribution boils down to three main points: (1) power of subconscious processing is inordinate and can be used by all employees, (2) priming subconscious goals produces similar effects to those of conscious goals, and the former occurs at little to no cost to employee attentional processing, and (3) the idea of facilitating cognitive automation at work by priming some goals can bring not only competitive advantage of vast potential to organizations but it can also bring one that is hard to imitate.

We proceed as follows. In Chapter 1, we examine the competitive landscape of today's organizations. We emphasize that extant approaches to competitive advantage are unequipped to tackle employee cognitive overload. To address it directly, new approaches are needed. In Chapter 2, we present goals, the main variable in this book. We review goal literature and stipulate how conscious goals guide self-regulation adaptively, both in life and at work. Because primed goals operate on the subconscious platform, which predicates automaticity, we discuss the workings of the subconscious and automaticity in Chapter 3.

From there, we move the theoretical narrative forward by connecting conscious and primed subconscious goals. In Chapter 4, we describe four conceptual models of goal priming. These models explain how goal-behavior associations are formed in the subconscious and how such associations are primed into automatic behaviors that can accomplish outcomes similar to those accomplished by conscious goals. The first four chapters complete the theory foundations of the cognitive automation framework.

In Chapters 5 to 8, we present the latest empirical research that was conducted on the basis of the four conceptual models of goal priming. In Chapter 9, we discuss the limitations of the conceptual cognitive automation framework and of extant research on goal priming, followed by suggestions for future research to address the constraints and push theory development forward. In Chapter 10, we zero in on the application of goal priming in the workplace. We conclude with seven rules for adaptive self-regulation that are better automated than free-willed, accompanied by some mild humor.

References

Bargh, J. A. (1990). Auto-motives: Preconscious determinants of social interaction. In E. T. Higgins & R. M. Sorrentino (Eds.), *Handbook of motivation and cognition: Foundations of social behavior* (Vol. 2, pp. 93–130). New York, NY: Guilford Press.

Bargh, J. A. (1990). Auto-motives: Preconscious determinants of social interaction. In E. T. Higgins & R. M. Sorrentino (Eds.), *Handbook of motivation and cognition: Foundations of social behavior* (Vol. 2, pp. 93–130). New York, NY: Guilford Press, Touchstone.

Bargh, J. A. (2017). *Before you know it: The unconscious reasons we do what we do*. New York, NY: Touchstone.

Bargh, J. A., Gollwitzer, P. M., Lee-Chai, A., Barndollar, K., & Trotschel, R. (2001). The automated will: Nonconscious activation and pursuit of behavioral goals. *Journal of Personality and Social Psychology, 81*, 1014–1027.

Bruder, J. (2013). The psychological price of entrepreneurship. *Inc. 5000.*

Cappelli, P. (2012). *Why good people can't get jobs: The skills gap and what companies can do about it*. Philadelphia, PA: Wharton Digital Press.

Chartrand, T. L., & Bargh, J. A. (2002). Nonconscious motivations: Their activation, operation and consequences. In A. Tesser, D. A. Stapel, & J. V. Wood (Eds.), *Self and motivation: Emerging psychological perspectives* (pp. 13–41). Washington, DC: American Psychological Association.

Davis-Laack, P. (2014, March 17). Maxed out doctors: The high cost of burnout in medicine. *Psychology Today*. Retrieved from www.psychologytoday.com/blog/pressure-proof/201403/maxed-out-doctors-the-high-cost-burnout-in-medicine

Dijksterhuis, A., Chartrand, T. L., & Aarts, H. (2007). Effects of priming and perception on social behavior and goal pursuit. In Bargh, J. A. (Ed.), *Social psychology and the unconscious* (pp. 51–131). New York, NY: Psychology Press.

Flores, R., & Arce, M. (2014, January 20). Why are lawyers killing themselves? *CNN*. Retrieved from www.cnn.com/2014/01/19/us/lawyer-suicides/index.html

Gustafson, J. P. (2005). *Very brief psychotherapy*. New York, NY: Routledge.

James, W. (1890). *The principles of psychology*. New York, NY: H. Holt & Company.

Kierkegaard, S. A. (1956). Purity of heart is to will one thing (D. Steere, Trans.). New York: Harper. (Original work published 1847).

Lam, B. (2015, August 27). The secret suffering of the middle manager. *The Atlantic*. Retrieved from www.theatlantic.com/business/archive/2015/08/middle-managers-stress-depression/402193/

Latham, G. P., Stajković, A. D., & Locke, E. A. (2010). The relevance and viability of subconscious goals in the workplace. *Journal of Management, 36,* 234–255.

Locke, E. A., & Latham, G. P. (2013). Goal setting theory: The current state. In E. A. Locke & G. P. Latham (Eds.), *New development in goal setting and task performance* (pp. 623–630). New York, NY: Taylor & Francis.

Miner, J. B. (2003). The rated importance, scientific validity, and practical usefulness of organizational behavior theories: A quantitative review. *Academy of Management Learning & Education, 2,* 250–268.

O'Keefe, P. A., Dweck, C. S., & Walton, G. M. (2018). Implicit theories of interest: Finding your passion or developing it? *Psychological Science, 29*(10), 1653–1664.

Postle, B. R. (2015). *Essentials of cognitive neuroscience*. New York, NY: Wiley-Blackwell.

Swenson, R. A. (2003). *A minute of margin: Restoring balance to overloaded lives*. Colorado Springs, CO: NavPress.

Tutton, M. (2010, March 12). Why being a CEO should come with a health warning. *CNN*. Retrieved from www.cnn.com/2010/BUSINESS/03/12/ceo.health.warning/index.html

Weingarten, E., Chen, Q., McAdams, M., Yi, J., Hepler, J., & Albarracín, D. (2016). From primed concepts to action: A meta-analysis of the behavioral effects of incidentally presented words. *Psychological Bulletin, 142,* 472–497.

Wickens, C. D. (1980). The structure of attentional resources. In Nickerson, R. (Ed.), *Attention and performance VIII* (Vol. 8, pp. 239–257). Cambridge, MA: Bolt Beranek and Newman Inc.

Part I

The Problem and Proposed Solution

1 Skyrocketing Cognitive Load Versus the Snail's Pace of Attentional Adaptation

We open this chapter by illustrating the contrast in job demands in the last five decades. Consider the clarity of description in this job advertisement, posted 50 years ago. In 1968, Radio Manufacturing Company placed a job ad in the London press stating the following:

> South city requires intelligent young man, 21–25, as Trainee Supervisor. Applicant should have Leaving Certificate standard of education and some mechanical experience.

Compare the above simplicity to a posting for a similar position at Rite Aid in 2019:

> Learn to lead store associates though the execution of company business plans and objectives to drive sales, be profitable, and provide a superior customer and associate experience . . . Learn to manage an individual store while meeting store retail budgeted sales, margin, labor, expenses, and overall P&L monthly results to ensure operating EBITDA and income are achieved.

The characteristics of yesterday's jobs are quite different from the job demands of today. In this chapter, we examine how the multifaceted and amorphous nature of modern-day jobs contributes to employee cognitive overload.

Why should you care about cognitive overload? We will provide empirical evidence from multiple sources indicating that employee cognitive overload is causing alarming levels of psychological distress and related health problems.

Could leaders tackle this issue with the existing tools in their wheelhouse? We will describe the competitive landscape of organizations and contend that traditional ways in which companies compete are inadequately equipped to tackle employee cognitive overload. Though these traditional practices have economic benefits, they are too remote to be convincing when it comes to remedying psychological problems.

Overall, data suggest we need new approaches to mitigate employee cognitive overload directly. One approach, as-of-yet unexplored in organizations, is cognitive automation.

The Old-New Jobs Gap

Work of the Past Was Clear and Predictable

By and large, jobs in the first part of the 20th century were clear; people knew what had to be done. Products were manufactured, packed, sold, and shipped. Fields were plowed, and crops were planted and harvested. Those with little formal education had a recourse in industrial jobs that were mostly unvarying and required little in the way of elevated cognitive processing. Once requisite job skills were acquired, performance was largely a matter of execution. Because work behaviors were pre-identified, more often than not, effort led to success; hence, "work hard and play by the rules" was the foundation of the American dream.

Work of Today Is Multifaceted and Amorphous

Those types of employment options are rapidly shrinking. Jobs that were once well-defined are now multifaceted. In terms of macro-economic forces, businesses are progressively shaped by transnational interdependencies. New realities are placing a premium on cognitive processing to fulfill increasingly complex occupational roles. Indeed, because of virtually all-embracing global interconnectedness, what happens in one part of the globe affects the welfare of organizations on the other side of the world. These global economic and cultural forces pressure organizations to adopt shifting missions and customized responses that can be hard for employees to fully understand, let alone to functionally control.

In terms of micro-foundations of daily work, a premium is placed on rapid acquisition of technology. The gap between technological innovation and work adaptation is shrinking. For example, elevator mechanics at Otis are now required to use iPhones to document malfunctions and order spare parts online in real time, even though smart phones may not be their forte. Likewise, employees are faced with expanding communication and cooperation across units. Let us not forget about emails, as there is a general expectation to answer them. Figuring out how the goals of yesterday morphed into new targets today because of new market entries and customer acquisitions, and how this shakes up a unit or an organization, takes another intellectual toll. Shifting work priorities call for added deliberations about new choices and data needed to support completion of a project; this is all wrapped into shrinking margins of error. Moreover, the best laid plans can be undone with one unexpected email from the boss which is why many employees feel that success today requires sleeping with an iPhone. Taken together, the cognitive processing burden placed on today's employees is accelerating.

To claim that society has not made strides to automate various job demands would be uninformed. By the same token, to ignore the psychological cost of cognitive overload in the modern workplace would be equally foolish. Apropos, we next review evidence from multiple sources, indicating that employee cognitive overload across professions appears to be causing alarming levels of psychological distress and related health problems.

Cognitive Dissonance and Psychological Distress

Compared with tasks employees used to perform, characteristics of the modern-day workplace demand higher levels of information processing. Because adaptation to, and management of, mounting cognitive load requires a corresponding psychological makeover, many employees fear whether they can handle it all (Stajković, Lee, Greenwald, & Raffiee, 2015). A survey conducted by the Institute of Leadership and Management in the United Kingdom found that about 40% of employees reported self-doubt about their performance and career (Flynn, Heath, & Holt, 2011). This discrepancy between job demands and employees' perceived inability to handle them results in a psychological phenomenon known as cognitive dissonance (Festinger, 1957), in which reality does not match one's perception of it. When dissonance is reduced, predictability fosters adaptive preparedness, making it more likely a person will surmount predicaments. However, "inability to exert influence that adversely affect one's life breeds apprehension, apathy, or despair" (Bandura, 1995, p. 1).

The U.S. Department of Health and Human Services (DHHS) uses the term *psychological distress* to refer to a range of psycho-somatic symptoms, where "psychological distress includes mental health problems severe enough to cause moderate-to-serious impairment in occupational functioning, and they may require treatment" (Weissman, Pratt, Miller, & Parker, 2015, p. 1). Based on the wide-ranging data DHHS collects (Weissman et al., 2015; Pratt, Dey, & Cohen, 2007), this agency concluded that psychological distress in the U.S. is not only rising, but it is at an all-time high. Yet, the education level of the U.S. workforce and living conditions today are far better than ever before (Pinker, 2018).

Employee cognitive overload is not limited to a few high-stress industries. Moderate-to-serious impairments in work functioning caused by psychological distress have been reported across occupations including arts, construction, entertainment, entrepreneurship, management, military, maintenance services, sports, and trucking (Allen et al., 2012; Bruder, 2013; Fan et al., 2012; Gu et al., 2013; Jacobsen et al., 2013; Ng, Eby, Sorensen, & Feldman, 2005; Shockey, Zack, & Sussell, 2017).

Neither is cognitive overload limited to just the U.S.; work-related psychological distress affects employees around the globe (Hassard et al., 2014), imposing an economic cost of $200 billion in the U.S. (SAMHSA, 2016), €617 billion in Europe (Hassard et al., 2014), and CA$11 billion in Canada (Chiu, Lebenbaum, Cheng, de Oliveira, & Kurdyak, 2017). Markedly, despite a 65% increase in antidepressant prescriptions for psychological distress in the last 15 years (Pratt, Brody, & Gu, 2017), suicide rates have risen by 25% (Curtin, Warner, & Hedegaard, 2016).

Traditional Ways in Which Companies Compete Are Inadequate to Address the Problem

Although the practices we review next unquestionably reap economic benefits, they do little to nothing to recognize and mitigate employee cognitive overload. We neither venerate nor dismiss these traditional approaches to gaining a sustainable competitive advantage. We simply underscore that these strategies have been leapfrogged by time when it comes to cognitive overload and consequences for employees' mental health.

Historically, because one purpose of forming an *organiz*ation was to *organize*, efficiency was paramount. Efficiency involves making a product or offering a service with the least amount of time, material, and labor. Frederick Taylor's *Scientific Management* was the high point of the efficiency focus at the turn of the 20th century. The first cousin of efficiency is scale. Economies of scale have consolidated many industries through mergers and acquisitions since the mid-20th century. As sources of a competitive advantage, efficiency and scale are about competing on lower unit cost. In the 1980s, Edward Deming pushed quality as a new focus in competitive business battles, which manifested itself in two ways. One is that products and services of high quality, e.g., certified by six sigma quality control processes, are more likely to be sold, *ceteris paribus*. The other is that higher quality products allow for a pricing premium. For every Southwest Airlines that earns margins via cost austerity, there is an Emirates Air that competes on luxury.

Many organizations still concentrate on these traditional sources of competitive advantage. The economic benefits of these strategies are undeniable. At the same time, they are tangential to substantively addressing mounting employee cognitive overload.

At a more micro level of analysis, organizations offer, almost in unison, more education as an answer to calls for *continual growth*, *doing more with less*, and *above and beyond performance*. Upgrading existing skills, mastering more academic subjects, and regulating learning by finding new ways of thinking are sensible alternatives; except, each one elevates the demand on attentional processing. Minimizing the frequencies of task switching, providing clearer and more instrumental feedback, being more careful in delivering negative evaluations, and reducing work interruptions can help reduce cognitive load (Demerouti, Bakker, Nachreiner, & Schaufeli, 2001), when feasible. The extent to which these procedures are enacted regularly is uncertain in light of escalating competitiveness and decreased time spent by companies on employee development (Cappelli, 2012). That is, research continues to show that employee cognitive load still impacts risk aversion (Benjamin, Brown, & Shapiro, 2013), impulsive behavior (Getz, 2013), unethical choices (Gino, Schweitzer, Mead, & Ariely, 2011), and stereotyping (van Boven & Robinson, 2012), and it also impairs judgement (Duffy & Smith, 2014).

New Approaches Are Needed

Given the pervasive negative effects of cognitive overload on a host of outcomes, a skeptic might conclude the extant approaches to mitigate load are not being used, not being used properly, or are not working. Because employee attentional processing capacity appears to be maxed out and because human "broadband" capacity is neither easily nor rapidly upgradable, conscious remedies can exasperate the already undulating employee cognitive load. It may be a bitter pill to swallow, but business professionals must recognize the biological fact that the attentional processing band employees have today is not all that broad, and it will not change during our lifetime. Instead, we call for consideration of a new employee "broad" band—subconscious processing via cognitive automation.

This proposal sets up the spontaneous question, "Why not use artificial intelligence instead of exploring the workings of the subconscious mind?" The future may bring brain-boosting power, for example, via CRISPR designer-minds. Someday, brains might be upgraded with new genes or with 3-D printed younger brain components. So, why go into the "unknown" depths of the subconscious when technical solutions appear auspicious?

First, we retort by asking, "Why is "artificial" intelligence better than real human intelligence?" Was it the oversight of God or evolution that human processing be inferior to an artificial commingle? If so, is it the responsibility of businesses to fix human cognitive shortcomings with mechanical solutions, for profit, of course? As it stands, the effectiveness of blending the mind with artificial "intelligence" (AI) in organizations is untested, to say nothing of it being legally unregulated and morally unclear. These concerns do not nurture implementation anytime soon.

Second, development of AI requires investment, is expensive to purchase and use, and requires electricity or batteries at all times. Using AI instead of human constituents could even be awkward. For example, a person can carry an iPhone on a date, but imagine if he asked Siri for advice midstream because the situation changed. Even if our parody of today becomes the reality of tomorrow, what if the gadget runs out of juice?

Third, the perpetual need to sell something coupled with the need to recuperate the sunk cost of investments has made businesses occasionally impervious to social considerations. Although many professionals are mesmerized by AI, few discuss if the fusion of human brains and AI would deepen social divisions. Given the rapid pace of AI advancement, it is not far-fetched to foresee a moral quandary where natural giftedness of a poor child is relegated by an artificially enhanced mind of a wealthier child. How would this scenario play out in standardized testing? If the scores should be adjusted, then what is the point of using AI in the first place? Many forget that when IQ testing was first used in Great Britain, it was meant to identify kids with high IQ who were from the lower social strata to afford them greater opportunities in society than what their social status would otherwise predict.

Fourth, maybe insistence on AI is drawn from a perception that artificial processing that costs millions is decidedly more powerful than the natural, God- or evolution-given human brain. The reasonableness of this assertion depends on what is compared. If AI is equated to conscious processing, AI wins. But, we have long known that consciousness is limited. Subconscious processing, though, outperforms AI. For instance, in 2013, the technology company Fujitsu used one of the most powerful super-computers at the time to simulate human brain processing. Even though this "super" computer connected 83,000 of the fastest processors, it took it 40 minutes to simulate 1 second of 1% of human brain activity.

Until a society agrees on how to handle the possibility of purchasing genetic upgrades, perhaps *real* human processing ought to be considered before going "all in" on *artificial*. To be sure, we are not dismissing the benefits of technology. Instead, we are asserting that a premature emphasis on AI-brain blend warrants scrutiny. If AI-brain enhancements become a market reality, it will check-mate human existence as we know it. The wealthy will buy artificial upgrades and outperform the rest. A multitude of quandaries will follow.

AI-brain fusion becomes even more dicey in light of the biological reality that humans have a mechanism within their existing arsenal of processing that can be employed instead. Subconscious processing is a source of remarkable cognitive capacity all humans possess. Though understudied, this alternative processing is available for exploration, not to mention that the subconscious offers the greatest human processing capacity on this planet.

Consider these neuroscience facts. About one million fibers leave the human eye at any given moment to scan the environment; this sensory information input approximates 1 megabyte (Koch & Tsuchiya, 2006). Conscious processing can handle only about seven chunks of information in any input stream from all senses (Miller, 1956). To enumerate these differences, the subconscious processes about 200,000 times more information than the conscious (Dijksterhuis, Aarts, & Smith, 2005), and it does not stop processing when the conscious is preoccupied; it operates non-stop even during sleep (Dijksterhuis, 2009).

In light of this biological evidence that subconscious processing is available to all people at all times, does not require electricity, and comes at little to no cost, it is unclear why organizations spend so much attention and dollars on the seeming apotheosis of artificial processing when real human processing of copious capacity is staring them in the face.

Summary

Employee cognitive overload causes psychological distress, which leads to health issues and performance impairments. This chain of events is a problem in today's organizations. Traditional approaches to competitive advantage are economically sound but unequipped to directly confront this psychological problem. AI-brain fusion is promising but frothed with unresolved regulatory and moral issues. For now, we have insufficient information to predict where this merge will go, let alone how the application will look in organizations. We are not against upgrading human species, but we are apprehensive about the nightmare scenarios that will accompany it. To mitigate employee cognitive overload directly, we propose a solution not yet explored in organizations: cognitive automation of some, not all, employee conscious goal processing by priming goals that operate on the subconscious platform. The latter cognitive system exists within all humans and has vast information processing capacity. The latest research demonstrates that primed subconscious goals can produce similar performance effects as assigned conscious goals.

In the next chapter, we introduce our main variable, goals. We describe how conscious goals guide self-regulation, and then draw parallels between conscious and primed goals.

References

Allen, T. D., Johnson, R. C., Saboe, K., Cho, E., Dumani, S., & Evans, S. (2012). Dispositional variables and work-family conflict: A meta-analysis. *Journal of Vocational Behavior, 80,* 17–26.

Bandura, A. (Ed.). (1995). *Self-efficacy in changing societies.* New York, NY: Cambridge University Press.

Benjamin, D. J., Brown, S. A., & Shapiro, J. M. (2013). Who is 'behavioral'? Cognitive ability and anomalous preferences. *Journal of the European Economic Association, 11,* 1231–1255.

Bruder, J. (2013). The psychological price of entrepreneurship. *Inc. 5000.*

Cappelli, P. (2012). *Why good people can't get jobs: The skills gap and what companies can do about it.* Philadelphia, PA: Wharton Digital Press.

Chiu, M., Lebenbaum, M., Cheng, J., de Oliveira, C., & Kurdyak, P. (2017). The direct healthcare costs associated with psychological distress and major depression: A population-based cohort study in Ontario, Canada. *PloS One*, *12*, e0184268.

Curtin, S. C., Warner, M., & Hedegaard, H. (2016). Suicide rates for females and males by race and ethnicity: United States, 1999 and 2014. *National Centre for Health Statistics*, 5.

Demerouti, E., Bakker, A. B., Nachreiner, F., & Schaufeli, W. B. (2001). The job demands-resources model of burnout. *Journal of Applied Psychology*, *86*, 499–512.

Dijksterhuis, A. (2009). The beautiful powers of the unconscious thought. *Psychological Science Agenda*, *23*, 1–4. Washington, DC: American Psychological Association.

Dijksterhuis, A., Aarts, H., & Smith, P. K. (2005). The power of the subliminal: On subliminal persuasion and other potential applications. In R. Hassin, J. Uleman, & J. Bargh (Eds.), *The new unconscious* (pp. 77–106). New York, NY: Oxford University Press.

Duffy, S., & Smith, J. (2014). Cognitive load in the multi-player prisoner's dilemma game: Are there brains in games? *Journal of Behavioral and Experimental Economics*, *51*, 47–56.

Fan, Z. J., Bonauto, D. K., Foley, M. P., Anderson, N. J., Yragui, N. L., Silverstein, B. A. (2012). Occupation and the prevalence of current depression and frequent mental distress. *American Journal of Industrial Medicine*, *55*, 893–903.

Festinger, L. (1957). *A theory of cognitive dissonance*. Stanford, CA: Stanford University Press.

Flynn, J., Heath, K., & Holt, M. D. (2011). Four ways women stunt their careers unintentionally. *Harvard Business Review*, *20*.

Getz, S. J. (2013). *Cognitive control and intertemporal choice: The role of cognitive control in impulsive decision making* (Ph.D. Dissertation), Princeton University.

Gino, F., Schweitzer, M. E., Mead, N. L., & Ariely, D. (2011). Unable to resist temptation: How self-control depletion promotes unethical behavior. *Organizational Behavior and Human Decision Processes*, *115*, 191–203.

Gu, J. K., Charles, L. E., Burchfiel, C. M., Andrew, M. E., Ma, C., Bang, K. M., & Violanti, J. M. (2013). Associations between psychological distress and body mass index among law enforcement officers: The national health interview survey 2004–2010. *Safety and Health at Work*, *4*, 52–62.

Hassard, J., Teoh, K., Cox, T., Dewe, P., Cosmar, M., Grundler, R., . . ., Van den Broek, K. (2014). *Calculating the cost of work-related stress and psychosocial risks*. Luxembourg: Publications Office of the European Union.

Jacobsen, H. B., Caban-Martinez, A., Onyebeke, L. C., Sorensen, G., Dennerlein, J. T., & Reme, S. E. (2013). Construction workers struggle with a high prevalence of mental distress, and this is associated with their pain and injuries. *Journal of Occupational Environmental Medicine*, *55*, 1197–1204.

Koch, C., & Tsuchiya, N. (2006). Attention and consciousness: Two distinct brain processes. *Trends in Cognitive Sciences*, *11*, 16–22.

Miller, G. A. (1956). The magical number seven, plus or minus two: Some limits on our capacity for processing information. *Psychological Review*, *63*, 81–97.

Ng, T. W., Eby, L. T., Sorensen, K. L., & Feldman, D. C. (2005). Predictors of objective and subjective career success: A meta-analysis. *Personnel Psychology*, *58*, 367–408.

Pinker, S. (2018). *Enlightenment now: The case for reason, science, humanism, and progress*. New York, NY: Viking.

Pratt, L. A., Brody, D. J., & Gu, Q. (2017). *Antidepressant use among persons aged 12 and over: United States, 2011–2014*. US Department of Health and Human Services, Centers for Disease Control and Prevention, National Center for Health Statistics.

Pratt, L. A., Dey, A. N., & Cohen, A. J. (2007). *Characteristics of adults with serious psychological distress as measured by the K6 scale, United States, 2001–04*. US Department of Health and Human Services, Centers for Disease Control and Prevention, National Center for Health Statistics.

SAMHSA, Substance Abuse and Mental Health Services Administration. (2016). *Behavioral health and spending use accounts. Substance abuse and mental health services administration. Behavioral health spending and use accounts, 1986–2014*. HHS, SMA-16–4975, Rockville, MD.

Shockey, T. M., Zack, M., & Sussell, A. (2017). Health-related quality of life among US workers: Variability across occupation groups. *American Journal of Public Health*, *107*, 1316–1323.

Stajković, A. D., Lee, D., Greenwald, J. M., & Raffiee, J. (2015). The role of trait core confidence higher-order construct in self-regulation of performance and attitudes: Evidence from four studies. *Organizational Behavior and Human Decision Processes*, *128*, 29–48.

van Boven, L., & Robinson, M. D. (2012). Boys don't cry: Cognitive load and priming increase stereotypic sex differences in emotion memory. *Journal of Experimental Social Psychology*, *48*, 303–309.

Weissman, J. S., Pratt, L. A., Miller, E. A., & Parker, J. D. (2015). *Serious psychological distress among adults, United States, 2009–2013*. US Department of Health and Human Services, Centers for Disease Control and Prevention, National Center for Health Statistics.

Part II

Theory Foundations

In Part I, we provided evidence that employee cognitive overload is worsening. We argued that extant approaches to organizational competitive advantage are unequipped to resolve overload because these approaches have been outpaced by change in the modern workplace. We proposed cognitive automation of some conscious processing by priming subconscious goals as an alternative method of mitigating employee cognitive overload.

In Part II, we unpack this proposal theoretically. In Chapter 2, we elaborate on goals, the key variable in our theory. Goals come in two forms: conscious and subconscious. We first discuss conscious goals as a foundation to help understand subconscious goals. In Chapter 3, we explain what the subconscious is, how it interacts with the conscious, and how it produces automaticity. In Chapter 4, drawing from the goal priming literature, we introduce four conceptual models to explain how formation and priming of subconscious goals can unfold in organizations.

2 Self-Regulation Guided by Conscious Goals

The formulation and pursuit of goals is "so fundamental to the Western way of thinking, that the circumvention of the *set a goal and then take action* model is "considered a violation of the rational ideal" (Bourgeois, 1980, p. 228). Social psychology aims to understand, predict, and influence behavior in a social context. A way to do it is to observe people in their social milieu and infer the causes of their behavior. People make observations daily, and some conclude that humans behave randomly. Given the plethora of things people go for, and that some respond to life by trial and error, we can see how a skeptic could conclude that behavior of humans is not guided by any organizing principle.

If we increase the number of observations and make them systematic, then patterns of behavior will emerge. Some people are motivated by reinforcers. Others act primarily on the basis of their personality. Some prefer the guidance of moral principles. For example, financial reinforcers motivate action, trait conscientiousness keeps us organized, and the principle of treating others with *a priori* respect sets the general guardrails for the journey.

At a higher level of abstraction, though, many humans seem to act in service of a future aim. People first represent mentally what they want, then they direct behavior in line with the representation, and, finally, they ponder what else can help them succeed. For this reason, most researchers and casual observers of behavior agree, to a large extent, that human behavior in a dynamic world is often envisioned and directed by goals.

What is a goal? The answer appears self-evident. After all, goals are a protuberant causal current in human affairs, and people have a lifetime of experience with them. Thus, many are self-taught goal psychologists. Further probing, such as asking, "How does the mind represent goals?" "How do goals traverse cognitive space from mental abstractions to behavior?" "What are the underlying psychological mechanisms connecting the two book-ends?" and "Under what guiding self-regulatory principles do such progressions unfold?" typically is answered with silence. This chapter focuses on conscious goal pursuit in which goals are selected, set, and implemented as a result of deliberate mental contemplation.

The presumption that having a goal leads to pursuing a goal is obvious enough, but selecting and setting a goal guiding effective execution is deeper. The following dialogue, adapted from *Aristophanes* in *The Clouds* (419 B.C.), illustrates the pertinence of this point:

STREPSIADES: Have you seen a transparent stone with which you may kindle fire?
SOCRATES: You mean a crystal lens?
STREPSIADES: Yes. Do you know that if I placed this stone in the sun, I could make the wax, upon which the words were written, melt?
SOCRATES: If it were only that easy.

Even on a sunny day, if Strepsiades shifts the position of the crystal magnifying glass, the wax will not melt. Only when he holds the glass steady, aims it at the specific target, and persists in this undertaking will the writing be erased. This story from the Antiquity illuminates the difference between just having a goal and setting it in a way to be effective.

Since Tolman (1932) started the conversation on goals in scientific psychology, research has identified distinct mechanisms involved in goal operations. We review goal literatures in social psychology and organizational behavior to elucidate what goals are and how they adaptively guide self-regulation. "A goal is a self-regulatory mechanism for monitoring, evaluating, and adjusting behavior" (Locke & Latham, 2009, pp. 19–20). Self-regulation relates to psychological processes that underlie behavior (Carver & Scheier, 1998). Through these processes, cognitive resources are gauged, allocated, and recalibrated given activity demands (Powers, 2005). Adaptive self-regulation is a hallmark of successful functioning (Carver & Scheier, 1998) because it allocates resources for a calibrated activity level following the principle of least necessary effort (Kukla, 1972). It is not adaptive to allocate less cognitive resources than needed, nor is it adaptive to use more resources for a task that can be accomplished with less (Heatherton & Baumeister, 1996).

Social Psychology Underpinnings of Goal Pursuits

A delineation between social psychology and organizational behavior goal literatures is in their emphases—social versus organizational behavior. Social psychology is concerned primarily with how people select a goal, whereas organizational behavior focuses more on how employees implement a goal. We organize the ensuing narrative along these lines.

Sources of Goals

One source of goals is *needs*, defined as a physiological or a psychological deficiency. Many scholars view goal pursuit as a matter of need satisfaction (McClelland, Atkinson, Clark, & Lowell, 1953; Weiner, 1972). Goals aimed at satisfying an autonomy need (want goals) lead to greater intrinsic motivation and better coping with failure (Deci & Ryan, 1985) compared with goals that guide behavior toward satisfying a duty need (must goals).

Dweck and colleagues (Dweck, 2008; Elliott & Dweck, 1988; Grant & Dweck, 2003) introduced perception of ability as another category of goal sources. People who perceive ability to be fixed tend to set performance goals for familiar undertakings and rarely pursue risky goals. This is because to fixed-mindset individuals, failure signals inadequate ability—a scenario they avoid at all cost. Those who perceive ability as acquirable are more likely to set learning goals. These individuals welcome feedback about what went well, where they made mistakes, and how they can improve. People that perceive ability as acquirable are more likely to recover from failure by setting a new goal because they believe that ability is an acquirable skill that can be improved incrementally.

A third source of goals is feedback related to progress. Feedback helps us understand what goals to approach or avoid next time (Higgins, 1998). Approach (promotion) goals launch behavior toward a desirable outcome, whereas avoidance (prevention) goals steer behavior away from undesirable outcomes. The general conception of feedback regulating responses to a pre-established value/referent/goal has existed in physics, cybernetics, and psychology for decades (Miller, Galanter, & Pribram, 1960; Tolman, 1932; Wiener, 1948).

Powers (1973), a physicist turned psychologist, discussed the role of feedback in control of mechanical systems (e.g., thermostat) to explain human behavior. The model has multiple names (e.g., cybernetic model, control theory, principles of feedback control, negative feedback loop), but in all linguistic modes there are four fundamental and sequentially situated components: input function, a reference point, a comparator, and an output function. In psychology of human regulation, an input function constitutes incoming information. As people cognitively process input information, it intercepts with the reference value (e.g., a standard, personal value, goal, and attitude) to which it is then compared. The output function is manifested by subsequent behavior, regulated by discrepancies from the preceding comparison. A feedback loop is created from the comparison. This loop is negative if input is below the standard and is positive if input is above the standard (Carver & Scheier, 1986, 1998).

Stajković, Lee, Greenwald, and Raffiee (2015) modified this model concerning the reference point and automaticity of responses. Here, we reiterate their main contentions. First, not all standards are goals, as described by Carver and Scheier (1998, p. 35):

> Many types of standards exist. Instructions, social comparison information, the norms of society or group, a person's attitudes—all these

are standards. Consider attitudes. A person's belief that something is desirable or undesirable can serve as a point of reference for that person, value around which to regulate behavior.

A goal is a desired end, but it is not a semantic for every end. A *theory of goal systems* in social psychology clarifies (Kruglanksi et al., 2002) that the hallmark of goals is a pursuit of new ends positively valenced for any given person (Aarts, Gollwitzer, & Hassin, 2004).

In a perfect world of mechanical functioning, a thermostat senses a change in room temperature from the preset reference point and adjusts automatically (Powers, 1973). Equating this with a "perfect" world of human functioning would mean that people hear, see, and experience an event (input), compare that information with a standard (referent point), and estimate exactly what resources are needed to proceed adaptively (output).

In reality, a reference point is not always a goal. It can be an attitude or a personal value (e.g., I want to espouse the values of my father). Understanding the reference point allows us to better predict the outcome. Consider the referent point, "I aim to walk in the footsteps of Jesus Christ," compared with, "I aim to earn a promotion at work at just about any cost." An individual with the first referent is likely to behave differently than one with the second.

When the performance output is below the reference point, a negative feedback loop is created. Closing the negative feedback loop and not exceeding the reference point is what the person wants in the "Jesus" referent point, whereas not only closing the negative feedback loop but also exceeding the reference point with a new goal of next-level promotion may be what the person desires in the "promotion" referent point. To understand an employee's reference point, a manager needs to understand these types of preferences. Sharing of personal preferences has increased dramatically with the advent of social media. Consequently, we call for nuanced gradation in determining a person's aim, especially before we attach arbitrary labels (e.g., "only low achievers aim for that").

Accordingly, Stajković et al. (2015) modified the automation mechanism of control theory, a key assumption of this theory that had been criticized. Specifically, Stajković et al. (2015) argued for two points: (1) a need to distinguish between reference points to frame reactions to feedback loops, which can both reduce the discrepancy or increase it, and (2) to understand that human reactions to feedback loops are volitional, not automatic.

Implying that a person's behavior is motivated by closing the negative feedback loop, and not wanting to exceed it, is likening humans to inanimate objects, e.g., a thermostat. This is an outdated notion that ignores the valence people attach to standards they *want to* pursue. Depending on the reference point people espouse, they may pursue closing the negative feedback loop only, the positive feedback loop only, neither, or both. Labeling a person as unmotivated because s/he espouses "walking in the footsteps of Jesus," no less and *no more*, disregards the valenced preferences of that particular individual.

By implication, positive discrepancy creation is not always desired. Furthermore, if an employee is outperforming continually the pre-set standard, s/he might be an uber achiever. However, the person might also be purposely miscalculating the goal at the onset. Perhaps s/he prefers to feel on top of things and intentionally sets the goal low. Or, maybe s/he does not set a goal at all and then back-fits the goal perceptually, as needed for comfort. As Michelangelo warned, "The greater danger for most of us lies not in setting our aim too high and falling short; but in setting our aim too low and achieving our mark."

Stajković et al. (2015) further clarified that whether reactions to a feedback loop are automatic or volitional will depend on the circumstances. For example, passengers on an aircraft want the reference parameters (e.g., speed, altitude, power) to align automatically for a safe flight. Automatic comparisons and reactions in human self-regulation, though, are the exception—not the norm. For example, imagine an assistant professor with a promotion goal to publish six top-tier articles within five years. After that time has passed, the professor is given feedback that his/her record is below the standard, and s/he is given another year to improve. The assistant professor's effort going forward will be volitionally regulated by personal preferences and perception of the circumstances. If s/he has other options and views the added effort to stay in the current school unjustified, then it is unlikely an attempt to close the negative feedback loop will be made. It could be that increased effort would take too much time away from the family, or maybe the professor perceives his/her input was not assessed fairly. For any of these reasons, this individual might willfully choose to leave instead of close the negative feedback loop. In contrast, s/he might desire to stay and believes s/he can do what it takes to close the loop. Here, the person will engage the feedback loop and work to reduce the discrepancy. Together, this example illustrates that output from feedback is far from an automatic course correction.

Setting goals without providing feedback is as nonsensical as giving feedback without *a priori* set goals. In our executive MBA classes, we hear about employers who assign goals, or require employees to self-set goals, but the process ends there; the feedback loop is never opened let alone closed. Employees who are assigned a goal need timely feedback. Else, how will they guide adaptive self-regulation? If their performance is not on track, how will they know? If performance created a positive feedback loop, will management know? Providing performance feedback without a pre-set goal is a slippery slope; employees are vulnerable to shifting goal posts by unscrupulous managers. Think of a manager who assumes a "do best" goal for employees. At the end of the time period, the employee expects positive reinforcement for increasing sales by 3%. Instead, the manager tells the employee he had expected a 5% boost in sales and offers no reinforcement. Fair?

To sum, people adopt varied standards as reference points, and comparisons to the standard inform their behavioral responses. In psychology of human, not mechanical, self-regulation, behavioral responses are not automatic; they depend on personal preferences.

Organizational Behavior Underpinnings of Goal Pursuits

Organizational behavior research is primarily concerned with setting and implementing goals. Employees generally know what to do, for goals generally pertain to performance levels. A manager at the strategic level can ponder goal pursuits in the marketplace; most employees do what they are told and have little leverage to choose or change goals. As our students remind us, if a loan-processing employee is hired, a level of loan processing is expected. We next discuss goal setting in organizational behavior and use goal-setting theory (Locke & Latham, 1990, 2002) to guide our narrative given its workplace focus.

Specific, Timebound, and Difficult Goal Attributes

Specific Goals

A goal must be specific. Vague goals spread attentional resources thin. We occasionally hear remarks that goal specificity in professional endeavors, such as law or medicine, is not as easily discernable as, for example, in manufacturing, which has specific levels of performance. True, but goals can relate to desired or undesired behaviors, such as do "this or that" to help win the litigation or to reduce medical errors. The frequency of such behaviors is quantifiable. When we conduct workshops on goal setting, we ask leaders to identify behaviors critical to their business. After they identify key behaviors, we make a list for supervisors to track the frequency to which their employees exhibit those behaviors.

One way to ascertain if your goal is specific enough is to ask, "Can someone unfamiliar with my situation decide if I achieved the goal?" For example, if you set a goal to "build my professional network," what indicates goal attainment after a month of progress? Use your answer to set the goal at the onset, e.g., *make 10 new professional connections on LinkedIn in one month*. Similarly, if your goal is to "have an open mindset," what marks goal attainment? Instead, why not set a goal to attend a pre-specified number of mindfulness workshops in some time period? The idea being, if you claim your goal cannot be specific, you are probably not thinking hard enough. To complicate matters, goal specificity is necessary but not sufficient. A specific goal does not affect performance *per se*, for goals vary in difficulty (further described later). Specificity is a precondition to move judiciously to the next attribute of specific, time-bound, and difficult (STD) goals, determining the time for goal pursuit.

Timebound Goals

Goals need reasonable time bounds. Absurdly short deadlines increase goal difficulty beyond the intended level and excessive time spans are not motivating. Visualize, for instance, setting a goal to earn your MBA in the next 20 years. Would that motivate you to make progress today? Probably not, because when people make decisions related to future events they discount the expected future benefits (Frederick, Loewenstein, & O'Donoghue, 2002). In other words, people have a present-biased preference; when considering trade-offs between two desired alternatives, the one that is most temporally proximate is given the most weight (O'Donoghue & Rabin, 1999). Though rarely discussed in goal literature, we see no reason why this economic principle of *hyperbolic discounting* would not apply to goals. After all, most of us have labored through being reminded that "it is better to have one bird in the hand than two in the bushes."

If a specific goal needs a lengthy timeline, then relevant sub-goals should be set. Why? First, they enable you to stay on track by providing "mile markers" (as Roman Legions discovered and implemented to their benefit centuries ago). This connects multiple sub-pursuits into a more discernable whole. Second, sub-goals allow for psychological "small wins," which reinforce a sense of accomplishment. Small wins also provide a floor; if you miss the next step, you will not fall too far back. Third, sub-goals in smaller units of time prevent an "out of sight, out of mind" issue and help keep the overall goal pursuit afloat.

Difficult Goals

A goal needs to be difficult, yet achievable, to be motivating. Easy goals hardly get competitive juices flowing. There is a positive linear relationship between goal difficulty and performance level. This is because difficult goals direct attention, intensify effort, and help to sustain persistence, especially in the face of obstacles (Locke & Latham, 2009). "Do best" goals have virtually no effect on performance because they carry idiosyncratic meanings. High achievers are likely to translate a "do best" goal to high levels of difficulty using a proven external referent, but many employees will view "do best" goals as whimsical targets assigned by uninformed managers.

The inevitable next questions are, "What is a difficult goal theoretically?" and "How is difficulty ascertained empirically?" Theoretically, the goal should be set right below the tipping point of an inverted

U curve, else, *this goal is too difficult, why bother?* We want to maximize performance, and this level represents the goal difficulty local optimum—the point at which the derivative of the goal difficulty and performance function equals zero.

Practically, this is easier said than done. The rule of thumb in the literature recommends setting the goal at the 90th percentile of difficulty, i.e., 10% of employees are performing at that level. For instance, if the top 10% of employees are assembling products at a 2% defect rate, then the manager should set goal difficulty at 2% for all employees. This makes an important assumption—that all employees *are capable* of performing at a 2% defect rate. Goal setting is a motivational technique; therefore, it assumes the other 90% are not performing at this level because of insufficient motivation—not lack of ability or skill. This may be incorrect. Monitoring performance in the next round will illuminate the circumstances. If it becomes clear that some employees lack the skills to meet the goal, training could help. If some do not have the ability, managers should not set them up to fail. Locke and Latham (2002) concluded that unless a difficult goal at the 90th percentile pushes past the limits of skill and ability, performance will improve, on average.

Pursuit of a specific, difficult goal can increase stress. If so, employee performance and leader effectiveness can suffer (Bardes & Piccolo, 2010). This is because goal specificity makes it apparent there is a level of performance to be reached, and difficulty of a goal makes it clear that failure is an option (Drach-Zahavy & Erez, 2002; Huber, 1985). Hence, stress arises from personal appraisals that demands exceed what one believes s/he can accomplish and worries about availability of resources (Folkman & Lazarus, 1985).

Is the employee exertion to perform at the 90th percentile worth the human costs? When economists talk about cost, they mean monetized value of resources needed to produce something. Marginal cost is the cost of producing one additional unit. Aside from the two studies on goals and stress we cited above, costs such as physical exertion, psychological distress, or medically documented illnesses caused by a goal pursuit are seldom discussed in relation to goal difficulty, let alone marginal human cost of achieving the next level of goal difficulty. Conventionally, the lens is performance, i.e., did it improve and how much? "What human toll does it take to reach difficult goal?" is typically not asked for goal theory supposes motivation basis of performance—employees could do more if they wanted to.

We call for a more quantitative approach to goal setting going forward. Do managers need to set the goal at the 90th percentile if arithmetic could reveal where the marginal benefit is maximized and the marginal cost is minimized on the performance distribution? Raising goal difficulty levels improves performance, but it almost certainly does so at a decreasing rate, which is rarely measured. At some goal level, goal difficulty will hit diminishing returns. A few calculations could reveal where that is. Companies can conduct surveys, if not medical exams, to estimate human exertion cost in relation to granular levels of goal difficulty. A bit of calculus can derive a function to enrich management's understanding of human costs and performance benefits of different goal levels over time.

Boundary Conditions

Self-Efficacy

Goal-setting theory specifies boundary conditions that moderate the effectiveness of conscious goals. First, even the most cherished goals are likely to be forsaken if one doubts s/he can do what it takes to attain them. This is one reason people behave sub-optimally in the pursuit of a goal even when they know full well what to do. Those beset by doubt have little incentive to act. In conceptions of human agency presented in social cognitive theory (Bandura, 1986), self-referent thought mediates the relationship between the environment and goals. Of these intermediary beliefs, and a transformative contributor to adaptive self-regulation by goals, is perceived self-efficacy—a malleable belief formed by an appraisal of how well one can execute action to succeed at performance. Generally speaking, higher self-efficacy increases the likelihood that people will favorably make their way through the transactions of work to achieve their desired goals (Stajković & Luthans, 1998).

For example, a recent survey of 600 successful small business owners in the U.S. (reported in Frohwein, 2019) found that 41% started a business in an industry unrelated to their previous profession. For these 246 entrepreneurs, despite knowing what they wanted to achieve, whether they would take action to pursue their goal came down to their "can-do" belief. When asked, 82% of these entrepreneurs said they were confident they would be successful, despite 65% reporting they were unsure if they even had enough to start the business. Indeed, 93% of all respondents calculated a run rate of shorter than 18 months. Yet, all business owners (in this survey) favorably made their way through the risky and bold transactions and have been operating a successful business for 11 years, on average.

Goal Acceptance and Commitment

Just because you believe you can attain a goal, it does not mean you will pursue it. Instead, people pursue goals they value, as signaled by goal acceptance (Erez & Zidon, 1984) and commitment (Locke & Latham, 2009). Goal commitment is "viewed as the more inclusive concept in that it refers to one's attachment to or determination to reach a goal, regardless of where the goal came from" (Locke & Latham, 1990, p. 125). Goal

commitment strengthens the relationship between the goal and performance and this link is amplified for (a) assigned goals, as buy-in may not
be immediate, and (b) difficult goals, for they necessitate more effort but
have a lower probability of attainment than do easy goals. If employees
are not committed to their goals and/or do not believe they have what it
takes to achieve them, then their performance will suffer.

Consider the story about a senior vice president (SVP) at Microsoft
described by Shaw (2004). During a meeting with the recruiting director, the SVP was asking for a number of new hires as a specific goal for
next year. The recruiting director resisted, and instead preferred a target
range. Frustrated at the reluctance of the manager to set a specific and
difficult goal, the SVP exclaimed, "If you won't give me a number, then
I'm going to give you one." The goal was then set at twice the current
year's hiring goal—much higher than the recruiting team thought possible to attain. In this example, the acceptance and commitment of the
goal by the recruiting team is not guaranteed. To increase the likelihood
of goal commitment, the SVP attached positive reinforcement by agree-
ing to throw a huge party for the recruiting team if the goal was met.
Fortunately, the team found the incentive motivating. They committed to
the specific goal and even exceeded it.

Figure 2.1 depicts graphically a goal-setting model, as described in this
section.

Feedback

Feedback aids performance primarily by clarifying the task; it provides
knowledge about prior performance, quantity and quality of outcomes,
and ways to improve next time. Feedback ought to lead to setting a
revised STD goal for the next performance period.

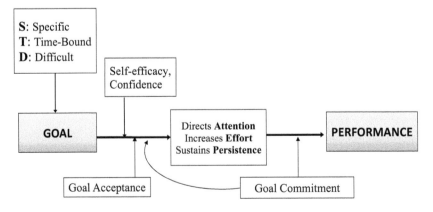

Figure 2.1 A model of goal setting.

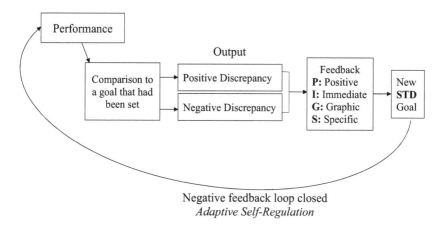

Figure 2.2 Model of feedback regulation in relation to a goal set. See also Stajković et al. (2015).

To operationalize systematic delivery of knowledge of results (outcome feedback) and suggestions for improvement (process feedback), we recommend Positive, Immediate, Graphic, and Specific (PIGS) feedback (Luthans & Stajković, 1999). Positive stands for being positive in the manner of delivery. We do not call for managers to fabricate facts to sound and be positive, just rudimentary social decorum indicating personal respect for the person regardless of performance level. Immediate follows the principle of reinforcement theory: the closer feedback is to performance, the more likely it is to be connected with the related behavior. A graphic feedback provides for an easy visual comparison. Finally, specific feedback has a similar meaning as specific goals.

The model of goal-feedback relationships is shown in Figure 2.2.

Goal Types

Goal-setting theory outlines several goal types. Performance goals are set for a level of proficiency. They should be set when employees have the ability and knowledge to attain them. Otherwise, difficult goals may set employees up to fail. When an employee lacks the capacity to perform a task, a specific and difficult learning goal should be assigned.

Learning goals divert attention from reaching a performance level to discovering proper procedures and strategies to successfully perform. If employees are instructed how to handle elements in the learning process, then a specific and difficult performance goal should be set. If a behavior guided by a learning goal has poorly unfolded, resulting in the wrong procedures or unsuitable strategies, then setting a performance goal will impede progress (Locke, 2000). Given these nuanced effects, we suggest setting a performance goal only when employees have previously mastered the task. Otherwise, in the learning phase of skill acquisition, we recommend setting and emphasizing learning goals.

If goals cannot be set for performance or learning, then behavioral goals can be used. Sometimes called action goals, behavioral goals are outcome driven (Albarracín, Hepler, & Tannenbaum, 2011). They include goals to be ethical, engage in organizational citizenship behaviors, and pursue cooperative versus competitive behaviors (Bargh, Gollwitzer, Lee-Chai, Barndollar, & Trötschel, 2001). Health and relationship goals fall into this category as well (Avivi, Laurenceau, & Carver, 2009). Another type of goal is attitudinal, such as stay positive or do not create waves at work (Veenhoven, 2002).

Goal-Setting (In)Effectiveness

Goal-setting theory has accumulated empirical support in about a thousand studies; goal setting is an evidence-based way to regulate employee behavior (Locke & Latham, 2002, 2013). A survey of business professors rated goal-setting theory first in both scientific rigor and practical importance out of 73 theories of organizations (Miner, 2003).

Critics have espoused skepticism concerning the effectiveness of goal theory (e.g., Ordóñez, Schweitzer, Galinsky, & Bazerman, 2009a, 2009b). They insist that when goal setting is "over-prescribed," there are harmful side effects. Though perhaps well intended, this is more of a criticism of wrongful application rather than of the psychological principles behind goal effectiveness. As both purposeful and negligent over-prescription of even the best medications can lead to side effects, inadequate application of goals will also lead to unwanted side effects. As Locke and Latham (2009a, 2009b) pointed out in their responses to these critics, uninformed application is not evidence against the effectiveness of goal setting as a reliable predictor of work behavior.

Aside from misguided application, at least three potential shortcomings of setting goals can arise. First, difficult goals tied to lucrative reinforcement, lax oversight, and an organizational culture that makes it easy to rationalize unethical practices, together, can lead to cutting corners to reach the goal. These practices comprise inaccurate charges to boost revenues toward the goal (e.g., charging for unnecessary services, inflating billable hours, putting extra weight in shipments to increase chargeable weight), lying about the progress toward the goal (e.g., "cooking the books" as in falsifying financial statements, opening fake customer accounts), and moral disengagement to justify unethical decisions (Bandura, 2016; Bardes & Piccolo, 2010; Barsky, 2008; Schweitzer, Ordóñez & Douma, 2004; Ordóñez et al., 2009a, 2009b). We summarize these malfeasance practices under the banner of false positives, or Type I error; simply, what is claimed to be there is not there.

Second, goal setting increases focus. Think of a radiologist who is trained to spot tumors in his/her area of expertise. In a study by Drew, Võ, and Wolfe (2013), 24 radiologists were asked to perform a lung-nodule detection. The researchers inserted a photo of a gorilla that was 48 times larger than the size of the average nodule into the x-rays. Shockingly, 83% of the radiologists did not see the inserted gorilla. Too much focus can create tunnel vision, causing people to miss important factors. For instance, eye tracking software in the Drew et al. (2013) study showed that the majority of radiologists who missed the gorilla looked directly at its location, as they are supposed to, but that also caused inattentional blindness.

Issues related to goal-caused tunnel vision are false negatives, or Type II error; there was an effect, but we missed it. Tunnel vision also relates to *confirmation bias*, or "unwitting selectivity in the acquisition and use of evidence" (Nickerson, 1998, p. 175). The notion that humans are attuned to information in support of their preset beliefs and are unattuned to disconfirming evidence has permeated human affairs for centuries:

> The human understanding when it has once adopted an opinion (either as being the received opinion or as being agreeable to itself) draws all things else to support and agree with it. And though there be a greater number and weight of instances to be found on the other side, yet these it either neglects and despises, or else by some distinction sets aside and rejects.
>
> (Frances Bacon, 1620/1939)

Third, goals can override behavior that are otherwise expected because goal striving is goal-dependent. The study of taxi drivers in New York City (NYC) on rainy days illustrates the point (Camerer, Babcock, Loewenstein, & Thaler, 1997). NYC is home to many people, and traffic gridlock is a daily nuisance. If it rains in NYC, people who normally walk are more likely to take a taxi. This increases demand for taxi drivers and presents an opportunity for drivers to earn more, and there should be more taxis on rainy days. Yet, a study by Camerer et al. (1997) found this not to be the case. When researchers examined why, they found that most drivers in NYC rent the taxi car and set a goal to double their daily rent. On rainy days, drivers reach the goal sooner and go home.

Finally, another issue with difficult goals is expectancy of success. On one hand, difficult goals increase the average performance, but employees assigned difficult goals also have a low success expectancy (Locke & Latham, 2002). On the other hand, consider the following conversation we had with two students. They acknowledged the motivation potential of difficult goals but questioned the wisdom of setting 90th percentile goals at work. Paraphrasing, "Why go out on a limb with 90th percentile goals, fail, and look bad? Why not set easy goals, accomplish them, and look good?" We have several answers. First, if we do that, on average, society loses. Second, for how long can employees bend the reality before it weighs back in on them? Third, if you invested all you had into a business and labored daily to keep it afloat, would you set low goals? Why do it in organizations?

Summary of the Section on Conscious Goals

Notwithstanding special circumstances, hardly anyone wanders aimlessly for more than a short time. Perpetual aimlessness speeds up doomsday. Instead, people set goals, plan how to achieve them, go for it, hopefully get feedback, and adapt accordingly for the next time. The better people get at this process, the more adaptive and productive they will be.

Transitioning From Goal Setting to Goal Priming

Until Bargh's (1990) article, goals were mostly treated as conscious determinants of action that were identified and operationalized through fastidious deliberation. Interest in the effects of primed subconscious goals and their automatic influence on behavior has been reinforced by studies showing causal effects of primed goals in addition to the effects of conscious goals on outcomes. How do we connect conscious to subconscious goals?

Experiences and knowledge accumulate over a lifetime; these memories do not reside in our conscious mind at all times. Childhood memories of a friend next door playing with your dog are probably not active in your consciousness currently. You can, however, bring these memories into consciousness. Information flows into and out of consciousness, and it can be initiated by priming. For example, if you meet your next-door friend or see photos of your dog, those memories can automatically spring up. You would not proclaim to yourself: "I am deliberately setting the goal to recall this memory from my childhood. Instead, when the memory is cued, it automatically "comes back" to you.

These connections at work can be illustrated as follows. In pursuit of a goal, employees first draw from their arsenal of skills. If they have the needed skill, they can automatically apply it toward a new goal. For example, when loggers were assigned a goal to cut more logs, they achieved it automatically by exerting more effort (Latham & Kinne, 1974). The new goal, to cut (more) logs, primed prior goal-behavior associations. The goal was new, but the goal-related behaviors were not. When, however, the loggers were assigned a goal to increase the average weight of the truckloads, new skills were required. The loggers now needed to mull over new strategies for stacking logs more efficiently and find ways to more accurately estimate the weight of a truck load before driving to the weighing station (Latham & Baldes, 1975). When a goal is substantively new and prior goal-behavior associations for it do not exist, conscious deliberation is necessary for the task.

Similar arguments have been made for more complex tasks (see Stajković & Luthans, 1998, for detailed discussion of task complexity), which allow for multiple paths to success and require strategy development for execution (Wood & Bandura, 1989). Consider being assigned the goal to grow your company's business in Cambodia. If activities germane to this goal have not been previously experienced or observed, conscious processing will be instrumental. If, however, your company recently underwent a similar expansion in Vietnam under your guidance, goal-strategy associations from the past were probably stored in the subconscious. If so, they can be primed for similar expansion in Cambodia.

A Primer on Goal Priming

How can these connections be explained theoretically? Ellen Langer (1978) claimed that behavior is under control of environmental cues and behavioral responses are carried out without conscious involvement. These automatic responses have been documented to occur even under conditions of information overload (Bargh & Thein, 1985; Bargh & Tota, 1988) and when people were actively trying to prevent the responses from unfolding (Bargh & Pratto, 1986). Bargh (1990, p. 96) questioned the cue-to-behavior theory:

> As to whether the social environment directly controls behavior, there exists no evidence in favor of—but compelling logical arguments against—the notion that social-interactive behavior can occur without an interposed intent or goal.

Self-regulation theorists joined this bandwagon given their emphasis on automaticity in control theory. In their view, utility of a conscious goal is, at least partially, derived from the absence of an automated response to a pursuit (Carver & Scheier, 1998). Accordingly, subconscious goals could be viewed as more fundamental than conscious goals, because if behavior was overlearned to the point of automation, it was critical. A goal-behavior association that is automated needed to be dealt with early and often in the past (Higgins, 1997). Thus, per this view, it could be said that automatic pursuits primed by subconscious goals represent "goal seeking for issues that are critically important . . . and that are now automated, deeply embedded in the fabric of the self" (Carver & Scheier, 1998, p. 270).

In 1990, social psychologist John Bargh questioned the orthodoxy of conscious goal origins. Though granular goal contemplation is priceless when appropriate, it leaves a lot unsaid about goal origin on a moment-to-moment basis when decisions are needed now.

> Conventional models by and large do not deal with this issue of where goals come from. . . . In the real world, at least as much work

is involved in determining what one wants to do as in determining how to do it.

(Wilensky, 1982, p. 13)

Bargh (1990) introduced goal-dependent behavioral automaticity. He theorized that automatic behavioral responses depend on *goal* activation. For example, thirst (need) is automatically associated with hydration (behavior), but a thirst cue can lead to different behaviors depending on the goal it activates in the interim, e.g., turn the faucet on, buy bottled water, or ask a colleague out for drinks. This conceptual view allowed for an array of behaviors to be automated. Bargh (1990) notes that we form goal-behavior associations through repetition. Because these pursuits are instrumental to functioning, they get stored in the subconscious. For example, a child who reads a book after being frequently reminded by his mother to study can create an association among the goal to study, the behavior of reading, and the cue of his mother. When the environmental cue is encountered (mother enters room), a goal is primed (study), which automatically triggers associated behavior (read a book). The child will consciously know he is engaged in the act of the reading a book, but he may be unaware of the primed subconscious goal to study.

One difference between attainments guided by conscious versus primed goals is that conscious goal strivers know why they want to achieve a goal and how to master behaviors needed. For example, if one competes with a goal to win, s/he is consciously trying to triumph. In contrast, a primed goal affects accomplishments without gaining conscious assistance. There are two types of priming. Subliminal priming presents a stimulus below the threshold of visibility to influence subsequent success. Supraliminal priming presents a stimulus within visibility, but the connection between the prime and its effect goes unnoticed. To demonstrate, trace the lines in the following figure without lifting your pencil. Your goal is to completely trace the entire figure without retracing any lines.

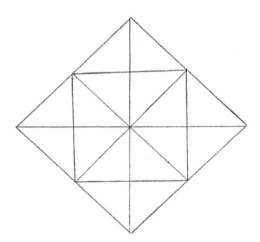

Were you able to solve it? Perhaps more importantly, how long did you persist before stopping? Versions of this puzzle were used in experiments on persistence. Unbeknown to participants, this puzzle is unsolvable. However, because goals increase persistence, participants primed with a goal persist longer, on average, than people who are not primed with a subconscious goal. Now, look back at the paragraph leading up to the puzzle. Out of 100 words in that paragraph, 12 related to achievement: *attainment, strive, achieve, master, thrive, compete, win, triumph, prevail, accomplishment, gaining,* and *success.* We took this ratio and words from Stajković, Locke, and Blair (2006) to prime a subconscious achievement goal. Because you probably were not paying attention to themes when you first read the paragraph, you were unaware of the supraliminal primes embedded within it. Nonetheless, the primed goal presumably influenced your persistence on the puzzle task. If it did, your subconscious connected the pattern of achievement-related words to activate a subconscious goal "to achieve." Again, you consciously saw the words, but when you first read the passage, it is unlikely you consciously connected the achievement theme.

Extending this to work, we published a field study using these same 12 achievement words embedded in a 100-word email sent from a CEO to his employees:

> All,
>
> I want to take a minute to celebrate our **accomplishments** at [one-word, name of the company]. As we move past the holiday season, let's remember our **successes**. I see you **master** what you do, **strive** to overcome obstacles, and **prevail**. With such mindset, sky is the limit to what we can **achieve**. As you live our motto—have fun, make money, grow your career—please know that your **triumphs** are appreciated! Our **attainments** are impressive. How we continue to **thrive** is in our hands. I hope we continue to **compete** each day, **gain** customers, and **win** together. Thank you for your service!
>
> Thank you for your commitment to [one-word, name of the company],
>
> CEO name

Employees who received the email with the prime words performed, on average, 15% more effectively and 35% more efficiently over one week compared to employees who received the neutral email shown below, without prime words (Stajković, Latham, Sergent, & Peterson, 2018):

> All,
>
> I want to take just a few minutes out of your day to thank you for all that you do for [one- word, name of the company]. As we move past the holiday season, I want to remind you that we need to do our best and take advantage of all that we have built over the

last several months. When you come to work each day, you need to remember what is important to our business. As you live our company motto—have fun, make money, grow your career—know that you are appreciated. Thank you for your service to [one-word, name of the company].

Thank you for your commitment to [one-word, name of the company],

CEO Name

This study illustrates priming in the real world and is discussed in detail in Chapter 6.

Summary of the Section on Primed Goals

People do not relearn goal-behavior associations every time they face the same situation. There is no need for it if the circumstances are the same. Think of a farmer getting ready to harvest cranberries. S/he has harvested cranberries in Wisconsin for the last 50 years. Does s/he reiterate every morning what the goal is, how to attain it, and what resources are needed? Sure, if something drastically changed that morning. But what if the activities that morning are similar to those performed each morning for the past five years, let alone 50? Chances are the farmer automated many of the goal-behavior associations. This allows him/her to conduct business with little deliberate contemplation about steps of this goal pursuit. Imagine the waste of attentional resources if people had to relearn goal-behavior associations daily (see Corkin, 2013). How are these associations formed? The literature on goal priming identifies four conceptual models that explain formation and priming of subconscious goals. These models are theoretically predicated on subconscious processing causing automaticity of goal-behavior associations. Therefore, in Chapter 3 we explain what the subconscious is, how it interacts with conscious, and how cognitive automaticity is created. In Chapter 4, we pick up the conversation on models of goal priming.

References

Aarts, H., Gollwitzer, P. M., & Hassin, R. R. (2004). Goal contagion: Perceiving is for pursuing. *Journal of Personality and Social Psychology, 87*, 23–37.

Albarracín, D., Hepler, J., & Tannenbaum, M. (2011). General action and inaction goals: Their behavioral, cognitive, and affective origins and influences. *Current Directions in Psychological Science, 20*(2), 119–123.

Avivi, Y. E., Laurenceau, J. P., & Carver, C. S. (2009). Linking relationship quality to perceived mutuality of relationship goals and perceived goal progress. *Journal of Social and Clinical Psychology, 28*(2), 137–164.

Bacon, F. (1620/1939). Novum Organum. *The English Philosophers from Bacon to Mill*, 24–123.

Bandura, A. (1986). *Social foundations of thought and action: A social cognitive theory*. Englewood Cliffs, NJ: Prentice-Hall.

Bandura, A. (2016). *Moral disengagement: How people do harm and live with themselves*. New York, NY: Worth Publishers.

Bardes, M., & Piccolo, R. F. (2010). Goal setting as an antecedent of destructive leader behaviors. In Schyns, B. & Hansbrough, T. (Eds.), *When leadership goes wrong: Destructive leadership, mistakes and ethical failures* (pp. 3–22).

Bargh, J. A. (1990). Auto-motives: Preconscious determinants of social interaction. In E. T. Higgins & R. M. Sorrentino (Eds.), *Handbook of motivation and cognition: Foundations of social behavior* (Vol. 2, pp. 93–130). New York, NY: Guilford Press.

Bargh, J. A., Gollwitzer, P. M., Lee-Chai, A., Barndollar, K., & Trötschel, R. (2001). The automated will: Nonconscious activation and pursuit of behavioral goals. *Journal of Personality and Social Psychology, 81*, 1014–1027.

Bargh, J. A., & Pratto, F. (1986). Individual construct accessibility and perceptual selection. *Journal of Experimental Social Psychology, 22*(4), 293–311.

Bargh, J. A., & Thein, R. D. (1985). Individual construct accessibility, person memory, and the recall-judgment link: The case of information overload. *Journal of Personality and Social Psychology, 49*, 1129–1146.

Bargh, J. A., & Tota, M. E. (1988). Context-dependent automatic processing in depression: Accessibility of negative constructs with regard to self but not others. *Journal of Personality and Social Psychology, 54*, 925–939.

Barsky, A. (2008). Understanding the ethical cost of organizational goal-setting: A review and theory development. *Journal of Business Ethics, 81*(1), 63–81.

Bourgeois, L. J. (1980). Performance and consensus. *Strategic Management Journal, 1*, 227–248.

Camerer, C., Babcock, L., Loewenstein, G., & Thaler, R. (1997). Labor supply of New York City cabdrivers: One day at a time. *Quarterly Journal of Economics, 112*, 407–441.

Carver, C. S., & Scheier, M. F. (1986). Self and the control of behavior. In L. M. Hartman & K. R. Blankstein (Eds.), *Perception of self in emotional disorder and psychotherapy* (pp. 5–35). New York, NY: Plenum.

Carver, C. S., & Scheier, M. F. (1998). *On the self-regulation of behavior*. New York, NY: Cambridge University Press.

Corkin, S. (2013). *Permanent present tense: The unforgettable life of the amnesic patient, H. M.* New York, NY: Basic Books.

Deci, E., & Ryan, R. M. (1985). *Intrinsic motivation and self-determination in human behavior*. New York, NY: Plenum Press.

Drach-Zahavy, A., & Erez, M. (2002). Challenge versus threat effects on the goal—performance relationship. *Organizational Behavior and Human Decision Processes, 88*(2), 667–682.

Drew, T., Võ, M. L. H., & Wolfe, J. M. (2013). The invisible gorilla strikes again: Sustained inattentional blindness in expert observers. *Psychological Science, 24*(9), 1848–1853.

Dweck, C. S. (2008). *Mindset: The new psychology of success*. New York, NY: Random House Digital, Inc.

Elliott, E. S., & Dweck, C. S. (1988). Goals: An approach to motivation and achievement. *Journal of Personality and Social Psychology, 54*(1), 5.

Erez, M., & Zidon, I. (1984). Effect of goal acceptance on the relationship of goal difficulty to performance. *Journal of Applied Psychology*, 69, 69–78.

Folkman, S., & Lazarus, R. S. (1985). If it changes it must be a process: Study of emotion and coping during three stages of a college examination. *Journal of Personality and Social Psychology*, 48(1), 150–170.

Frederick, S., Loewenstein, G., & O'Donoghue, T. (2002). Time discounting and time preference: A critical review. *Journal of Economic Literature*, XL, 351–401.

Frohwein, R. (2019). No, it's not money—this is the one thing small businesses need to succeed, according to survey. *Business Insider*, March 22, 2019. Retrieved from https://www.businessinsider.com/small-businesses-need-confidence-to-succeed-kabbage-survey-2019-3

Grant, H., & Dweck, C. S. (2003). Clarifying achievement goals and their impact. *Journal of Personality and Social Psychology*, 85(3), 541–553.

Heatherton, T. F., & Baumeister, R. F. (1996). Self-regulation failure: Past, present, and future. *Psychological Inquiry*, 7(1), 90–98.

Higgins, E. T. (1997). Beyond pleasure and pain. *American Psychologist*, 52, 1280–1300.

Higgins, E. T. (1998). Promotion and prevention: Regulatory focus as a motivational principle. In M. P. Zanna (Ed.), *Advances in experimental social psychology* (Vol. 30, pp. 1–46). Cambridge, MA: Academic Press.

Huber, V. L. (1985). Effects of task difficulty, goal setting, and strategy on performance on a heuristic task. *Journal of Applied Psychology*, 70, 492–504.

Kruglanksi, A. W., Shah, J. Y., Fishbach, A., Friedman, R., Chun, W. Y., & Sleeth-Keppler, D. (2002). A theory of goal systems. In M. P. Zanna (Ed.), *Advances in experimental social psychology* (Vol. 34, pp. 331–378). San Diego, CA: Academic Press.

Kukla, A. (1972). Foundations of an attributional theory of performance. *Psychological Review*, 79, 454–470.

Langer, E. J. (1978). Rethinking the role of thought in social interaction. *New Directions in Attribution Research*, 2(1), 35–58.

Latham, G. P., & Baldes, J. J. (1975). The "practical significance" of Locke's theory of goal setting. *Journal of Applied Psychology*, 60(1), 122–124.

Latham, G. P., & Kinne, S. B. (1974). Improving job performance through training in goal setting. *Journal of Applied Psychology*, 59(2), 187–191.

Locke, E. (2000). Motivation, cognition, and action: An analysis of studies of task goals and knowledge. *Applied Psychology*, 49(3), 408–429.

Locke, E. A., & Latham, G. P. (1990). *A theory of goal setting & task performance*. Englewood Cliffs, NJ: Prentice-Hall, Inc.

Locke, E. A., & Latham, G. P. (2002). Building a practically useful theory of goal setting and task motivation: A 35-year odyssey. *American Psychologist*, 57, 705–717.

Locke, E. A., & Latham, G. P. (2009). Has goal setting gone wild, or have its attackers abandoned good scholarship? *The Academy of Management Perspectives*, 23, 17–23.

Locke, E. A., & Latham, G. P. (Eds.). (2013). *New developments in goal setting and task performance*. New York, NY: Routledge.

Luthans, F., & Stajković, A. D. (1999). Reinforce for performance: The need to go beyond pay and even rewards. *Academy of Management Perspectives*, *13*(2), 49–57.

McClelland, D. C., Atkinson, J. W., Clark, R. A., & Lowell, E. L. (1953). *Century psychology series. The achievement motive*. East Norwalk, CT: Appleton-Century-Crofts.

Miller, G. A., Galanter, E., & Pribram, K. H. (1960). *Plans and the structure of behavior*. New York, NY: Henry Holt and Co.

Miner, J. B. (2003). The rated importance, scientific validity, and practical usefulness of organizational behavior theories: A quantitative review. *Academy of Management Learning & Education*, *2*, 250–268.

Nickerson, R. S. (1998). Confirmation bias: A ubiquitous phenomenon in many guises. *Review of General Psychology*, *2*, 175–220.

O'Donoghue, T., & Rabin, M. (1999). Doing it now or later. *The American Economic Review*, *89*, 103–124.

Ordóñez, L. D., Schweitzer, M. E., Galinsky, A. D., & Bazerman, M. H. (2009a). Goals gone wild: The systematic side effects of overprescribing goal setting. *Academy of Management Perspectives*, *23*(1), 6–16.

Ordóñez, L. D., Schweitzer, M. E., Galinsky, A. D., & Bazerman, M. H. (2009b). On good scholarship, goal setting, and scholars gone wild. *Academy of Management Perspectives*, *23*(3).

Powers, W. T. (1973). *Behavior: The control of perception*. Oxford, England: Aldine.

Powers, W. T. (2005). *Behavior: The control of perception* (pp. 34–37). New Canaan: Benchmark Publications.

Schweitzer, M. E., Ordoñez, L., & Douma, B. (2004). Goal setting as a motivator of unethical behavior. *Academy of Management Journal*, *27*, 422–432.

Shaw, K. N. (2004). Changing the goal-setting process at Microsoft. *Academy of Management Executive*, *18*, 139–142.

Stajković, A. D., Latham, G. P., Sergent, K., & Peterson, S. (2018). Prime and performance: Can a CEO motivate employees without their awareness? *Journal of Business and Psychology*.

Stajković, A. D., Lee, D., Greenwald, J. M., & Raffiee, J. (2015). The role of trait core confidence higher-order construct in self-regulation of performance and attitudes: Evidence from four studies. *Organizational Behavior and Human Decision Processes*, *128*, 29–48.

Stajković, A. D., Locke, E. A., & Blair, E. S. (2006). A first examination of the relationships between primed subconscious goals, assigned conscious goals, and task performance. *Journal of Applied Psychology*, *91*, 1172–1180.

Stajković, A. D., & Luthans, F. (1998). Self-efficacy and work-related performance: A meta-analysis. *Psychological Bulletin*, *124*(2), 240–261.

Tolman, E. C. (1932). *Purposive behavior in animals and men*. New York: Appleton-Century-Crofts.

Veenhoven, R. (2002). Why social policy needs subjective indicators. *Social Indicators Research*, *58*(1–3), 33–46.

Wiener, N. (1948). *Cybernetics; or control and communication in the animal and the machine*. Oxford, England: John Wiley.

Weiner, B. (1972). *Theories of motivation: From mechanism to cognition.* Oxford, England: Markham.

Wilensky, R. (1982). Points: A theory of the structure of stories in memory. In W. G. Lehnert & M. H. Ringle (Eds.), *Strategies for natural language processing* (pp. 345–374). New York, NY: Psychology Press.

Wood, R., & Bandura, A. (1989). Impact of conceptions of ability on self-regulatory mechanisms and complex decision making. *Journal of Personality and Social Psychology, 56*(3), 407–415.

3   Subconscious Processing and Cognitive Automation

There is an ancient fable about gods deciding where to hide the greatest power of the world from humans so they cannot find and ruin it. One of the gods said, "Let's hide it on top of the highest mountain." They decided against it, for they were certain curiosity would lead humans to climb the highest mountain, sooner or later. Another god then said, "Let's hide it at the bottom of the deepest ocean," and a third suggested, "In the middle of the Earth." They agreed that humans would eventually conquer the oceans and the earth. Finally, the wisest of them all said, "Let's hide the greatest power of the world within the mind of man. He will never think to look there!"

It has long been speculated that the subconscious sphere of the mind has substantial processing power and that its presence and operations are unobvious to us. From a scientific psychology perspective, how we understand subconscious cognitive processing vis-à-vis the conscious depends first on definitions. Thus, we start this chapter with a discussion of definitions and the nature of influences between the two cognitive processes.

Etiology of Subconscious and Conscious Processes

Definitions

Subconscious and conscious cognitive processes are different, but they are part of one mind, whose unified purpose is to help us survive and prosper (Bargh, 2017). Despite the everyday vernacular of a conscious mind and a subconscious mind, humans do not have two minds. Pathologies of the mind occur and can cause severe consequences, but no part of the mind is intended to make human life more difficult.

The conscious apparatus is at the surface of cognitive processing; it is the mental system at the intersection of us and the external world. On an evolutionary timeline, conscious processing is the latest add-on to our subconscious wheelhouse. A point often overlooked is the addition of conscious processing did not cause our original subconscious machinery to go away; it still exists. Unless you believe that God and/or evolution created redundant cognitive systems on purpose, or somehow made a mistake in guiding human adaptation and development, *sub*conscious predicates cognitive processing *below* awareness.

In terms of their interplay, consciousness is transitory—a conscious thought now can disappear in a moment (Corkin, 2013). In this instance, the conscious thought has transitioned to the *subconscious* for the time being. For example, a teacher heading to class transfers relevant materials from the subconscious to the conscious. When the class ends, the material reverts back to the subconscious. The information does not disappear from memory nor does it have to be relearned before every class. Why does it not remain in consciousness? If all information resided in our conscious mind, it would get "clogged up," given its finite capacity. Psychologists generally agree that information flows between the conscious and subconscious as needed to aid adaptive behavior.

Where definitions diverge is on assumptions about which kinds of information in the subconscious can rise into conscious versus remain below awareness. For instance, Freud (1900) prefers the term *preconscious* for the cognitive system that we refer to as subconscious. Freud also defined *un*-conscious to denote both a process and a sphere in the mind that can never become conscious. We describe Freud's terms in the section on his contributions presented later in this chapter. Several terms indicating lack of awareness of cognitive processing are presented in Table 3.1.

Nature of Influences

How precisely the conscious and subconscious interact to influence thought and behavior is a weighty question in 21st-century psychology. To introduce the reader to this literature, we stick to the mostly agreed-upon postulates about the workings of both processes.

> The unconscious must be assumed to be the general basis of [mental] life. The unconscious is the larger sphere, which included within it the smaller sphere of the conscious.
>
> (Freud, 1899, 1955 translation, p. 607)

We know that the subconscious automates physiological functions; humans cannot ask their livers to up the ante on Friday nights. Despite the niceties of "free will," to ensure we do not jeopardize our survival with wishful thoughts, God and/or evolution safeguarded all critical biological processes with automaticity guided by the subconscious.

> If the grace of God miraculously operates, it probably operates through the subconscious door.
>
> (William James, 1902, p. 270)

Table 3.1 Definitions of Terms With a Common Conceptual Thread Indicating Lack of Awareness

Term	Source	Definition	Can it become conscious?
Preconscious	Freud (1923) Moskowitz, Gollwitzer, Wasel, and Schaal (1999)	"latent but capable of becoming conscious" (p. 5) "preconscious stages in which categorization occurs and stereotypes are activated" (p. 167)	Yes. Thoughts in the preconscious are "one-step" away from consciousness. Same as above.
Unconscious	Freud (1933)	"we call a psychical process unconscious whose existence we are obliged to assume—for some such reason as that we infer it from its effects—but of which we know nothing" (p. 70)	No. The unconscious is repressed and is inadmissible to consciousness. It can be inferred from behavior and interpreted by psychoanalysis, or accidentally revealed by verbal, a.k.a., Freudian, slips.
	Bargh and Morsella (2008)	"unconscious processes are defined in terms of their unintentional nature and the inherent lack of awareness is of the influence and effect of the triggering stimuli and not of the triggering stimuli" (p. 78)	No. People are not aware of the mental processes that are activated by stimuli in the environment and guiding behavior.
Id	Freud (1933)	"It is the dark, inaccessible part of our personality . . . chaos, a cauldron full of seething excitations" (p. 73)	No. "The id has intercourse with the external world only through the ego" (p. 79) (see also Figure 3.1 in this chapter).
Ego	Freud (1933)	"The ego represents what may be called reason and common sense" (p. 19); it's a buffer zone between id and super-ego	Yes (see also Figure 3.1 in this chapter).
Super-ego	Freud (1933)	Battles the id from moving up to reason.	No (see also Figure 3.1 in this chapter).
Non-conscious	Bargh (2005)	"Nonconscious control of individual social behavior—behavior induced to occur by environmental factors and not by the individual's conscious awareness and intentions" (p. 38)	Minimal. "This research is showing, to a startling degree, just how unaware we are of how we move and make movements in space" (Bargh, 2005, p. 45).

(Continued)

Table 3.1 (Continued)

Term	Source	Definition	Can it become conscious?
Not conscious	Bargh and Morsella (2008)	"efficient procedures that can run outside of consciousness, but nonetheless are intentional processes (one doesn't sit down to type without meaning to in the first place, and the same applies to driving a car)" (p. 74)	Yes. People can become aware of these processes.
* *Subconscious*	Stajković, Locke, and Blair (2006)	"Subconscious goals operate automatically, without intention, awareness, and conscious guidance" (p. 1172)	Yes. Current subconscious constructs can become conscious, for there is constant flow between conscious and subconscious.
Intuition	Jung (1933)	"That psychological function transmitting perceptions in an unconscious way" (pp. 567–568)	No. "One defining characteristics of intuitive processing is that it is nonconscious" (p. 33).
	Dane and Pratt (2007)	"intuition draws on our inborn ability to synthesize information quickly and effectively" (p. 33)	Not addressed.
Implicit	Schacter (1987)	"Implicit memory is revealed when previous experiences facilitate performance on a task that does not require conscious or intentional recollection of those experiences" (p. 501)	No. "[N]eural correlates of explicit and implicit memory differ qualitatively" (Rugg et al., 1998).
Tacit	Polanyi (1966)	"cannot be put into words, nor even conveyed by pictures" (p. 5)	Yes. "wherever some process in our body gives rise to consciousness in us, tacit knowing will make sense of the event" (p. 9)

* Throughout this book, we use the term *subconscious* (as have Latham, Stajković, & Locke, 2010; Shantz & Latham, 2009; Stajković et al., 2006), because it clearly indicates that the locus of a process being considered is below the conscious level. By analogy, Londoners call their transportation system that operates below ground *subway*, not unway or nonway.

The subconscious automates functions critical for survival and prosperity. For the most part, natural selection influenced general behavioral tendencies; our thoughts and actions are not randomly determined nor are they always the product of "free" will. Human decision-making predates consciousness (Dijksterhuis, 2009). Humans survived and prospered because our brains developed mechanisms to help us adaptively self-regulate. In particular, information that helped us in the past to adaptively self-regulate was fed forward as a starting point for next time. This cumulative knowledge building became an automated *a priori* mental "shortcut" (Campbell, 1974) to save us from having to ponder what is dangerous or advantageous every time we needed these answers, especially when we were in a hurry. For example, back in our early days as *Homo sapiens* in Eastern Africa, if we encountered a lion, the automated response that was naturally selected to be fed forward was to run away fast. People who wondered if the lion was friendly and went to pet it were selected out of the gene pool by the lion.

Automation is really no different in the buzz of social and working life, though that claim is more challenging to sell than an automated instinct to run away from danger. The hard sell is caused by human pushback against the notion that thoughts and actions are beyond our immediate control, let alone that they are predetermined by "illusory" forces of which we are unaware. Yet, research shows that deciding every second on the most efficient and effective behavioral and emotional response to any given environmental stimuli would mentally deplete us in a matter of seconds. If something was critical to human existence but was not automated, we would get overwhelmed with decision-making between the time we wake up and actually get up. The subconscious processing is a cognitive system streamlined by natural selection to save us from deliberating every dilemma and using up limited attentional resources. We believe this is the least understood piece of information in the public based on our experience of presenting on these topics.

Importantly, subconscious processes are not stale leftovers from the bygone years. They are adaptive like conscious processes. The subconscious has a much longer evolutionary timeline and is responsible for keeping some human basics intact (e.g., love, trust, altruism) amid drastic perturbations in external living conditions. Despite the environmental changes since antiquity, has anyone ever contended that love of a parent for a child is wrong? Having children is a pure economic loss, for most parents, yet most people still choose to have kids. Even economists acknowledge the power of love over money in this case. Has there ever been a thoughtful writing suggesting that interpersonal trust is a superfluous invention and we should simply monitor everyone's actions instead of trust some of them to save us from mental exhaustion? Has there ever been a mindful writing about altruism in a group being a bad thing? Regardless of the surface appeal of deliberate contemplation, some basics have been fed forward and are here to stay.

Said differently, we argue that humans cannot bend social reality as a matter of daily willfulness and get away with it, at least in the long run. What is social reality? The mix of subconsciously ingrained social axioms that most acknowledge (e.g., love, trust, altruism) and willful contemplation of surrounding circumstances. The former may change in the future, but not overnight. As often said in the monotheistic religious traditions, fear of God is the beginning of wisdom, where God embodies in the abstract the truths of human prosperity. Violating willfully ingrained social axioms fed forward by natural selection (c.f., hate your kids, mistrust everyone, be selfish to those close to you) might make you feel in control now, but it will cost you in the long run. If people disregard these subconsciously ingrained basics, regardless of their assumed origin, they are either insufficiently attentive or are misunderstanding them; either way it is a perilous choice.

What was not automated in the subconscious is handled by the conscious. Although "in nature, the unconscious mind is the rule, not the exception" (Bargh & Morsella, 2008, p. 78), the unique capacity of the conscious to interpret new information is unparalleled compared to the mental powers of any other biological dweller on this earth. Along the lines of *this is too good to last long*, the amount of information the conscious can process is limited. For example, a study showed that contemplating eating radishes or chocolates impaired cognitive performance on a subsequent task (Baumeister, Bratslavsky, Muravn, & Tice, 1998). The authors concluded, "conscious, free choice must remain at best restricted to a very small portion of human behavior" (1998, p. 1263). Others agree.

> [M]ost of a person's everyday life is determined not by their conscious intentions and deliberate choices but by mental processes that . . . operate outside of conscious awareness and guidance.
> (Bargh & Chartrand, 1999, p. 462)

This is not an underhanded sucker-punch to imply conscious processing is ineffective, but only to point out it should be used sparingly. Protecting consciousness from unnecessary deployment and wasteful use is a *sine qua non* of adaptive self-regulation.

> Conscious acts of self-regulation occur only rarely in the course of one's day . . . only 5% or so of the time.
> (Baumeister et al., 1998, p. 464)

Consider the following metaphor in the Bible:

> Look at the ships; though they are so great and are driven by strong winds, they are guided by a very small rudder wherever the will of the pilot directs.
> (James, 3:4)

This Bible passage illustrates why the two systems were designed to "talk to each other." A mighty force (ship) without a steering mechanism (captain) is as useless as a steering mechanism without a ship. The ship has might but no directional will, and the captain has will but no power. Either one alone is otiose, but together they get us home. In the same way, the subconscious cannot support new behavior without consciousness steering it first. Although consciousness has reached virtual deification today, its consideration in isolation from the subconscious foundation is as nonsensical as expecting the subconscious to respond to sarcasm. Philosopher A. N Whitehead gives us his two cents on this topic:

> Operations of thought are like cavalry charges in a battle—they are strictly limited in number, they require fresh horses, and must only be made at decisive moments.
>
> (quoted in Bargh & Chartrand, 1999, p. 464)

Progression of Theory Development

Humans have long speculated about the subconscious and have sought to understand it. In the following section, we provide a brief history of the theory development progression.

From Aristotle to Freud

Aristotle is credited with initial thoughts about the interaction between sensory input and consciousness in his *Idea of the Mind*. He argued that the soul (psyche) and nature manifest themselves in a "double character" within the mind. Homer picked up the mantle with many depictions of the interplays between a visible and an invisible mind in both *The Iliad* and *The Odyssey*. Plato basically described priming in *The Republic* almost in the way we define it today by suggesting that light activates preexisting capabilities within a person.

In the Middle Ages, religion in Europe influenced social perceptions. The Bible teaches us that humans were created in God's image; thus, if we heard voices or jabbered to ourselves, the community perceived this as soul's demonic possession. Said differently, mental perturbations were seen as an evil force of a dark spirit to cause aberrant actions, because God does not mumble to himself. Early 17th-century philosopher René Descartes "canonized" this social perception in the literature by affording consciousness God-like qualities. When he wrote *Je pense, donc je suis* (French) or *Ego cogito, ergo sum* (Latin), we are, however, not sure he meant "I think, therefore I am," as is typically back-fitted.

By extension, what was not perceived as conscious was non-God-like and spurned. Later in the 17th century, another philosopher, John Locke, fell for Descartes's mental typecasting in his analysis of the acquisition of knowledge in *An Essay Concerning Human Understanding*. He theorized eloquently that humans acquire input from the natural world, which the mind then examines and condenses as needed. However, he then concluded, erroneously per Freud, that sensory input cannot be stored without conscious filtering first.

> To say a notion is imprinted on the mind, and yet at the same time to say, that the mind is ignorant of it, and never yet took notice of it, is to make this impression nothing. No proposition can be said to be in the mind which it never yet knew, which it was never yet conscious of.
>
> (J. Locke, 1690, p. 15)

For every musing of Descartes ossifying the conscious, there is one from St. Augustine stating, "I cannot grasp all that I am," meaning that no human totality can be grasped at any given moment in time. J. Locke's *carte blanche* to consciousness has been rather undermined by the meticulous analysis of Leibniz (founder of calculus contemporaneously with Newton) who made a case for the interaction between the conscious and subconscious parts of the mind. Rather than conceptually confronting the genius of Leibnitz (also credited with discovering binary arithmetic, a language used by all computers of today), J. Locke mounted ad hominem attack by allegedly responding:

> Mr. L's great name had raised in my expectation which the sight of his paper did not answer. This sort of fiddling makes me hardly avoid thinking that he is not the very great man as has been talked of him.

We encourage the reader to consider Tallis's (2012) Chapter 1 in which the author details many intermediary contributors to subconscious theory before Darwin came to the scene with his seminal take. In particular, in his classic *On the Origin of Species*, Darwin (1859) referred to *unconscious selection* in nature and contrasted such automatic selection with *purposeful selection*, e.g., by animal breeders. Similar arguments about unconscious natural selection were discussed in the book *The Selfish Gene*, by Dawkins (1976).

In the instances described above, subconscious referred to automatic (unintentional) acts. Lack of awareness did not pertain to the stimuli; instead, it referred to lack of knowledge about their influences on automatic actions. For example, most traffic participants (c.f., notwithstanding bikers) automatically stop on a red light without deliberating much and concluding that stopping is a better idea than continuing. Today, we call these influences supraliminal; where the stimulus is clearly seen but its effects are subconsciously processed. Freud (1911, 1915) shifted the emphasis from the stimuli of which one is unaware to the subconscious etiology of their influences. In the next section, we describe briefly Freud's pioneering contribution to the study of the subconscious mind.

Freud's Contribution

For context, to discuss the subconscious without Freud would be to discuss the lyrics of the Doors without Jim Morrison, the performance of Queen without Freddy Mercury, or the orchestral comprehensiveness of Led Zeppelin without Jimmy Page. To consider this entire literature sans Freud is to consider 1980s music without Michael Jackson.

Around the turn of the 20th century, Pierre Janet in Paris and Sigmund Freud in Vienna argued independently that psychological malfunctions have roots in physiological causes. Indeed, the English word *trauma* owes its origin to the Greek *trauma*, which connotes "physical" wound. Janet brushed off this causation to atypical brain functioning. Freud, however, examined this causal chain to a deeper extent. In short, he formulated a locus of psychological maladies in the subconscious as the root cause of most mental problems.

Based on his psychiatry practice, Freud concluded that some people have psychological issues. He then argued, logically, that if these people recognized the existence of their problem and knew its cause, they would have remedied it. Therefore, if people suffer from mental mores but have no clear basis to infer their origins, Freud argued that the causes of psychological problems are in the unconscious sphere of the mind. And, there is perhaps a good reason as to why such causes remain in the unconscious; if they surfaced, they could cause more issues by bringing to light dark sides we harbor.

Freud's preferred word was *unconscious*, and he defined two modes of it. The first mode represents thoughts that can vacillate between being conscious and unconscious. Freud called this mode of processing the *latent unconscious*, or *preconscious*. Specifically, this terminology differentiates thoughts that can become conscious from those that are repressed permanently in the unconscious. Freud believed repressed thoughts cannot become conscious on their own. This is not to say these unconscious thoughts can *never* become conscious; they can (as explained in the next section), but they are restrained from volitionally rising to conscious. Freud formulated this view from a pathological theory of repression that already existed. In this sense, *unconscious* is a depository of deep, often sexual, desires and painful emotions that were subjugated out of consciousness. Otherwise, if they were allowed to surface to consciousness, they would cause more mental damage than from the subterranean space. Thus, according to Freud, not all that is unconscious is repressed for such thoughts can be preconscious, but all that is repressed is unconscious.

The repression in the unconscious can occur by the conscious, where unwanted desires are pushed down because of their inconvenient nature. Freud also allows for the possibility that unconscious desires came directly from the external world bypassing conscious filters. One way or another, despite being buried, these thoughts still exert influence—they are not "dead" but repressed. They "want to be heard" and cause psychological maladaptation and mental conflict inexplicable to self. To address deep-seated desires, per Freud, is to bring them into consciousness and then sort them out more conveniently. This can be done with psychoanalysis/therapy, or such memory traces can be revealed by verbal, Freudian slips. In Figure 3.1, we depict our best understanding of Freud's theory in its basic form.

Few objections have been raised to the general framing and topology of mental processing espoused by Freud. Numerous claims of Freud have

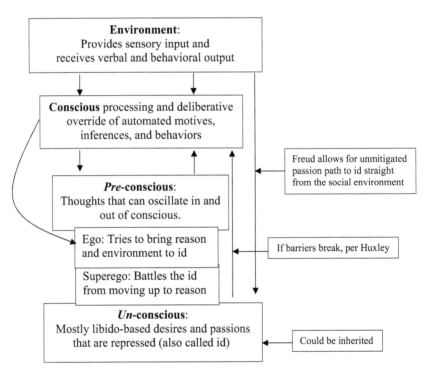

Figure 3.1 Freud's basic model. Freud argued that repressed mental states are mostly libido based, and he called them id. He also introduced two mechanisms between preconscious and the id, ego, and superego. Ego is a coherent organization of mental processing through which conscious operates, and it tries to bring the nature and facts into the battle against id. Superego is the first line of defense (or bottom part of ego) against the forces of id. Superego is closer to id in its nature than to preconscious and vice versa with regard to ego.

even been empirically supported (e.g., Briere & Conte, 1993; Dijkster-huis, 2009; Eagle, 1998; Westen, 1998). A puzzling question, then, is why has Freud attracted copious contention?

> One reason why Freud generated such emotive contention is that he shatters our cherished ideals—what we hold most dear . . . Freud ultimately threatens us with knowledge of ourselves—what we wish to know nothing about at all, knowledge that can potentially disrupt the way we experience and understand our inner worlds.
>
> (Mills, 2004, p. 10)

One of Freud's contentions was to argue vehemently that not only mental patients but all people have an unconscious repository of opaque desires. One example that sent critics over the edge was Freud's claim that *all* people experience the *Oedipus complex*. This refers to a child's subconscious sexual desire for the opposite-sex parent, often a son for a mother, while at the same time hating the same-sex parent. As we read this literature, the biggest adversaries of such arguments were not scholars, as few, aside of Jung, have reached Freud's depth of thought. It was not empirical evidence either, for none has really disproved his conceptualization. Perhaps the more fundamental question is if Freud meant sexual desire in a sense that a child unconsciously wishes to have sex with the parent. Instead, Freud may have been referring to a deep bond that creates another level of love between a child and the opposite sex parent. The strength of this bond can generate jealousy of the child toward the same sex parent. Yet, these emotions reside in the uncon-scious, as consciously the child loves each parent equally. Because "sex" is another term for gender, sexual desires as stated by Freud can be inter-preted to simply mean a connection between a child and the opposite gender parent—not necessarily a desire to engage in a sexual act. Jung (1933) explains this more eloquently than Freud, but the damages was already done.

Evolutionary logic would support the latter interpretation versus the more grotesque one (see Bargh, 2017). Though parts of mind can veer off-course, that was not the evolutionary aim. Consequently, if the *Oedi-pus complex* is a daily phenomenon, then it is hard to surmise how these unadaptive tendencies survived natural selection. If these multiplexities exist within humans but cause no trouble, then they are irrelevant to the daily discourse of life.

A similar take was offered by philosopher Aldous Huxley (1954) in his work *The Doors of Perception* (this title inspired Jim Morrison to name his legendary band *The Doors*). Huxley argued that the proverbial doors of perception include both "heaven and hell," because life witnesses both good and bad. The latter is tucked away in the unconscious to save us from its vitriol. It cannot make the trip up because consciousness overrides it.

If, however, consciousness gets exhausted, or is altered through alcohol, love, or other mind-altering drugs, cracks emerge, allowing subconscious to push through the conscious filter. According to Huxley, this can lead to debauched experiences but also worthy ones when the peek is offered into realms of promise that were unreachable via consciousness alone.

In sum, one of Freud's key claims is as follows:

> When making decision of minor importance, I have always found it advantageous to consider all the pros and cons. In vital matters however . . . the decision should come from the unconscious, from somewhere within ourselves.
>
> (cited by Dijksterhuis, 2009, p. 1)

In supposing this, Freud turned upside down the argument that humans only automate bodily functions and simple repetitive tasks. He cleverly contended that automating simple things in social life makes little logical sense, for it generates only a meager evolutionary advantage. Simple tasks can be dispensed virtually toll-free to conscious resources. The value-added contribution to humans from the subconscious comes instead in processing complex tasks, because the subconscious processes more information. Consider a couple contemplating a job offer to relocate to another continent. After a prolonged conversation of apparent pros and cons, they decide to "sleep on it" until tomorrow. The act of "sleeping on it" is an allegory for "let the subconscious process all the facts." The subconscious is a powerhouse that can simultaneously comprehend and connect underlying pros and cons, ultimately arriving at a decision without consuming limited attentional resources.

Cognitive Automaticity

Continuing with post-Freud theory development, we next unpack automaticity. We explain why automaticity is important in human functioning and how it can be driven by cognitive structures, semantic networks, and norms. Several definitions of automaticity are provided in Table 3.2. Put simply, if a set of interrelated cognitions and actions is automated, then unified behavior unfolds (e.g., riding a bike). This presumes the individual does not have to consciously and concurrently ponder action selection, timing, sequencing, coordination, dynamic changes, and execution. As a result, cognitive automaticity saves humans both attentional resources and time, and makes them more functional, productive, and adaptive to the possibilities afforded by both the social and physical environments.

For example, learning to ride a bike can be an overwhelming experience. A person must simultaneously perform cognitive and motor acts, such as balancing body weight, pedaling both legs in speed unison, observing traffic and steering accordingly and temporaneously, to say

Table 3.2 Definitions of Automaticity and Related Terms

Process	Source	Definition
Automaticity	Bargh and Williams (2006, p. 1)	"Refers to control of one's internal psychological processes by external stimuli and events in one's immediate environment, often without knowledge or awareness of such control."
Automatic	Shiffrin and Dumais (1981, p. 111)	"Automatic processing does not necessarily demand processing resources, freeing the system for higher-level processing and alternative control processing."
Automatically	Aarts and Dijksterhuis (2000, p. 18)	"Behavior is elicited by environment, without a consciously expressed fiat or mandate."
Spontaneous	Hassin, Bargh, and Uleman (2002, p. 515)	"An inference is defined as spontaneous if: (1) it is not suggested by the experimental instructions, (2) people are usually unaware of their intentions to make it, and (3) people are usually unaware of the inference itself."

nothing of sequentially explaining this to a child who is eager to jump on the bike and speed down the driveway. With practice, kids learn to ride a bike "without thinking." They automatically coordinate and execute the component functions necessary to stay on top of wheels, illustrating the necessity, usefulness, and power of automated processing.

Consciousness can guide bike riding, in theory. In practice, it would become cognitively overwhelming to calculate the weight pressure on each pedal to thrust the bike forward but maintain balance, coordinate the requisite movements among eyes, hands, body weight tilt, legs, and feet, and put it all together to process the no-fall angle of turns. Add the consequences of "speeding," and it becomes apparent why cognitive automation operates on the subconscious platform and why its processing power is formidable. As mentioned, these automatic processes are critical to human survival and progress, but consciousness is irreplaceable for optimal adaptation when pertinent circumstances change suddenly.

Automaticity Underscored by Cognitive Structures

The automation mechanism has been labeled differently across literatures, including terms like *cognitive schemas*, *cognitive scripts*, and *cognitive categories*. They all, however, can be characterized as "cognitive knowledge structures held in memory that describe the appropriate sequencing of events in conventional or familiar situations" (Lord & Kernan, 1987, p. 266). Humans form cognitive knowledge structures that encompass sets of functionally interrelated behaviors that are (in)appropriate at certain places, events, or social situations. These mental systems are meant to guide recurring behavior effortlessly.

Examples include behaving professionally at work and more jovially at a party, being genuine with friends but not in-laws, and acting respectful in a religious institution but stimulated in an amusement park. The context triggers a particular cognitive structure that guides behavior automatically according to prior established patterns. Thus, cognitive automation saves mental energy and time in processing innumerable external cues.

Cognitive structures are enacted via habits, obsessive-compulsive disorder (OCD), traits, heuristics, mindsets, and mental shortcuts. A habit subconsciously guides "routine repetition of past acts" (Wood, Quinn, & Kashy, 2002, p. 1281). A habit is measured indirectly by the frequency of repeated acts (Ouellette & Wood, 1998). OCD has a similar definition and meaning, but the causes are different. One may pursue a habitual behavior because it brings positive reinforcement. In contrast, repetitive behaviors caused by OCD are driven by a chemical imbalance. Traits are innate personal dispositions; behaviors they predispose one to can vary across activities, social milieus, and time, but the behaviors are uniformly coherent with the trait (Stajković, Bandura, Locke, Lee, & Sergent, 2018).

Heuristics are decisional shortcuts. Consider Gigerenzer and Todd's (1999) example of a patient complaining of a heart attack. When the patient arrived at the hospital, he was assessed on 19 cues. To be useful, the cues need to be tabulated and condensed into a decision of high risk or low risk. Conscious processing would imply that 19 separate tests need to be deliberately evaluated, rank-ordered, and combined interactively to formulate a decision. Though logical, this approach could kill the patient, for it entails an inordinate number of computational permutations before a doctor even sees the patient. As a shortcut, a decisional-tree heuristic was developed to reduce evaluation to three questions.

A mindset refers to a mental attitude or general inclination. It is not focused on specific content. Examples include plan wisely, drive carefully, study hard, spend judiciously, be open-minded. Carol Dweck (2008) of Stanford University popularized the concept of mindset in her book, *Mindset: The New Psychology of Success*. In it, she defined mindset as "a simple belief about yourself" (p. *ix*). Studies on mindsets have shown they can be primed into automatic action. For example, participants were primed either with a deliberative mindset by being asked to contemplate a personal change or with an implementation mindset by being asked to prepare for the execution of a plan (Gollwitzer, Heckhausen, & Steller, 1990). Participants then had to describe a decision that should be made.

Those primed with a deliberative mindset exhibited more deliberative and less implementation intentions, and vice versa. These findings demonstrate that participants subconsciously transferred primed mindsets to other unrelated contexts. Terms, their definitions, and related examples discussed in this section are summarized in Table 3.3.

Finally, when we use mental shortcuts, we fill in missing information automatically, form snap judgements, and generate predictions without much information. For example, conscious and subconscious prejudice are forms of mental shortcuts. The word prejudice comes from the Latin word *praejudicium* (prejudgment) and it indicates that someone is prejudged, irrespective of facts, for better or worse (Allport, 1954). A discussion of subconscious prejudice is presented elsewhere (see Sergent & Stajković, 2018).

Automaticity Guided by Associations in Semantic Networks

Interrelated stimuli and behaviors can be organized and connected in semantic networks (Förster, Liberman, & Friedman, 2009). For example, many automatically connect nurse with hospital, professor with university, and car with travel. These associations have the same purpose as cognitive structures; they save mental energy and time in connecting cues.

Said differently, they eliminate the need to relearn associations every time a cue is encountered. In an intriguing study by Bargh, Chen, and Burrows (1996), participants who unscrambled sentences containing words related to old age, e.g., *Florida, wrinkles*, and *retirement*, walked down a hallway slower than did a control group without knowing speed was being measured. The semantic link affected behaviors associated with words.

Associations in semantic networks also affect judgements. For example, Higgins, Rholes, and Jones (1977) asked participants to memorize either a positive or a negative word. Those who memorized a positive word evaluated subsequently the description of a stranger more favorably than those who memorized a negative word. Similarly, Bargh and Pietromonaco (1982) primed participants with ascending exposure to hostility-related words and then asked them to evaluate an ambiguous behavior. The percentage of primed hostile words was related positively to the subsequent attribution of hostile actions.

Automaticity Driven by Norm Activation

Aarts and Dijksterhuis (2003) showed that norms can also guide automaticity, where norms "represent generally accepted beliefs about how to behave in particular situations and are learned by associating normative behavior to these situations" (p. 18). Norms are encoded in memory as a mental representation of appropriate behavior in a given setting. For

Table 3.3 Definitions of Categories of Cognitive Structures

Term	Source	Definition	Examples
Habit	Oullette and Wood (1998, pp. 54–55)	"habits denote one's customary ways of behaving . . . They are tendencies to repeat responses given a stable and supporting context"	Putting your phone away while at work. Making coffee while your computer is starting up.
Heuristic	Kahneman and Tverskey (1982, p. 2)	"cognitive rules that govern the mental undoing of past events"	Emphasizing confirmatory evidence. Weighting more immediate events stronger.
Mindset	Gupta and Govindarajan (2002, pp. 116–117)	"how people and organizations make sense of the world . . . our current mindset guides the collection and interpretation of new information"	Global mindset of openness to and awareness of diversity across cultures and markets.
Mental model	Johnson-Laird (1983, p. 365)	"models of the system's capabilities, predilections, and preferences"	Second-order thinking/connections, "If I do x, what will likely happen after that?"
Cognitive map	Ford and Hegarty (1984, p. 290)	"cause/effect maps that decision makers use as a basis for evaluating various options they have available"	Drawing a fish-bone diagram to analyze the root cause of a current problem.
Schema	Anderson (1980, p. 4)	"A schema can be conceived as a set of related propositions"	Choosing to work on tasks that conform to your supervisor's perceptions of you (e.g., detail-orientated versus abstract thinker).
Scripts	Abelson (1981, p. 715)	"embodying knowledge of stereotyped event sequences"	Expectations about the order or a ritualized event sequence for processing a bank loan.

example, Aarts and Dijksterhuis (2003) primed participants with a photo of a library. This caused participants to speak more quietly if they also were assigned a goal to visit the library that day. In other words, "environments are capable of priming normative behaviors when the environment is of immediate behavioral relevance" (Dijksterhuis, Chartrand, and Aarts, 2007, pp. 106–107). Other examples of situational norms include removing your hat when inside a church and raising your hand before speaking in a classroom.

Automaticity in OB Research

In organizational behavior, arguments in the early literature pertaining to subconscious and automaticity in human functioning were seen as too distal to be convincing and were eschewed by organizational scholars and managers. Organizational scholars, by and large, instead turned their attention to attitude and motivation surveys and interventions such as compensation systems, setting goals, and job design. These were viewed as more useful tools for increasing motivation and performance at work (see Latham, 2012; Latham et al., 2010, for reviews). It took 50 years for OB research to pick up on the ideas from early work on the subconscious (c.f., Freud, 1911; McClelland, 1961). Need for achievement (nAch) (McClelland, 1961) and implicit manager motives (Miner, 1960) were introduced as automatic motives relevant to organizations. These conceptualizations were deemed reasonable, but their measurement by projective tests did not receive a warm welcome.

Need for Achievement as an Automatic Motive in Organizational Studies

One clue that Freud left behind that was picked up by organizational scholars was the role of free associations—or, how one train of thought transitions to another freely. Based on this idea, McClelland and colleagues introduced "the achievement motive," also known as "need for achievement" (McClelland, 1961, 1985; McClelland, Atkinson, Clark, & Lowell, 1953). McClelland defined the motive as "goal-oriented free choice with habit and situational factored controlled" (p. 38). This definition emphasizes free choice in discerning motives from other automatic causes of behaviors, such as impulses, instincts, and learned responses, e.g., brushing your teeth.

How Need for Achievement Motive Is Formed

As people engage in different activities, they learn which ones bring them pleasure and they develop stronger motives for these activities. The positive feelings arise not only from engaging in the act, but also from anticipatory thoughts of future action and history of reinforcement. For instance, some people derive pleasure from anticipating and attending a sporting event. Others extract joy from pursuing and achieving goals. Because these behavior-reinforcement patterns are experienced starting in childhood (McClelland, Koestner, & Weinberger, 1989), a general tendency toward achievement is formed and gradually stored in the subconscious. Although nAch is a trait-like tendency, theory asserts that context can prime when and how it can be triggered and expressed (McClelland et al., 1989).

Measurement of nAch

Concepts such as nAch are recognized broadly; asking participants if they are high achievers invites measurement distortion caused by social desirability. Consequently, indirect measurement is used, where, instead of asking people, "Are you a high achiever?" projective measures prompt a person to "divulge deep-seated feelings and tendencies of which even he himself may be unaware, and without sensing that he is revealing personal data" (Rohde, 1946, p. 170). Projective measures supposedly capture a more accurate portrait of the motives that reside in the subconscious. The most commonly used projective measure is the *Thematic Apperception Test* (TAT) (McClelland et al., 1953; Murray, 1938, 1943). This measurement tool involves asking participants to write a story in response to a photo. The photos represent a variety of life situations. People who write stories with modal references to excellence, doing more, and achieving a goal are believed to have a higher nAch than those who do not illustrate these themes in their stories.

Outcomes Related to nAch

The effects of nAch are mixed (Collins, Hanges, & Locke, 2004). Because nAch is a broad construct, it was expected to predict broad outcomes. Hence, nAch failed to predict narrow achievement domains (see Low & MacMillan, 1988; McClelland, 1985). For narrow tasks, its predictive power depends on task complexity. On complex tasks, performance is initially similar between high and low nAch, but high nAch people improve as they progress. This is because their need to achieve encourages them to learn new task strategies, challenge their assumptions, and analyze their actions. For simple tasks, however, nAch is unrelated to performance as standards are obvious and easily achievable (McClelland, 1985). The criticism in this literature is not directed so much at the idea that high achievers outperform low achievers, but at the way nAch is measured.

Motivation for Managerial Role as an Automatic Motive

Role motivation theory (Miner, 1960, 1978b) proposed that managerial roles generalize across firms and industries and that individuals vary systematically in their motivation for engaging managerial roles.

Qualities associated with high managerial role motivation include respect for authority, competitive spirit, and visibility (Miner, 1978b). Individual differences for managerial roles predict type of managerial positions (e.g., staff vs. line), rate of managerial advancement, and overall career advancement level. Somewhat narrow in its emphasis, this theory only focuses on managerial roles and positions in organizations.

Measurement of Role Motivation

Similar to social desirability concerns about nAch, motivation for managerial roles is mostly measured with projective tests, such as sentence completion tests (Miner, 1960, 1978a; Rotter, Rafferty, & Schachtitz, 1949). Drawing on this literature, Miner (1960, 1965) developed a Miner Sentence Completion Scale (MSCS). In like manner with the TAT, the MSCS disguises the purpose of measurement to avoid social desirability, and it taps into role motivation as a subconscious motive (Miner, 1993).

Outcomes Related to Role Motivation

Findings reveal a positive relationship between role motivation and managerial success and a lack of support for this link in non-managerial domains (Miner, 1978b). Howard and Bray (1990) reported that a projective measure of subconscious advancement motivation predicted managerial level of Bell Systems managers after 20 years.

Summary

Humans have one mind, not two. This mind comprises two modes of operations to handle different aspects of cognitive processing and functioning, but their role is complementary. The subconscious draws connections among memories, knowledge, events, emotions, thoughts, and behaviors. Consciousness encodes and processes novel stimuli to help us make deliberate decisions and to understand the world in terms of its current content and context. At any given moment, the subconscious and conscious interact to determine optimal cognitive and behavioral outputs. The idea of this interaction has existed at least since Greek philosophers initially articulated them, although the specifics grew with the momentous conceptualizations of Freud and Jung. Social psychologists expanded these inquiries and discovered that goals are stored within knowledge structures, making them susceptible to priming by cues in the environment, to which we turn in the next chapter.

References

Aarts, H., & Dijksterhuis, A. (2000). Habits as knowledge structures: Automaticity in goal-directed behavior. *Journal of Personality and Social Psychology*, 78, 53–63.

Aarts, H., & Dijksterhuis, A. (2003). The silence of the library: Environment, situational norm, and social behavior. *Journal of Personality and Social Psychology, 84*(1), 18–28.

Abelson, R. P. (1981). Psychological status of the script concept. *American Psychologist, 36*(7), 715–729.

Allport, G. W. (1954). *The nature of prejudice.* Reading, MA: Addison-Wesley.

Anderson, J. R. (1980). *Concepts, propositions, and schemata: What are the cognitive units? (No. TR-80-2).* Pittsburgh, PA: Department of Psychology, Carnegie-Mellon University.

Bargh, J. A. (1982). Attention and automaticity in the processing of self-relevant information. *Journal of Personality and Social Psychology, 43*(3), 425–436.

Bargh, J. A. (2005). Bypassing the will: Toward demystifying the nonconscious control of social behavior. In R. R. Hassin, J. S. Uleman, & J. A. Bargh (Eds.), *The new unconscious* (pp. 37–60). New York, NY: Oxford University Press.

Bargh, J. A. (2017). *Before you know it: The unconscious reasons we do what we do.* New York, NY: Touchstone.

Bargh, J. A., & Chartrand, T. L. (1999). The unbearable automaticity of being. *American Psychologist, 54*(7), 462–479.

Bargh, J. A., Chen, M., & Burrows, L. (1996). Automaticity of social behavior: Direct effects of trait construct and stereotype activation on action. *Journal of Personality and Social Psychology, 71*(2), 230–244.

Bargh, J. A., & Morsella, E. (2008). The unconscious mind. *Perspectives on Psychological Science, 3*(1), 73–79.

Bargh, J. A., & Pietromonaco, P. (1982). Automatic information processing and social perception: The influence of trait information presented outside of conscious awareness on impression formation. *Journal of Personality and Social Psychology, 43*(3), 437–449.

Bargh, J. A., & Williams, E. L. (2006). The automaticity of social life. *Current Directions in Psychological Science, 15*(1), 1–4.

Baumeister, R. F., Bratslavsky, E., Muraven, M., & Tice, D. M. (1998). Ego depletion: Is the active self a limited resource? *Journal of Personality and Social Psychology, 74*, 1252–1265.

Briere, J., & Conte, J. (1993). Self-reported amnesia for abuse in adults molested as children. *Journal of Traumatic Stress, 6*(1), 21–31.

Campbell, D. T. (1974). "Downwards causation" in hierarchically organized biological systems. In F. Ayala & T. Dobzhansky (Eds.), *The problem of reduction in biology.* Berkeley, CA: University of California.

Collins, C. J., Hanges, P. J., & Locke, E. A. (2004). The relationship of achievement motivation to entrepreneurial behavior: A meta-analysis. *Human Performance, 17*(1), 95–117.

Corkin, S. (2013). *Permanent present tense: The unforgettable life of the amnesic patient, HM.* New York, NY: Basic Books.

Dane, E., & Pratt, M. G. (2007). Exploring intuition and its role in managerial decision making. *Academy of Management Review, 32*(1), 33–54.

Darwin, C. (1859). *On the origins of species by means of natural selection* (p. 247). London: Murray.

Dawkins, R. (1976). *The selfish gene.* New York, NY: Oxford University Press.

Dijksterhuis, A. (2009). The beautiful powers of the unconscious thought. *Psychological Science Agenda, 23*, 1–4. Washington, DC: American Psychological Association.

Dijksterhuis, A., Chartrand, T. L., & Aarts, H. (2007). Effects of priming and perception on social behavior and goal pursuit. In J. A. Bargh (Ed.), *Frontiers of social psychology. Social psychology and the unconscious: The automaticity of higher mental processes* (pp. 51–131). New York, NY: Psychology Press.

Dweck, C. S. (2008). *Mindset: The new psychology of success.* New York, NY: Ballantine Books.

Eagle, M. N. (1998). Freud's legacy. Defenses, somatic symptoms and neurophysiology. In G. Guttmann & I. Scholz-Strasser (Eds.), *Freud and the neurosciences: From brain research to the unconscious* (pp. 87–101). Vienna, Austria: Verlag der Österreichischen Akademie der Wissenschaften.

Ford, J. D., & Hegarty, W. H. (1984). Decision makers' beliefs about the causes and effects of structure: An exploratory study. *Academy of Management Journal, 27*(2), 271–291.

Förster, J., Liberman, N., & Friedman, R. S. (2009). What do we prime? On distinguishing between semantic priming, procedural priming, and goal priming. *Oxford Handbook of Human Action*, 173–193.

Freud, S. (1899). *The interpretation of dreams.* (J. Stracehy, Trans., 1955). New York, NY: Basic Books.

Freud, S. (1911). Formulations on the two principles of mental functioning. In *The standard edition of the complete psychological works of Sigmund Freud, Volume XII (1911–1913): The case of Schreber, Papers on technique and other works* (pp. 213–226). London, UK: Hogarth Press.

Freud, S. (1915). Thoughts for the times on war and death. In *The standard edition of the complete psychological works of Sigmund Freud, Volume XIV (1914–1916): On the history of the psycho-analytic movement, Papers on metapsychology and other works* (pp. 273–300).

Freud, S. (1923). The ego and the id. In J. Strachey (Ed.) (1961), *The standard edition of the complete psychological works of Sigmund Freud, Volume XIX (1923–1925): The ego and the id and other works* (pp. 1–66). London, UK: Hogarth Press.

Freud, S. (1933). The dissection of the psychical personality In J. Strachey (Ed.) (1964), *The standard edition of the complete psychological works of Sigmund Freud, Volume XII (1932–1936): The ego and the id and other works* (pp. 57–80). London, UK: Hogarth Press.

Gigerenzer, G., & Todd, P. M. (1999). Fast and frugal heuristics: The adaptive toolbox. In *Simple heuristics that make us smart* (pp. 3–34). New York, NY: Oxford University Press.

Goldsmith, M. L. (1934). *Franz Anton Mesmer: A history of Mesmerism.* Doran, Incorporated: Doubleday.

Gollwitzer, P. M., Heckhausen, H., & Steller, B. (1990). Deliberative and implemental mind-sets: Cognitive tuning toward congruous thoughts and information. *Journal of Personality and Social Psychology, 59*(6), 1119–1127.

Gupta, A. K., & Govindarajan, V. (2002). Cultivating a global mindset. *Academy of Management Perspectives, 16*(1), 116–126.

Hassin, R. R., Bargh, J. A., & Uleman, J. S. (2002). Spontaneous causal inferences. *Journal of Experimental Social Psychology, 38*(5), 515–522.

Higgins, E. T., Rholes, W. S., & Jones, C. R. (1977). Category accessibility and impression formation. *Journal of Experimental Social Psychology, 13*(2), 141–154.

Howard, A., & Bray, D. W. (1990). Predictions of managerial success over long periods of time: Lessons from the Management Progress Study. In K. E. Clark &

M. B. Clark (Eds.), *Measures of leadership* (pp. 113–130). West Orange, NJ: Leadership Library of America.

Huxley, A. (1954). *The doors of perception.* New York, NY: Harper & Row.

James, W. (1902). *The varieties of religious experience.* Cambridge, MA: Harvard University Press.

Johnson-Laird, P. N. (1983). *Mental models: Towards a cognitive science of language, inference, and consciousness.* Cambridge, MA: Harvard University Press.

Jung, C. G. (1913). The theory of psychoanalysis. *The Psychoanalytic Review (1913–1957), 1,* 1.

Jung, C. G. (1933) (First published in 1921). *Psychological types.* New York, NY: Harcourt, Brace, and Company.

Kahneman, D., & Tverskey, A. (1982). The simulation heuristic. In D. Kahneman, P. Slovic, & A. Tversky (Eds.)., *Judgement under uncertainty: Heuristics and biases.* New York, NY: Cambridge University Press.

Kahneman, D., & Tversky, A. (2000). *Choices, values, and frames.* Cambridge, NY: Cambridge University Press.

Latham, G. P. (2012). *Work motivation: History, theory, research, and practice.* Los Angeles, CA: Sage.

Latham, G. P., Stajković, A. D., & Locke, E. A. (2010). The relevance and viability of subconscious goals in the workplace. *Journal of Management, 36,* 234–255.

Locke, J. (1924). 1690. *An essay concerning human understanding.* New Jersey: Claredon Press.

Lord, R. G., & Kernan, M. C. (1987). Scripts as determinants of purposeful behavior in organizations. *Academy of Management Review, 12*(2), 265–277.

Low, M. B., & MacMillan, I. C. (1988). Entrepreneurship: Past research and future challenges. *Journal of Management, 14*(2), 139–161.

McClelland, D. C. (1961). *The achievement society.* Princeton, NJ: Von Nostrand.

McClelland, D. C. (1985). How motives, skills, and values determine what people do. *American Psychologist, 40*(7), 812–825.

McClelland, D. C., Atkinson, J. W., Clark, R. A., & Lowell, E. L. (1953). *Century psychology series. The achievement motive.* East Norwalk, CT: Appleton-Century-Crofts.

McClelland, D. C., Koestner, R., & Weinberger, J. (1989). How do self-attributed and implicit motives differ? *Psychological Review, 96*(4), 690–702.

Mills, J. (2004). *Rereading Freud: Psychoanalysis through philosophy.* New York, NY: SUNY Press.

Miner, J. B. (1960). The effect of a course in psychology on the attitudes of research and development of supervisors. *Journal of Applied Psychology, 44,* 224–232.

Miner, J. B. (1965). *Studies in management education.* Atlanta, GA: Organizational Measurement Systems Press.

Miner, J. B. (1978a). The Miner sentence completion scale: A reappraisal. *Academy of Management Journal, 21*(2), 283–294.

Miner, J. B. (1978b). Twenty years of research on role-motivation theory of managerial effectiveness. *Personnel Psychology, 31*(4), 739–760.

Miner, J. B. (1993). *Role motivation.* New York, NY: Routledge.

Moskowitz, G. B., Gollwitzer, P. M., Wasel, W., & Schaal, B. (1999). Preconscious control of stereotype activation through chronic egalitarian goals. *Journal of Personality and Social Psychology, 77*(1), 167–184.

Murray, H. A. (1938). *Explorations in personality.* Oxford, England: Oxford University Press.

Murray, H. A. (1943). *Thematic apperception test.* Cambridge, MA: Harvard University Press.

Ollendick, T. H., Finch, A. J., & Ginn, F. W. (1974). Comparison of Peabody, Leiter, WISC, and academic achievement scores among emotionally disturbed children. *Journal of Abnormal Child Psychology, 2*(1), 47–51.

Ouellette, J. A., & Wood, W. (1998). Habit and intention in everyday life: The multiple processes by which past behavior predicts future behavior. *Psychological Bulletin, 124*(1), 54–74.

Polanyi, M. (1966). The logic of tacit inference. *Philosophy, 41*(155), 1–18.

Rohde, A. R. (1946). Explorations in personality by the sentence completion method. *Journal of Applied Psychology, 30*(2), 169–181.

Rotter, J. B., Rafferty, J. E., & Schachtitz, E. (1949). Validation of the rotter incomplete sentences blank for college screening. *Journal of Consulting Psychology, 13*(5), 348–356.

Rugg, M. D., Mark, R. E., Walla, P., Schloerscheidt, A. M., Birch, C. S., & Allan, K. (1998). Dissociation of the neural correlates of implicit and explicit memory. *Nature, 392*(6676), 595.

Ruhland, D., Gold, M., & Feld, S. (1978). Role problems and the relationship of achievement motivation to scholastic performance. *Journal of Educational Psychology, 70*(6), 950–959.

Schacter, D. L. (1987). Implicit memory: History and current status. *Journal of Experimental Psychology: Learning, Memory, and Cognition, 13*(3), 501–518.

Sergent, K., & Stajković, A. D. (2018). Prime and prejudice. *Applied Psychology, 0*(0), 1–58.

Shantz, A., & Latham, G. P. (2009). An exploratory field experiment of the effect of subconscious and conscious goals on employee performance. *Organizational Behavior and Human Decision Processes, 109*, 9–17.

Shiffrin, R. M., & Dumais, S. T. (1981). The development of automatism. *Cognitive Skills and Their Acquisition*, 111–140.

Stajković, A. D., Bandura, A., Locke, E. A., Lee, D., & Sergent, K. (2018). Test of three conceptual models of influence of the big five personality traits and self-efficacy on academic performance: A meta-analytic path-analysis. *Personality and Individual Differences, 120*, 238–245.

Stajković, A. D., Locke, E. A., & Blair, E. S. (2006). A first examination of the relationships between primed subconscious goals, assigned conscious goals, and task performance. *Journal of Applied Psychology, 91*, 1172–1180.

Tallis, F. R. Hidden Minds: A History of the Unconscious. New York, NY: Arcade Publishing.

Tversky, A., & Kahneman, D. (1974). Judgment under uncertainty: Heuristics and biases. *Science, 185*(4157), 1124–1131.

Westen, D. (1998). The scientific legacy of Sigmund Freud: Toward a psycho dynamically informed psychological science. *Psychological Bulletin, 124*, 334–371.

Wood, W., Quinn, J. M., & Kashy, D. A. (2002). Habits in everyday life: Thought, emotion, and action. *Journal of Personality and Social Psychology, 83*(6), 1281–1297.

4 Four Conceptual Models of Goal Priming

We next discuss formation of goals in the subconscious and their priming into automatic behaviors. Four conceptual models of goal priming are introduced: the auto-motive, goal contagion, means-goal, or "bottom up," and a model in which a history of reinforcement creates associations between goals, behaviors, and reinforcers from the environment.

The Auto-Motive Model

How are subconscious goals formed? Bargh's (1990) theory of goal automaticity, called the auto-motive model, addressed the origin of subconscious goal-behavior associations. Bargh (1990) explained that as people pursue goals in similar environments, they gradually encode an association between the cues in the environment and the goal. As people strive for the same goal under similar circumstances, links among the environmental cue, the goal, and the associated behaviors become automatic and get stored in the subconscious. When a stored cue from an environment is encountered, it primes a mental representation of the related goal. Once primed, the goal representation triggers associated behaviors. This process, from an environmental cue-to-goal and then from goal-to-behavior, unfolds automatically, without conscious assistance and awareness.

For example, consider a CEO who chronically pursues a competition goal in the boardroom. Subsequently, an environmental cue (e.g., boardroom table) primes the competition goal, which activates competitive or even aggressive behaviors in the CEO without him/her recognizing that s/he is pursuing a competition goal. As a personal illustration, Alex is from Serbia, and Serbian is his native language. Both Cyrillic and Latin (English) alphabets are interchangeably used in Serbia, and children are taught both concurrently. When Alex visits Serbia he reads his favorite local newspaper (*Politika*) even though the print is in Cyrillic (Политика). One day an American colleague asked him, in surprise, "You can read that?" Alex's answer was not only "Sure, why not?" but, upon self-reflection, he realized he mentally switches between the alphabets automatically. There is no conscious prompt to switch or guidance on how to switch, it just unfolds automatically without conscious attention or awareness. The Cyrillic alphabet does not reside in Alex's conscious perpetually; it is stored in his subconscious, and he accesses it automatically as needed. This type of cognitive automation resembles that used for conversing in different languages, especially when switching between tongues is needed in real time.

Goal Contagion Model

People deduce intentions of others pursuant to observed actions (Aarts, Gollwitzer, & Hassin, 2004). Because humans are social creatures, understanding the cause of a person's behavior provides insight into his or her intentions. Consider a colleague of the opposite sex who is being overly nice to you. Maybe s/he is affable? Maybe s/he wants a favor? Maybe s/he is flirting? Identifying a behavior is informative, but ascertaining the goal behind the behavior is more illuminating (Hassin, Bargh, & Uleman, 2002). Inferred goals are important because they signal diverse motives with varying responses and consequences. Generally, people automatically back-fit goals to other people's behaviors, as described by Hassin et al. (2002, p. 515):

> Inferring causal relations . . . is one of the most important tasks the cognitive system has to perform. Moreover, in a dynamic world, full of shifting conditions and sudden surprises, inferring causes is a task that the cognitive system has to perform frequently and swiftly.

Automatic goal inference is called *goal contagion* and is defined as "the automatic adoption and pursuit of a goal that others are perceived to strive for" (Aarts et al., 2004, p. 24). Observing, conversing, or corresponding with others can prime inferred goals. To illustrate, consider the following scenario used in an experiment by Aarts et al. (2004, p. 37):

> Bas is meeting a former college friend called Natasha while having a beer at his favorite pub. They are having a chat, and Bas tells her about his new job. The atmosphere in the pub is great, and a lot of people have been showing up. At the end of the evening Bas walks Natasha home. When they arrive at her home, he asks her, "May I come in?"

After reading this passage, men in this experiment were more likely to give feedback to a female experimenter than men who read a goal-neutral passage. This is because primed participants automatically adopted the inferred goal of Bas (e.g., a hookup) and behaved accordingly in the next, unrelated scenario (e.g., help the female confederate). Yet, they were unaware they had adopted the goal, and they had no knowledge they were acting in pursuit of the goal. When this experiment was repeated with a male experimenter, the men who read this passage were no more likely to help him compared with those in the control group.

People sometimes communicate goals explicitly to ensure nothing is "lost in translation." More often, though, in naturally occurring social encounters goals are neither openly nor clearly conveyed. Reasons include hedging bets to avoid embarrassment if the intent is unwelcome, to conceal unethical goals, or to keep the "cards close to the vest." Because people learn not to ask about underlying goals or because they question the sincerity of response, they develop their own inferences by automatically back-fitting action-to-goal conclusions, for better or worse. Our cognitive system attaches a perceptual "causal goal tag" to actions when objective goals are unknown. This logic aligns with a line often heard in political circles: "Get on top of the message immediately or others will frame it for you."

Automatic inference allows for adaptive responses in direct interactions, as well as for adjusting flexibly to social surroundings (Tomasello, Kruger, & Ratner, 1993). For this reason, people can "catch a goal" by observing or interacting with others. Unlike mimicry, the inferred goal will not invariably lead to automatically executing the same behavior. Instead, people act automatically in a manner consistent with behaviors they encoded in memory associated with the inferred goal. In this way, the inferred goal behind other's behavior influences our own response. This illustrates one reason why goals "are everywhere" whether we recognize it or not and why they enrich any given social space with a variety of behavioral responses.

The probability of goal contagion transpiring is less tied to situational features, as in the auto-motive model, and is more related to the automated tendency to encode certain actions as related to certain goals and the acceptability of the goal (Uleman, 1999). For example, a third of male participants in the Aarts et al. (2004, p. 37) study read the following passage (the italics part is different from the similar example provided above):

> Bas is meeting a former college friend called Natasha while having a beer at his favorite pub. They are having a chat, and *Bas tells her about the upcoming birth of his child*. The atmosphere in the pub is great, and a lot of people have been showing up. At the end of the evening Bas walks Natasha home. When they arrive at her home, he asks her, "May I come in?"

Compared to the control group, there was no evidence of goal contagion for participants who read this passage. Comparing these results with the previous, the authors concluded that goal contagion is more likely to affect behavior when the inferred goal is personally desirable, which adds another layer of variation to goal pursuits.

At times, people can certainly consciously debate inferred goals. But, more often consciousness is uninvolved and automation draws the conclusions. For example, Hassin et al. (2002) had participants read this sentence, "Marci solved the mystery half way through the book." People automatically inferred an achievement goal. Markedly, when participants had to memorize the passage, they still automatically inferred the goal. During the debriefing, all participants responded that they were unaware of this goal inference.

Goal contagion is a mechanism facilitative of adaptive self-regulation if it points to correct and productive associations and if its automaticity prevents unnecessary attention involvement; in this case, the evolutionary purpose of cognitive automation is achieved. For instance, a new employee who observes a diligent co-worker striving to achieve an efficiency goal could associate the implied goal (e.g., efficiency), the observed action (e.g., diligence), and the cue (e.g., co-worker). When the employee interacts with this colleague, the interaction primes the efficiency goal. Reversing the correlates, though, many faux pas occur because of an automatic misperception of intentions behind actions. For example, a co-worker might automatically infer a colleague's goal is to gain favors if s/he arrives early to a meeting. Yet, another co-worker could infer that colleague is conscientious. Different goal inferences cause different reactions, causing people to treat the target person differently for the same behavior, and consciousness has nothing to do with this variance.

We believe organizations can use goal contagion to promote desired behaviors. For example, goals related to precision in medicine are frequently inferred by new residents. Priming precision could improve outcomes beyond assigning precision goals. Similarly, patient satisfaction is a useful goal in health care. Doctors are often assigned this goal, but priming it could lead to even higher satisfaction. Relatedly, priming goals has increased hand hygiene compliance in clinical and hospital environments (King et al., 2016). These studies primed hygiene goals by introducing a "clean" citrus smell with ScentAir aroma dispensers and by placing a visual prime (e.g., a photograph of eyes) above hand sanitizer dispensers. Both types of primes were effective at increasing hand hygiene (less transferred infections) outcomes. Another candidate for contagion is safety goals, for example, in organizations with exposure to toxins and/or maneuvers of heavy machinery.

Automatic contagion does not only apply to goals. Sergent and Stajković (2018) published a paper on priming subconscious prejudice. In it, they provided many examples of automated contagion related to work discrimination. For instance, if a minority person complains at work, colleagues view her/him as too sensitive (not for Whites); if a Black person pulls out a wallet in an ambiguous situation, most people perceive it as a gun (not for Whites); if a White person does something good, more often it gets attributed to internal factors such as ability and effort. If a minority person does the same good thing, people more often attribute the success to external factors such as luck. In contrast, when Whites make a mistake, people attribute it to external influences, such as poor luck. When Blacks make the same mistake, it is attributed to low ability and effort.

Means-Goal, or "Bottom-Up" Priming, Model

How can students improve their grades? By studying. How can employees earn more money? By getting a promotion. How can you meet more people at work? By networking. These links are established means-goal associations, e.g., studying–grades, promotion–money, networking–meeting others. In contrast to the auto-motive model, the links in the means-goal priming model are not built only on personal experienced. Instead, these links can be formed by reasonably agreed upon norms in one's social environment; therefore, means-related cues can prime associated goals they are perceived to serve.

This is because goals reside in memory and are nested within knowledge structures connected by functional links. In this view, goals exist within a cognitive system characterized by connections among lower-order activities (i.e., means) and the goals they assist (Kruglanksi et al., 2002). Means encompass "any activity, event, or circumstance perceived as likely to contribute to the attainment of a goal" (Shah & Kruglanski, 2003, p. 1109). This includes behavioral strategies to improve (e.g., exercise to get healthy) and cognitive means that increase likelihood of success (e.g., self-efficacy or confidence leading to initiating and sustaining goal striving). In means-goal priming, primed means bring to mind goals they relate to, automatically initiating behavior that had been associated with the goal. This sequence of events is also known as "bottom-up" priming (Shah & Kruglanski, 2003). The stronger the functional connection between a means and a goal, the greater the likelihood that means will prime the goal (Bayer, Achtziger, Gollwitzer, & Moskowitz, 2009). Consider, for example, the following statements:

1.   Edwin puts forth long hours at work.
2.   As she sits down to write, Alexa repeats to herself "I can do it."
3.   Sheldon spent all night preparing for tomorrow's board meeting.

In each of these examples, the goal was not stated. The sentence only described the means to achieve a goal (long hours, self-efficacy, preparation). Nonetheless, the goal served by these means probably came to mind when you first read the sentence. Edwin puts forth long hours to make more money. Alexa needs a confidence boost as she finalizes her first book. Sheldon prepares to impress the board of directors tomorrow. Even if you have no prior experience presenting to the board, the means

Table 4.1 Examples of Means-Goal Links

Means	Goal
Business attire	Be Professional
Eloquence	Make a Good Impression
Money	Be Self-Sufficient
Practice	Obtain Perfection
Wine	Truth*
Exercise	Good Health
Food	Comfort
Long hours	Earn a Promotion
Schmoozing	Obtain Perks
Confidence	Achievement
Study	Get Good Grades
Alcohol	Relax
Saving money	Retire
Vacation	Rest
Pitch	Sell
Manners	Be Friendly
Professor	Act Smart

* Based on the Latin phrase *in vino veritas*, with wine comes truth, or more literally, in wine is the truth.

(preparation) can nonetheless prime an achievement goal when you read this sentence. This is because means-goal associations are formed by the knowledge or perception that something, e.g., an activity, strategy, or opportunity, facilitates a goal. This is the key difference between means-goals priming and the auto-motive model: Prior practice of a specific behavior is unnecessary in the means-goal model of goal priming—only the knowledge of means-goal connection. In Table 4.1, we list a few examples of generally recognized means-goal functional links.

Priming History of Reinforcement Associated With Goal Pursuit

Consequences of achieving or not achieving a goal may be greater or lesser for one goal than for another goal, and reinforcers may be more immediate or more distal. Hence, reinforcement of goal-directed behavior creates mental associations among goals, behavior, and the contingent reinforcers. Three of the commonly used reinforcers in OB are money, social recognition, and feedback (Stajković & Luthans, 1997, 2001, 2003).

Money

People exchange money for virtually everything they want, and money also carries semiotic meanings (Aarts & Bijleveld, 2014; Furnham &

Argyle, 1998). Ostensibly, money has been an indispensable component of human affairs since antiquity. Despite the ubiquitous presence of money in social discourse, cultural anthropology research shows people's perception of money has been anything but impervious; across cultures (Mead & Stuppy, 2014) the perception of money ranges from "the root of all evil" to "the almighty dollar." For example, in the Old Testament, King Solomon recognized the importance of money but warned people against living "life as a festival held for profit." Greek Philosopher Sophocles lamented that "nothing so evil as money ever grew to be key current among men." During the Enlightenment era, empiricists such as John Locke viewed money as instrumental, but poets and playwrights ridiculed it, as in Oscar Wilde's sarcastic avowal: "When I was young, I used to think that money was the most important thing in life; now that I am old, I know it is." In June of 2018, a search of the Google database returned 686 million hits for the phrase "articles about money," which topped even the number of hits for a search on the phrase "articles about love" (487 million).

Priming Money

Compared to the "trite" effects of real money, an interest in more thought-provoking effects of primed money emerged at the dawn of the 21st century in social psychology (Vohs, Mead, & Goode, 2006). To illustrate, take a moment to answer the following question: Which rectangle below would you choose for a new $10 and $20 bill?

Merely introducing the concept of money, such as in the above task, supposedly activates a goal to make money automatically, which leads to thoughts and behaviors associated with money. Vohs et al. (2006) stated that priming the concept of money alters cognitive and behavioral responses in two ways. One is an increase in motivation, performance, and self-sufficiency, as assessed by measures of greater autonomy (Vohs et al., 2006), uptake in endurance (Mogilner, 2010), and more self-control (Boucher & Kofos, 2012). The other is a decrease in concern for others, as assessed by measures of decline in cooperation (Pfeffer & DeVoe, 2009), empathy (Molinsky, Grant, & Margolis, 2012), and ethical behaviors (Kouchaki, Smith-Crowe, Brief, & Sousa, 2013). All things considered, this research suggests that priming money increases individual motivation and productivity, while simultaneously making people less cooperative and ethical.

Social Recognition

Social recognition can be both formal (e.g., receiving plaques awarded by a committee) or informal, such as personal attention conveyed freely through expressions of interest, approval, and appreciation of a job well done (Luthans & Stajković, 2000). People engage in behaviors that receive social recognition and they avoid behaviors that lead to disapproval from others (Stajković & Luthans, 2001). To illustrate, when the legendary comedian, Bob Hope, was asked at his 90th birthday why not retire and go fishing, he responded, "Because fish don't clap." Interest in how others' reactions influence our own pursuits has existed for well over 100 years (see Triplett, 1898). In OB, the focus has been on conferment of recognition from one party to the other, either physically or electronically. In contrast, the social psychology literature assumes that social influences extend to mental representations of others, such that an "inner audience" can automatically trigger a related goal. This is because thoughts of a person increase salience of goals socially reinforced by that person in the past (Shah, 2003a). Models of self-regulation and goal setting assume that the value of goal pursuit is, at least partially, derived from its construed importance to significant others (Heckhausen, 1977; Locke & Latham, 1990).

Fitzsimons and Bargh (2003) primed participants with mental representations of close significant others and found it activated achievement goals. Andersen, Reznik, and Manzella (1996) found people were motivated to approach others who resembled a positive significant other and avoided someone who resembled a negative other. Shah (2003a) reported that seeing the face or name of a significant other primed goals associated with that person. The greater the number of goals associated with a person, the less likely an individual invoked any one goal strongly. In a subsequent study by Shah (2003b), goal performance and persistence improved when participants were primed with the name of others who had high expectations of them compared with names of others with low expectations. Goal pursuit was enhanced if the primed significant other highly valued the goal. Extrapolating these findings to the workplace, if a supervisor provides social recognition as reinforcement for many goals, interacting with or observing the supervisor is less likely to prime any one goal. If, however, the supervisor holds high expectations and gives frequent social recognition for valued goals, exposure to his or her name and face is likely to impact positively employees' future goal pursuits.

Feedback

If associated with goal pursuit, feedback can automatically guide behavior when primed. For example, Baldwin, Carrell, and Lopez (1990) primed psychology graduate students with a scowling photograph of

Table 4.2 Work-Related Examples of Each of the Four Models of Goal Priming

Goal Priming Model	Definition	Work Examples		
Auto-motive	Goal is chronically pursued in a certain way in a given environment, and the prime-goal association turns automatic over time.	**Prime:** Manager walks over to your desk **My goal:** Impress the manager **My behavior:** Use formal business language		**Prime:** Business dinner with key customer **My goal:** Close the deal **My behavior:** Act professionally
		You learned that your boss reacts positively to business lingo. She appears impressed by it. Now, you use this language automatically every time you see her. Importantly, you don't consciously use formal language, it unfolds automatically because it formed over time.		As you see the customer approach the table, you straighten your tie, button-up your jacket, stand up, and put a smile on. During the dinner, you focus on evidence devoid of personal musings. This happens automatically due to prior experiences with customers, business dinners, and closing the deals.
Goal contagion	Automatic inference of goals based on observed actions.	**Prime:** Co-worker was commissioned beyond expectation **My inferred goal:** Focus on sales volume instead of "wasting time" on quality of customer service **My behavior:** Attention turns to sales volume		**Prime:** Boss's office door is closed **My inferred goal:** Do not bother the boss **My behavior:** Stay away, ask no questions
		Despite an assigned conscious goal for "quality of customer service," when you observe a well-compensated co-worker sell high volumes, you automatically adopt a goal to "focus on sales quantity."		During performance evaluation, my boss gives me feedback that I do not say hello nor seek guidance from him. Upon reflection, I agree, though it was not my intention and I didn't realize I was exhibiting these behaviors. When I mention the closed door, the boss replies that traffic/noise from the nearby stairwell distracts him, hence the closed office door.

Means-goal, "bottom-up"

Perception that a specific means facilitates a goal.

Prime: Government-issued poster showing Rosie the Riveter

Goal: Encourage women to join the workforce

Behavior: Women joined the workforce and helped the war effort immensely despite meager prior work participation!

Believing that you can do something helps you initiate effort, focus, and sustain persistence. Priming women with "We can do it!" increased their participation but without obtrusive debates about gender stereotypes. Their automatic reaction was "Of course, we can!" Means-goal priming worked on a large scale, rather smoothly, and virtually cost-free.

It also did not hurt that Rosie was young and cute, priming men that the influx of women to the workforce may help their dating prospects, which was yet another way of subtle means-goal priming.

History of reinforcement

Certain reinforcers lead to certain desired outcomes and the reinforcer-goal-behavior link becomes automatic over time.

Prime: Colleagues are discussing money

My goal: Make more money

My behavior: Work longer hours

You learned in life that you are reinforced for more effort, which often means long hours. Today, you walk past colleagues discussing money. Overhearing a money reference automatically primed a goal to make more money, and you worked longer than anticipated that day. Yet, you did not consciously register the conversation nor did you deliberately analyze it.

Prime: Sight of a grumpy boss

My goal: Avoid criticism

My behavior: Stress and anxiety

After receiving frequent negative feedback from your boss, you become stressed and anxious at any sign of contact with the boss. These outcomes occur automatically, even if you just saw the boss out of your peripheral vision walk by on his way to a meeting without talking to him or making any contact.

their department chair. This transferred a message of negative feedback and adversely influenced students' assessments of their research ideas. Similarly, practicing Catholics primed with a scowling picture of the Pope rated themselves more harshly than those primed with a scowling photo of an unknown other. This effect was not found for non-practicing Catholics. This implies that feedback can prime goals when it comes from a recognized and relevant party to a goal pursuit.

Summary

In this chapter, we discussed four conceptual models that explain how goals in the subconscious are formed, how goals are primed, and how cue-goal and goal-behavior associations become automatic over time. To recap, the auto-motive model holds that as people repeatedly pursue goals in the same environment, the association between contextual cues, the goal, and behavior become stored in memory. When encountered, the cue primes the goal, which triggers automatic behavior. People can vicariously learn and store goal-behavior associations through goal contagion, a process that involves observing behaviors of others and spontaneously inferring goals behind actions. The means-goal model of priming involves automatic associations created by the perception that a specific behavioral or cognitive means facilitates goal attainment. Finally, history of reinforcement associated with specific goals causes the association between the goal, behavior, and reinforcer to turn automatic. In the reinforcement model of priming, money, social recognition, and feedback can prime associated goals. Table 4.2 presents more work-related examples for each of the four conceptual models of goal priming.

References

Aarts, H., & Bijleveld, E. (2014). *The psychological science of money*. New York, NY: Springer.

Aarts, H., Gollwitzer, P. M., & Hassin, R. R. (2004). Goal contagion: Perceiving is for pursuing. *Journal of Personality and Social Psychology, 87*, 23–37.

Andersen, S. M., Reznik, I., & Manzella, L. M. (1996). Eliciting facial affect, motivation, and expectancies in transference: Significant-other representations in social relations. *Journal of Personality and Social Psychology, 71*(6), 1108–1129.

Baldwin, M. W., Carrell, S. E., & Lopez, D. F. (1990). Priming relationship schemas: My advisor and the Pope are watching me from the back of my mind. *Journal of Experimental Social Psychology, 26*(5), 435–454.

Bargh, J. A. (1990). Auto-motives: Preconscious determinants of social interaction. In E. T. Higgins & R. M. Sorrentino (Eds.), *Handbook of motivation and cognition: Foundations of social behavior* (Vol. 2, pp. 93–130). New York, NY: Guilford Press.

Baumeister, R. F., Heatherton, T. F., & Tice, D. M. (1994). *Losing control: How and why people fail at self-regulation*. San Diego, CA: Academic press.

Bayer, U. C., Achtziger, A., Gollwitzer, P. M., & Moskowitz, G. B. (2009). Responding to subliminal cues: Do if-then plans facilitate action preparation and initiation without conscious intent? *Social Cognition, 27*(2), 183–201.

Boucher, H. C., & Kofos, M. N. (2012). The idea of money counteracts ego depletion effects. *Journal of Experimental Social Psychology, 48*(4), 804–810.

Fitzsimons, G. M., & Bargh, J. A. (2003). Thinking of you: Nonconscious pursuit of interpersonal goals associated with relationship partners. *Journal of Personality and Social Psychology, 84*, 148–164.

Furnham, A., & Argyle, M. (1998). *The psychology of money.* Florence, KY: Taylor & Frances.

Hassin, R. R., Bargh, J. A., & Uleman, J. S. (2002). Spontaneous causal inferences. *Journal of Experimental Social Psychology, 38*(5), 515–522.

Heckhausen, H. (1977). Achievement motivation and its constructs: A cognitive model. *Motivation and Emotion, 1*(4), 283–329.

King, D., Vlaev, I., Everett-Thomas, R., Fitzpatrick, M., Darzi, A., & Birnbach, D. J. (2016). "Priming" hand hygiene compliance in clinical environments. *Health Psychology, 35*(1), 96.

Kouchaki, M., Smith-Crowe, K., Brief, A. P., & Sousa, C. (2013). Seeing green: Mere exposure to money triggers a business decision frame and unethical outcomes. *Organizational Behavior and Human Decision Processes, 121*(1), 53–61.

Kruglanksi, A. W., Shah, J. Y., Fishbach, A., Friedman, R., Chun, W. Y., & Sleeth-Keppler, D. (2002). A theory of goal systems. In M. P. Zanna (Ed.), *Advances in Experimental Social Psychology* (Vol. 34, pp. 331–378). San Diego, CA: Academic Press.

Locke, E. A., & Latham, G. P. (1990). *A theory of goal setting & task performance.* Englewood Cliffs, NJ: Prentice-Hall, Inc.

Luthans, F., & Stajković, A. D. (2000). Provide recognition for performance improvement. In E. Locke (Ed). *Handbook of principles of organizational behavior* (pp. 166–180). West Sussex, UK: Jon Wiley & Sons.

Mead, N. L., & Stuppy, A. (2014). Two sides of the same coin: Money can promote and hinder interpersonal processes. In *The psychological science of money* (pp. 243–262). Springer, New York, NY.

Mogilner, C. (2010). The pursuit of happiness: Time, money, and social connection. *Psychological Science, 21*(9), 1348–1354.

Molinsky, A. L., Grant, A. M., & Margolis, J. D. (2012). The bedside manner of homo economicus: How and why priming an economic schema reduces compassion. *Organizational Behavior and Human Decision Processes, 119*(1), 27–37.

Pfeffer, J., & DeVoe, S. E. (2009). Economic evaluation: The effect of money and economics on attitudes about volunteering. *Journal of Economic Psychology, 30*(3), 500–508.

Sergent, K., & Stajković, A. D. (2018). Prime and prejudice. *Applied Psychology, 0*(0), 1–58.

Shah, J. (2003a). Automatic for the people: How representations of significant others implicitly affect goal pursuit. *Journal of Personality and Social Psychology, 84*, 661–681.

Shah, J. (2003b). The motivational looking glass: How significant others implicitly affect goal appraisals. *Journal of Personality and Social Psychology, 85*, 424–439.

Shah, J. Y., & Kruglanski, A. W. (2003). When opportunity knocks: Bottom-up priming of goals by means and its effects on self-regulation. *Journal of Personality and Social Psychology, 84*, 1109–1122.

Stajković, A. D., & Luthans, F. (1997). A meta-analysis of the effects of organizational behavior modification on task performance, 1975–95. *Academy of Management Journal, 40*(5), 1122–1149.

Stajković, A. D., & Luthans, F. (2001). Differential effects of incentive motivators on work performance. *Academy of Management Journal, 44*(3), 580–590.

Stajković, A. D., & Luthans, F. (2003). Behavioral management and task performance in organizations: Conceptual background, meta-analysis, and test of alternative models. *Personnel Psychology, 56*(1), 155–194.

Tomasello, M., Kruger, A. C., & Ratner, H. H. (1993). Cultural learning. *Behavioral and Brain Sciences, 16*(3), 495–511.

Triplett, N. (1898). The dynamogenic factors in pacemaking and competition. *The American Journal of Psychology, 9*(4), 507–533.

Uleman, J. S. (1999). Spontaneous versus intentional inferences in impression formation. *Dual- Process Theories in Social Psychology*, 141–160.

Vohs, K. D., Mead, N. L., & Goode, M. R. (2006). The psychological consequences of money. *Science, 314*(5802), 1154–1156.

Part III

The Latest Empirical Research

In the next four chapters, we present a sampling of the latest research in organizational behavior guided by four models of goal priming introduced in Chapter 4. We demonstrate how primed goals are guided by the auto-motive (Chapter 5), goal contagion (Chapter 6), means-goal associations (Chapter 7), and a history of reinforcement (Chapter 8) models.

Before we present this research, we reiterate several premises guiding our choices. First, each upcoming chapter is about priming goals. We do not venerate goals, but we focus on them because of the robust scientific evidence supporting their effectiveness. Research should likewise examine ways to automate other important variables in the workplace. Second, we do not call for indiscriminate use of the subconscious to replace conscious processing. Instead, we cultivate a consideration of priming established functional goal-behavior associations to reduce reliance on conscious goals for those same behaviors. Third, we propose cognitive automation by priming goal-behavior associations because it saves attentional processing while potentially generating the same results.

Fourth, we do not have all the answers to all practical problems in organizations. The research we present only shows that priming can trigger automated goal pursuits, and that, by doing so, cognitive load can be reduced and performance enhanced. In the archetypal *if-then* matrix of organizational *problems-answers*, we show that some cells can be filled with primed goals. As research on cognitive automation advances, more *if-then* answers will be priming-based.

Consider the following cognitive automation example that guided a split-second decision to save the lives of over 200 people. On a flight to San Francisco (SFO), near the landing approach the wind shear was extraordinarily strong. Nearly every passenger was vomiting, some in bags but most all over themselves. The turbulence was frightful. Several passengers with unfastened seat belts flew up and hit the ceiling as the plane approached landing. Terror was painted on the flight attendants' faces. The plane finally touched down. As a huge sigh of relief was permeating the cabin, the plane bounced and was back in the air. The next 15 minutes were a roller-coaster ride. As people prayed for their lives, the plane finally landed, and a wave of calm imbued the cabin. The captain came on over the intercom. Almost gleefully, he told us, "You were lucky today, you had a Navy pilot, ha! We had bad wind shear, but I've handled these situations on the Carrier. I had to bounce back into the air many times. I managed to land this baby in San Jose. Piece of cake, fun doin' some real flyin'!"

Cognitive automation of goal-behavior associations that were cemented in the past kicked in automatically and immediately as the situation triggered the goal to safely land the plane. This pilot had only a split second between the plane making the first contact with the ground during the bounce to decide to abort the landing or let the plane come down from the bounce. If he had not aborted the landing immediately, the plane likely would have tipped over or broke apart, as planes are not designed to bounce off the ground.

The more important/perilous/in-the-now decisions a person faces, the more important automatic goal-directed behaviors become. Consciousness is just too capricious.

5 Organizational Behavior Research on Priming Goals Guided by the Auto-Motive Model
Evidence From 15 Studies

In Game 6 of the 1998 NBA finals, the Chicago Bulls faced off against the Utah Jazz. With 40 seconds to go in the game, the Bulls were down by three points. Michael Jordan, the best basketball player of all time, took on Byron Russell. Jordan made a quick layup, cutting the deficit to one point. Utah had possession with seconds left on the clock. Jordan knocked the ball loose and flew down the court with six seconds left in the game. Seemingly effortless, he made a 20-footer to secure the NBA Championship. When later interviewed on NBA TV about this winning moment, 50-year-old Michael Jordan said:

> I practice as if I'm playing the game, so when the moment comes in the game, it's not new to me. . . . That's the reason why you practice . . . so when you get to that moment you don't have to think. Instinctively things happen.

This example illustrates the auto-motive model of goal priming. As Jordan explained, practice under similar conditions in pursuit of the same goal created an association between the goal (to close the game), the cue (seconds left on the clock), and the necessary behaviors (sink the shot). When the cue was encountered, this goal-association enabled Jordan's behavior to unfold automatically and flawlessly. If Michael Jordan had to deliberate consciously what to do in that moment, time could have run out or his nerves could have crippled him under the pressure. In many sports, goal-behavior associations are referred to as muscle memory; e.g., golf swing, tennis serve return; soccer goalie jolts at penalty kicks. We know, though, that muscles cannot store memories. Memories are stored in the mind. The aim behind creating "muscle memory," then, is to form automatic associations between the cue (looking down at the tee), the goal (a perfect swing), and the behavior (swinging the club). The purpose of practice is to automate these associations, so that in the moment when it matters the conscious mind is freed from vexations and the tried-and-proven goal-behavior associations unfold effortlessly. Increasingly, cognitive automation is a prerequisite for contending, let alone winning in sports. If you believe that Brazilian "soccer poetry" beats German soccer goal-behavior automation, recall the Brazil-Germany 1–7 game at the 2018 World Cup.

We next discuss goal priming research guided by the auto-motive model. We focus on reviewing research in OB. In addition to explanatory and predictive properties, theories in OB are evaluated by their power to improve employee functioning and positively affect organizational change. OB priming research has examined outcomes through tasks that demonstrably entail levels of performance, as is critical for proper goal setting at work.

Goal Priming in OB Laboratory Experiments

Following Locke and Latham's (2004) recommendation to start examining sources of subconscious motivation, Stajković and Locke (2004) proposed goal priming as a new approach to goal research. At that time, less was known about how primed goals operate, to say nothing of their interaction with conscious goals. As Bargh (2005, p. 41) reflected:

> [W]e still know little of how these [subconscious] effects occur, how they develop, and why so much in the way of complex, higher mental processes should take place outside of conscious awareness and control.

Positive Interaction of Primed Subconscious and Conscious Goals on Performance

Stajković, Locke, and Blair (2006) set out to examine a potential synergy between conscious and subconscious goals. The authors hypothesized a positive interaction of primed subconscious and set conscious goals on task performance, where both goals focused on achievement. The theory undercurrent was the premise that "There is a constant interaction or movement between the conscious and subconscious" (Locke, 2015, p. 410). Before we proceed to theory about interactive effects of primed and set goals, we offer a primer on the meaning of an *interaction*. Because an interaction has a specific statistical interpretation, we explain what a statistical interaction is and how it applies to goals.

What Is an Interaction?

In common lexicon, an interaction is associated with positive or negative synergy, where the interactive components generate greater or smaller effects compared with the sum of their parts. For example, imagine a mom and a dad playing ten matches of chess against their kids. On average, mom wins two matches and dad wins two matches. But, when mom

and dad team up, they win six matches. Mom and dad positively interacted to increase their winning percentage. Whether they explored new
gambits or enacted more effective monitoring of the board is irrelevant.
They did something better together than they did alone. If mom and dad
did not interact, their joined winning percentage would equal the sum
of their individual wins. In that case, their individual contribution to
the "mom and dad team" was additive (i.e., win four matches together).
A negative interaction would mean they do worse together than they do
individually, i.e., they drag each other down.

This rationale pertains to varied aspects of life. At work, an employee
can feel better at a meeting if their mentor is present vs. absent, people usually deliver a more impactful presentation following thorough vs.
surface preparation, and the negative impact of being reprimanded by a
supervisor may not be as burdensome on Friday afternoons as it would be
on Monday mornings. Socially, a person can be happier in the presence
vs. absence of significant others and consuming alcohol is more tolerable
with food than without it. Other examples of colloquial interactions that
kids would readily recognize include that Oreo cookies taste better with
milk than without milk, a peanut-butter sandwich tastes better with jelly
than without jelly, and enjoyment from watching a movie while eating
salted, buttery popcorn is beyond the pleasure derived from their discrete
tastes and consumption.

Statistically, a two-way interaction means that A affects C differently
for the levels of B. Let's assume that A is the first medication, B is the
second medication, and C is the dependent variable—e.g., improvement
in patient health shown by ascending numbers. Each A and B medication
is manipulated at two levels: administered or not. This scenario can be
quantified by simple arithmetic as follows:

	B, not administered	B, administered
A, not administered	3	5 = +2 (B alone)
A, administered	5	7 = +2 (adding B to A)
	+2 (A alone)	+2 (adding A to B)

The variance in health outcome when medication A is administered alone
(+2) is the same regardless of whether medication B was administered
or not (+2 adding B to A). Similarly, the effects of medication B are the
same regardless if medication A was administered or not (+2). Thus, we
conclude that medication A and B have separate "main effects" on the
dependent variable. To quantify main effects, we use the change in aver-
ages (i.e., marginal means). The main effect of medication A is calculated
by subtracting the average health when A is administered ((5 +7) / 2)) from
the average health when it is not administered ((3 + 5) / 2), i.e., (6 – 4 = 2).
Therefore, the effects of each medication on health are the same regardless
of the other medication. We conclude medication effects are additive.

In the prior example, both medications A and B have the same strength (+2). We can rewrite the example such that medication A has a stronger main effect than medication B, and vice versa. But, an interaction effect between the two medications is still not present:

	B, not administered	B, administered
A, not administered	3	4 = +1 (B alone)
A, administered	5	6 = +1 (adding B to A)
	+2 (A alone)	+2 (adding A to B)

As can be gleaned by the above numbers, medication A produces a benefit of (+2) regardless of whether it is administered alone or added to medication B. Likewise, medication B produces a benefit of (+1_ regardless of whether it is administered alone or added to medication A.

Now, consider the following scenario where medications A and B do interact.

	B, not administered	B, administered
A, not administered	2	5 = +3 (B alone)
A, administered	8	7 = -1 (adding B to A)
	+6 (A alone)	+2 (adding A to B)

Based on these numbers, adding medication A to medication B is helpful (+2), but adding medication B to medication A is harmful (-1). Therefore, we can conclude that the two medications together produce an interaction effect that depends on each other's levels. Unlike the prior examples where each medication brought its consistent benefit regardless of the other medication, in this example, the total net benefit depends on how the two medications interact together. Further differentiation is made based on the statistical significance of the interaction. If the interaction is significant, then the differences occurred beyond chance at some level (typically 95%) of Type I error rate (false positive).

What Is an Interaction Between Primed Subconscious and Conscious Goals?

People pursue both conscious and primed goals, but what psychological mechanisms underlie their simultaneous operations? How are cognitive resources allocated to the two goals? Are there cognitive trade-offs, and if so, do they come at a benefit or a cost? How do we manage these processes if "people do not and cannot have direct access to acts of causal intention" all the time (Bargh, 2005, p. 42)? There is no integrated theory about an interaction between primed and conscious goals (Dijksterhuis, 2014), though many scholars have made suggestive statements. For example, in his recent book on priming, Bargh (2017) seems to embrace the interplay between the conscious and the subconscious:

> Once we acquire the right frame for understanding the interplay of conscious and unconscious operations of our mind, new opportunities open up to us.
>
> (pp. 3–4)

Shortly thereafter, Bargh further argued:

> Only when we actively integrate both the conscious and unconscious workings of the mind, and listen to and make good use of both, can we avoid the pitfalls of being blind to half the mind.
>
> (p. 17)

In yet another attempt at convincing a skeptical reader, Bargh turned up the heat:

> We aren't mindless automatons at the total mercy of incoming stimuli that send us marching through life like windup dolls, but neither are we all-seeing masters of ourselves who control our each and every thought and action. Rather, there is a constant interplay between the conscious and unconscious operations of our brain.
>
> (pp. 33–34)

Focused theory development is needed to specify how cognitive resources are allocated when goal pursuit involves guidance of both a primed and a conscious goal. We make an initial attempt at cracking this theory nut by integrating points made previously and contributing our conceptual perspective.

Research has shown that both primed and conscious goals affect behaviors. For a theory of cognitive automation to overlook an interaction between primed and conscious goals would be to assume that the two goals are either inconsequential to each other or that one goal overrides the other. If they operate independently with no coordination, then what happens when these goals compete for cognitive resources?

First, adaptive self-regulation allocates the exact amount of cognitive resources needed for a calibrated activity level; no more and no less (Kukla, 1972). The mind gauges this resource allocation depending on the intensity and breadth of activities involved. This process does not presume independent processing of the same information, causing cognitive waste through redundancy. It is unclear why humans would have two goal systems that operate fully independently and double-up on operations. It is more logical that conscious and subconscious regulation of action switch as needed for most adaptive functioning, where goals at both levels "talk to each other" to coordinate resource allocation.

Second, if conscious and primed goals do not interact, then which one prevails? If they are of equal strength but are not communicating, would that distort behavior? For example, if your conscious goal was to drive to Walgreens to buy a notepad, but you pass a Target billboard on your drive, what will happen? Will the Target prime paralyze you and stop the car because of equal opposing forces? If the two levels of goals are unequal, which one takes over and when? Several scholars believe that the more sophisticated motive will prevail. This would be the conscious goal as it allows for mental functioning in its most recent evolutionary form. In this view, conscious goals will override primed subconscious goals. Others, however, assert a more nuanced position (e.g., Bargh, 2017, quotes earlier).

Third, a more contextualized argument can be construed for organizations. Rarely are employees devoid of conscious goals at work. By the same token, organizational context is rich with embedded cues that can prime goals (Kay, Wheeler, Bargh, & Ross, 2004). Accordingly, we deduce that rarely are conscious goals pursued in absence of primed goals at work. Hence, understanding self-regulation by goals is theoretically more perplexing than traditionally assumed. A uni-deterministic view of goals lacks theory gradation and paints an incomplete portrait of the interplay between conscious and primed goals in the mind. As Bargh, Gollwitzer, Lee-Chai, Barndollar, and Trötschel (2001, p. 1025) stated:

> In goal pursuit that is linked to the here and now through the automatic activation of internal goal representations, the cause of the resultant behavior is inherently interactional—not caused by either situation or person in isolation, but by their combination.

If a goal to achieve is primed and a goal to achieve is set, the two goals should generate better outcomes than either goal alone. Otherwise, conscious goals are irrelevant to primed goals even when aimed at the same outcome, and vice versa. We illuminate a flaw in this argument with a simple example. Imagine driving to work with the conscious goal to arrive on time. You pass a billboard picturing a bear. Do you veer off to the zoo? Hopefully not. If you continue to work without the detour, your conscious goal overrode the primed goal. As Baumeister, Heatherton, and Tice (1994) noted in their book *Losing Control*, a critical purpose of attentional resources is "conscious override" of subconscious impulses.

Now consider a similar example. You are driving to work with the goal to arrive on time. But, this time you see a pulled-over car and a woman is struggling to fix a flat while a baby cries in the backseat. Do you veer off course to help out? The answer is not as apparent as the prior example. In this scenario, the primed goal to help can more readily override the conscious goal to arrive to work on time because altruism is more deeply seated in the human psyche compared with going to the zoo on a whim instead of to work.

Thus, conscious and primed goals are not irrelevant to one another, and one does not always override the other. Instead, they interact as needed to guide human behavior adaptively. Switching regulation by goals from conscious to automatic control when appropriate is an adaptive way of saving scarce attentional resources at work. To benefit from cognitive automation in organizations, we need to understand which primed goals are effective, which are ineffective, and how much power they have when juxtaposed with conscious goals. Our review of the goal priming research literature shows many empirical findings pertaining to interactions between conscious and primed goals (see Table 5.1).

Returning to the Stajković et al. (2006) study, these authors hypothesized a positive interaction of conscious and primed goals when both goals aimed at achievement. The data supported the hypothesis. Priming an achievement goal augmented performance when combined with assigning a difficult and a do best achievement goal. The cognitive processes through which the goals interacted were not tested, but Stajković et al. (2006) proposed four mechanisms.

First, Stajković and colleagues theorized that motivation generated by both conscious and primed goals could be greater than motivation generated by one goal. Higher levels of motivation lead to higher performance. Shantz and Latham (2011, p. 3) concurred by stating, "the two goals together have a greater effect on performance than either one alone." This "motivation hypothesis" was supported in a study by Stajković, Latham, Sergent, and Peterson (2018), discussed later in this chapter.

Second, conscious and primed goals could increase task focus, hence a "focus hypothesis." The subconscious stores large sums of information (Schwarz, Strack, Hilton, & Naderer,1991). By coupling a conscious goal with a primed subconscious goal, people can apprehend information more effectively if the primed goal makes a greater amount of information accessible to consciousness. Third, goal commitment could increase when a goal is primed. The "commitment hypothesis" may hold water if humans associate goals in the subconscious with previous levels of commitment for that goal. In this way, priming a goal activates its commitment "tag" that increases determination to reach the goal.

Finally, when conscious and subconscious goals are congruent, Stajković et al. (2006) proposed that the primed goal frees up attentional resources, hence the "attentional resource hypothesis." After behavior is automated to operate without awareness, it no longer relies on cognitive resources (Webb & Sheeran, 2003). This explanation is consistent with the premise of *cognitive load theory*. This theory claims that as behavior is automated through repetition, working memory capacity is freed for other activities (see van Merriënboer & Sweller, 2005). From this

Table 5.1 Interaction Effects in Priming Research

Source	Interacting Variables	Interaction Explanation	Interaction Implication
Bargh, Raymond, Pryor, and Strack (1995)	Predisposition × primed power	Two-way and three-way (across two scales of predisposition). Predisposition to sexual harassment significantly interacted with primed power.	Those predisposed (top 25% in two surveys) to sexual harassment, when primed by power, were inclined to sexually harass, but those in the bottom 75% were not. Power does not corrupt everyone when it comes to sexual harassment.
Chartrand and Bargh (1996)	Honesty × primed impressions goal	Two-way. Honest behaviors differed depending on whether an impression formation goal was primed. Three-way. Honest behaviors differed depending on whether an impression formation goal was primed and on personality traits. Three-way. Honest behaviors differed depending on whether an impression formation goal was primed and when it was primed (trial).	Though many consciously strive to be honest, the related behaviors depend on whether social information processing goals are primed. This two-way interaction is further informed by several personality traits and by time passing.
Aarts and Dijksterhuis (2000)	Habit strength × primed travel goal	Two-way. In the absence of a primed goal, response latencies did not differ between people of high/low habit strength; but when a travel goal was primed in people with habitual travel behaviors, responses were significantly faster than those who were not primed.	Not all people respond in the same way to primed goals. Those with stronger habits are more likely to positively respond to primed goals that are consistent with their habits.

Bargh et al. (2001)	Task type × primed performance goal	Two-way. A primed performance goal significantly improved behavior on a performance task, but not on an impression-formation task. Three-way. Priming effects on both tasks were equally strong at no delay, but primed achievement-impressions became less extreme over time.	Primed goals work best on performance tasks and do not dissipate in strength over time, whereas primed perceptions impact judgement of others, but only in the short term.
Chen, Lee-Chai, and Bargh (2001)	Relationship orientation × primed power goal	Two-way. People with lower scores on Mach IV and SDO scales (i.e., communal) pursued social-responsibility goals after being exposed to power words; people who scored higher (i.e., exchangers) pursued self-interest goals after the same exposure.	Those predisposed to more communal vs. self-interested tendencies, when primed by power, were inclined to pursue social goals, but those predisposed to self-interest were not. Power does not corrupt everyone when it comes to cooperation versus competition.
Shah and Kruglanski (2002)	Goal relation × primed distraction goal	Two-way. The negative effect of a primed distraction (i.e., alternative) goal on performance and persistence was significantly greater when the between the focal and distraction goal were perceived as unrelated as to compared to related. Three-way. When the distraction and focal goal were perceived as unrelated, priming the distraction goal dampened positive reactions to feedback regarding progress toward the focal goal. When the goals were perceived as related, the primed goal enhanced positive mood in response to process feedback.	Incongruent (i.e., distraction goals), when primed, do not always undermine behavior on the focal task. Instead, it depends on how people perceive the relatedness between the focal and distraction goals.

(Continued)

Table 5.1 (Continued)

Source	Interacting Variables	Interaction Explanation	Interaction Implication
Fitzsimons and Bargh (2003)	Gender × interpersonal goal Conscious goal × subconscious goal	Two-way (Study 1). Men were more willing to help in the friend-priming condition than were women, and men were less willing to help in the coworker-priming condition than were women. Two-way (Study 3). Participants with a conscious goal of understanding behavior and a primed friend goal were more motivated to find underlying causes of behavior than were all other participants. Two-way (Study 4a). Participants with a conscious goal to make their mother proud and a congruent primed goal did better than all other participants on a cognitive performance task.	Men are more likely to automatically help others when exposed to personal social goals versus professional goals. When conscious and primed goals are aimed at the same outcome, behaviors related to the goal are likely to be better than those guided by either goal alone.
Smeesters, Warlop, Van Avermaet, Corneille, and Yzerbyt (2003)	Social value orientation × primed morality or power goal	Three-way. In people with low consistency in social value orientation, pro-social orientation leads to more cooperation than pro-self when no primed goal is present, but not when a morality or power goal is primed. In people with high consistency, pro-socials cooperated more than pro-selves with no primed goal, but not under a morality primed goal. Two-way. Pro-socials have higher expectations of a partners' cooperation than pro-self with no primed goal, but not when a morality/power goal is primed.	Although social value orientation affects cooperation versus competition, priming people with morality or power goals can negate the conscious effects of orientation. This is likely because it heightens the trade-offs even for those that have a pro-self orientation.

Study	Interaction	Findings	Implication
Fishbach, Friedman, and Kruglanski (2003)	Temptation goal × primed relevant goal	Two-way. Participants were faster to recognize goal-related words when primed with a relevant versus irrelevant goal. This relationship did not hold when the target word was a temptation word. Three-way. The more important that the goal of weight watching was, the faster successful (but not unsuccessful) self-regulators were to recognize diet words following primed food goals.	People who are more successful self-regulators are more likely to adhere to an important conscious goal when a temptation goal is primed.
Sheeran, Webb and Gollwitzer (2005)	Implementation intentions × speed primed goal	Two-way. When both implementation intentions and speed prime goal were present, speed of performance was the highest, but when there was no primed goal, implementation intentions had no effect on speed of performance.	Conscious intentions to implement goals are not always effective. Combining them with a congruent primed goal increases performance.
Sheeran, Aarts, Custers, Rivis, Webb, and Cooke (2005)	Drinking habit × primed socializing goal	Two-way. When strong drinking habits were combined with primed social goals, participants responded faster to drinking-related words.	Conscious habits combined with primed goals that are congruent with the habit heightened activation of the habit beyond either one alone.
Fishbach, Dhar, and Zhang (2006)	Subgoal × primed goal	Two-way. In the absence of a superordinate goal, completing an initial subgoal resulted in lower interest in pursuing another subgoal. However, when the superordinate goal was primed, completing an initial subgoal increased interest in pursuing another subgoal toward the same goal.	Priming a related subgoal can increase interest in the focal goal after one goal has already been completed. Thus, priming related goals helps keep people on track toward their bigger-picture goals.

(Continued)

Table 5.1 (Continued)

Source	Interacting Variables	Interaction Explanation	Interaction Implication
		Two-way. In the absence of a fitness prime goal, comparison to a low standard elicited lower interest in goal attainment (eating healthy). But, when a fitness goal was primed, comparison to a low standard increased interest in healthy eating.	
Custers and Aarts (2007)	Goal valence × primed socializing goal	Two-way. Effort increased significantly when positive affective goal valence was high and a socializing goal was primed, but this effect was absent when affective goal valence was low.	A more positive goal valence corresponds with increased effort to attain the goal state, but only when a congruent goal is primed.
Aarts, Custers, and Marien (2009)	Time lag × primed self-agency goal	Two-way. In a short time lag condition, the primed goal led to higher conscious agency ratings, but it had no effect in a long time lag condition.	Priming self-agency goals heightens outcome expectancy, which increases conscious feelings of self-agency in the short term, but not in the long term.
Hassin, Bargh, and Zimmerman (2009)	Environment × primed goal	Two-way. When primed with a goal, people were more flexible than when not primed, as they more successfully disengaged from their favorite location following changes in their environment.	Under certain circumstances, self-regulation dilemmas can be resolved automatically with primed goals.

Bipp and Kleingeld (2011)	Feedback ×primed achievement goal	Two-way. When no feedback about prior performance was given, priming an achievement goal enhanced performance. When negative feedback was given, though, the primed goal undermined performance compared to control.	Priming an achievement goal does always not enhance performance. Instead, if negative feedback is received, activating a primed achievement goal can undermine performance.
Marien, Hassin, Custers, and Aarts (2012)	Conscious goal × primed social goal	Two-way. Responding to a recent negative probe was more difficult for participants who had no conscious goal and were primed with a social goal. Two-way. When a primed social goal was considered highly important, people were less accurate in detecting errors compared to when the primed social goal was considered less important.	Incongruent primed goals hurt behavior more in the absence of a counter-active conscious goal. Moreover, incongruent goals seem to undermine performance more when the incongruent goal is considered important.

perspective, if the automatic system knows how to respond, it can activate behavior and carry it out without a need for conscious assistance.

Fishbach, Friedman, and Kruglanski (2003) found that under induced high cognitive load, performance *declines* were not affected by primed goals. If primed goals consumed limited cognitive resources, we would have expected performance to suffer even more when high cognitive load was combined with primed goals. Because this effect was not found, the authors concluded that primed goals can enhance performance without adding to cognitive overload. This finding supported the view of Stajković et al. (2006, p. 1174):

> [S]ubconscious priming may free up space in the conscious memory; thus, more of its capacity can be dedicated to performance, other pressing demands of the task, or both . . . Simply, the conscious mind is not limitless, and the more of it that is readily available, the better the performance.

Integrating Fishbach et al.'s (2003) findings and the attentional resource hypothesis of Stajković et al. (2006), if a conscious and primed goal are congruent, then demands on cognitive resources are reduced. This is because the conscious goal allocates resources to initiate and execute actions to attain the goal. When a congruent subconscious goal is subsequently primed, there is no need for additional allocation of cognitive resources because the activities underlying the goal are the same as those put in motion by the conscious goal. Consider the following example from the TV show *Breaking Bad*:

> A man is talking to his wife. He appears to be in trouble. His cell phone rings; he looks at the caller ID and does not answer. Shortly thereafter, he leaves and is declared missing a few days later. Police get involved with a conscious goal to investigate. Hypothetically, let us assume the conscious goal of investigation consumes 100 attentional resources. The cops meet with the distraught wife, and she mentions the husband's phone call. The cops examine records and find no call made to that number.
>
> When the evidence of no call to husband's cell was discovered, two sets of reactions ensued. The wife strongly urged the cops to "go back out there and figure this out." If the cops had followed the advice to consciously "figure this out," let us assume conscious deliberation of the conundrum would have consumed 20 mental resources. Instead, upon seeing there was no call, the answer came automatically to the cops: The husband must own a second cell phone, unknown to wife.
>
> Prior training engrained this association and it took the cops merely seconds to arrive at this conclusion when they encountered the cue. This automatic processing saved the cops 20 attentional resources that otherwise would have been spent to arrive at the same conclusion. These resources can now be redirected elsewhere.

This story exemplifies cognitive automation of some attentional processing to arrive at the same conclusion. Learning and professional practice created a goal-cognition association in memory. A cue primed the association, and the police officers reached a conclusion with little attentional involvement. The automated conclusion was correct, but that may not always be true. We do not advocate undiscerning use of primed goals. Instead, we advocate priming goals that have established, reliable, and useful cognitive and/or behavioral associations.

How, then, are goals primed in experimental research? To prime an achievement goal, Stajković et al. (2006) used two approaches, each frequently used in prior goal priming research (Bargh & Chartrand, 2000). In study 1, a word-search puzzle primed an achievement goal. To illustrate this priming technique, try completing the word-search puzzle shown in Figure 5.1.

P	M	A	L	N	A	Z	P	T	Q
S	A	G	N	I	D	L	I	U	B
T	S	H	B	W	A	J	V	R	E
R	T	D	Y	N	Q	N	Z	T	V
I	E	B	T	K	F	E	B	L	E
V	R	C	O	M	P	E	T	E	I
E	L	P	A	T	S	R	R	G	H
A	T	T	A	I	N	G	I	V	C
Q	B	S	L	J	F	W	O	E	A
R	D	E	E	C	C	U	S	Z	D

Building	Succeed	Plant
Win	Staple	Achieve
Turtle	Strive	Master
Compete	Lamp	
Green	Attain	

Figure 5.1 There are 13 words in this word-search puzzle. Words can appear with letters in a straight line either from left to right or from right to left, reading down or reading up, and diagonally reading either down or up. Please circle all the words in the puzzle. You have three minutes.

Did you notice the theme? Of the 13 words, seven related to achievement. For participants in the control group, all words were goal-neutral. After the priming task, participants listed as many uses as possible in two minutes for a wire-coat hanger. Duplicate uses, such as "to hang clothes" and "to hang pants" were counted as one use. Participants primed with achievement performed significantly better than those who received a neutral puzzle. In study 2, the authors used the scrambled sentence task to prime a goal. In the primed goal group, the authors embedded achievement-related words in the sentences. Figure 5.2 presents the scrambled sentences.

In the control group, all words were content-neutral. Figure 5.3 presents these neutral sentences. We encourage you to try to unscramble these sentences per instructions. Can you discern the differences in the underlying theme between the two groups?

Next, the authors manipulated the conscious goal to examine how goal difficulty interacted with the primed achievement goal. Specifically, they set a conscious goal at three levels: easy, do best, and difficult. Then, participants performed the brainstorming task. In the easy conscious goal group, the instructions assigned the goal of listing four uses. In the "do best" goal group, no goal was assigned; participants were told to do their best. The instructions in the difficult goal group stated the goal was to brainstorm 12 uses in two minutes (10% expectancy of success). Both priming and setting a goal improved performance. More importantly, these two goals positively interacted to affect performance. The primed goal boosted performance more when combined with a difficult and do best goal compared with an easy goal. The next day, the authors asked the participants to "recall what they did yesterday." Then, the participants performed another brainstorming task. The effects from the prior day were replicated.

What it would mean if Stajković et al. (2006) had not found an interaction? Imagine steering a sailboat on a windy day. Is it not more productive for two sailors to cooperate rather than for each to chart independently the ship's course? It is simply unclear why God/evolution would set conscious and primed goals at cross-purposes within the same mind. Rather, understanding how subconscious goals influence conscious pursuits leads to a richer understanding of how behavior unfolds at work. The findings from Stajković et al. (2006) inform us that when primed goals are in tandem with conscious goals, participants perform better than if they were only assigned or primed with a goal.

Sergent (2018) conducted a conceptual replication and extension of Stajković et al.'s (2006) experiments to examine the positive interactive effect of conscious and primed achievement goals on performance. In addition, this study tested the "attentional resource hypothesis" to see if cognitive load mediates the effects of primed goals on performance. The study design was similar to Stajković et al. (2006), but with several modifications. First, Stajković et al. (2006) manipulated a conscious goal

For the next task, you will be provided with several word sets. Each word set contains five words. Your task is to make a grammatically correct sentence using **FOUR** of the five words in each set. In doing so:

a) You cannot change the tense of the verbs (e.g., "flew" to "fly"), and
b) The sentence must make sense without any punctuation except an end period.

<u>An example:</u>
flew   eagle   the   water   around   (set of five words)
<u>The eagle flew around.</u>   (correct **four**-word sentence)

1. was	Bob	visits	yesterday	married
2. prevail	mirror	team	will	the
3. accomplished	he	green	the	task
4. melts	water	when	butter	heated
5. get	to	compete	mountain	promoted
6. pet	soccer	the	gently	dog
7. obstacles	car	strive	against	tough
8. by	highlighter	work	thrive	they
9. wood	eating	pie	she	likes
10. despite	notebook	triumphed	she	obstacles
11. on	sleeping	turn	the	lamp
12. to	study	hard	achieve	Daisy
13. mastered	Joe	the	piano	sunshine
14. an	aspirin	Suzie	clock	took
15. wins	he	race	superficial	the
16. a	trees	fly	kite	go
17. her	enjoys	swear	success	she
18. by	sunny	money	effort	gain
19. sang	sweetly	robin	the	scratching
20. attain	import	perfection	to	try

Figure 5.2 Achievement goal priming sentence unscrambling task.

1. was	Bob	visits	yesterday	married
2. spicy	wind	likes	he	food
3. the	push	wash	well	clothes
4. melts	water	when	butter	heated
5. somewhat	type	prepared	was	I
6. pet	soccer	the	gently	dog
7. maintain	river	to	composure	try
8. a	what	worse	smile	great
9. wood	eating	pie	she	likes
10. good	likes	I	deals	he
11. on	sleeping	turn	the	lamp
12. studies	she	history	we	ancient
13. sunshine	Joe	the	guitar	plays
14. an	aspirin	Suzie	clock	took
15. always	she	race	worried	was
16. a	trees	fly	kite	go
17. her	drives	swear	car	she
18. shoes	easy	replace	old	the
19. sang	sweetly	robin	the	scratching
20. are	try	courteous	often	we

Figure 5.3 Scrambled sentences for the neutral (control) group.

at three levels (easy, do best, and difficult). In Sergent (2018), a conscious goal was manipulated at two levels (do best, difficult), as done by Shantz and Latham (2009). Second, instead of a laboratory, this study was conducted online using Qualtrics. Third, unlike Stajković et al. (2006) in which participants were students at a large Midwestern university, participants in Sergent (2018) were recruited from a general population sample. Qualtrics was responsible for recruiting, managing, and stopping data collection once the target sample size was reached.

The same task and scrambled sentences with the same words as in Stajković et al. (2006) were used to prime the achievement goal, as well as the same brainstorming task. Participants were then given the *Paas Cognitive Load Scale* to assess mental effort (Paas, van Merriënboer, & Adam, 1994). This unidimensional scale with a nine-point Likert anchor is sensitive to small differences in load, is validated and reliable, and is unobtrusive, which ensures the measurement itself does not artificially inflate cognitive load. Next, participants were given instructions for the *Stroop task*, which was used to measure mental efficiency. The instructions stated that the next screen would present the word of a color and it would either be printed in a "congruent" or an "incongruent" color to its meaning. The instructions told participants to identify quickly whether the word and color combination were congruent or incongruent. Correct identifications assessed their mental efficiency.

The findings replicated those of Stajković et al. (2006). In particular, participants in the difficult conscious goal condition listed 1.07 more uses, on average, than those in the do best goal group. Participants primed with an achievement goal listed 0.87 more uses, on average, than those in the control group. More importantly, the primed and conscious goal positively interacted; when participants were both assigned and primed with an achievement goal, a synergistic effect boosted performance by an additional 1.21 uses. Figure 5.4 illustrates this interaction. In looking at Figure 5.4, notice the far-right column in which both a difficult goal was assigned and an achievement goal was primed. If the effects were additive, we would expect to see a similar distance between the control (light grey) and subconscious goal (dark grey) bars as shown on the left. Instead, the bars on the right are separated by a much greater distance. This exemplifies the positive interaction.

In addition to replicating the Stajković et al. (2006) positive interaction, Sergent (2018) found that assigning a conscious goal increased mental effort, but priming a subconscious goal did not. Priming a subconscious goal also enhanced mental efficiency. These findings support

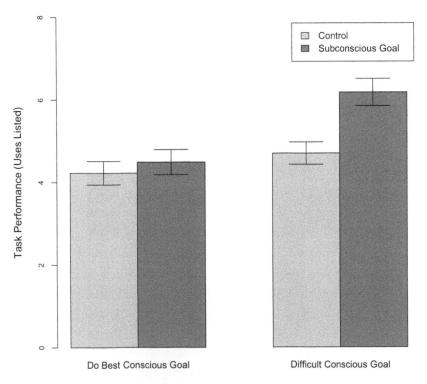

Figure 5.4 Predicted task performance means with corresponding error bars of the point estimates.

the "attentional resource" hypothesis that priming goals aids performance without increasing cognitive load. If both priming a goal and assigning a goal increased mental effort, then the data would have suggested both types of goals consume limited cognitive resources. Instead, the data showed that only the conscious goal drained resources, and, in fact, the primed goal also helped to improve efficiency of mental resource allocation. Together, these findings support the main contentions in this book—that priming goals can be used to increase performance like conscious goals without increasing cognitive load.

Negative Interaction Effect of Primed and Conscious Goals on Performance

Shortly after their 2006 publication, Stajković, Locke, and Blair (2007) posed an antithetical question: If primed and conscious goals can positively interact, can they likewise negatively interact? Said differently, if the aims of each goal are contrary to each other, will the incongruent primed goal impact how participants pursue the conscious goal?

The authors hypothesized a negative interaction of a primed goal for accuracy and a conscious goal for speed on task performance. The underlying theory premise was the foundational research on self-regulation by Carver and Scheier (1998, p. 95), who have long called for research on conflicted conscious and subconscious goals. Carver and Scheier believed goal conflict would spread attention resources too thin. The excerpt below encapsulates the conceptual foundation for the Stajković et al. (2007) study:

> An interesting question is whether multiple goals influence behavior outside of awareness more commonly than people realize. . . . There is only so much time and attention to be used. If too much has to go into one domain . . . concentration is necessarily removed from other domains. As attention is pulled away . . . progress in these domains begins to suffer.

Attempts to adaptively self-regulate can go awry. If two conscious goals are conflicted, employees can seek help. If primed and conscious goals are conflicted, however, a person is only aware of the conscious goal. The key downstream consequence is undetected goal conflict and an inability to rectify it deliberately. Because the conflict goes unnoticed, it can lead to compromised behavior inexplicable to self. By learning how primed goals may disrupt conscious goals, we can "clean up" our goal pursuits at work. In doing so, we can shrink inconsistencies between what we had in mind and what we end up doing.

To illustrate, the interference of a conflicted primed goal on a conscious goal is like an electromagnetism that automatically and imperceptibly deflects a ship's compass when it passes a mountain with ore. Subconscious goals, of course, are not electromagnetic, but this analogy exemplifies the point: self-regulation by conscious goals can guide behavior effectively, but understanding how deliberate aims can be indiscernibly undermined by primed subconscious goals offers new insights into some costly detours at work.

When conscious and primed goals are both active and incongruent, greater strains are placed on cognitive resources to self-regulate the concurrent demands. This logic is consistent with the premise presented by Marien, Custers, Hassin, and Aarts (2012, p. 412) that "unconscious and conscious goals both operate on a platform that usurps mental resources." These authors explained that priming subconscious goals automatically puts mental processes into motion. Once triggered, however, these processes need mental resources to execute goal-directed behavior. Theories of resource allocation initially viewed cognitive trade-offs as distinct disengage-engage functions (Posner & Petersen, 1990). More recent views assume competitive resource allocation (Vuilleumier, 2005).

Accordingly, contemporary self-regulation research also assumes people have limited cognitive resources, such that "attentional resource limitations characterize all deliberative cognitive functioning" (Kruglanksi et al., 2002, p. 333). This standpoint underlined early goal conflict research, showing that as people directed more cognitive resources toward one conscious goal, less resources remained for another conscious goal (Kanfer, Ackerman, Murtha, Dugdale, & Nelson, 1994; Kanfer & Kanfer, 1991). Research has evidenced trade-offs demanded by conscious goals when employees pursue multiple goals, when their goal is to work on two tasks simultaneously, when new goals differ from prior self-set goals, and when goals are assigned for different tasks.

Implications of prior research for self-regulation by primed subconscious goals across fields suggest a similarity in effects and processes of conscious and primed goals:

> [O]nce activated, the [subconscious] goals operate to guide subsequent cognition and behavior in the same way that consciously held goals do, all without the individual's awareness of the goal's guiding role.
>
> (Chartrand & Bargh, 2002, p. 15)

> [N]ot only should conscious and nonconscious goals produce the same effects, but they should also produce the same effects in the same way.
>
> (Chartrand & Bargh, 2002, p. 21)

> [N]onconsciously activated goals will cause the same attention to and processing of goal-relevant environmental information and show the

same qualities of persistence over time toward the desired end-state, and of overcoming obstacles in a way, as will consciously set goals.
(Bargh et al., 2001, p. 1015)

If resource limitations underlie self-regulation conflict by conscious goals, and if the same self-regulation processes govern conscious and primed goals, then we ought to consider cognitive trade-offs that may occur between conflicted conscious and primed goals.

Unlike a congruent primed goal, an incongruent primed goal will necessitate a division of attentional resources because activities to initiate and adaptively guide behavior differ from activities guided by the conscious goal. This disunion places greater demands on cognitive capacity, overloading the mental system and, ultimately, undermining performance.

In particular, we hypothesize an incongruent primed goal will compete for resources from the *same* pool of cognitive resources as the conscious goal. Both goals are operative and relevant to the task. We do not contend, however, that the primed goal occupies a superior position in the goal hierarchy, causing the conscious goal to be abandoned. Instead, people strive to achieve both goals, but this requires a mental compromise, which comes at a cost to performance.

This is not to say that people cannot accomplish both goals. Proofreaders can be both fast and accurate, but to successfully achieve both goals is more mentally draining. Pressure for allocation of attentional resources to incongruent goals results in less adaptive self-regulation. For example, think back to the employee who encountered a car with a flat tire on the side of the road. This appears to be a seemingly innocuous goal distraction in the morning, but his/her subconscious nonetheless picks up the altruism primed goal. The employee moves on with the day, is engrossed in work responsibilities, conscious thoughts are absorbed, and no attention is given to the morning dilemma. Nonetheless, the employee's behavior can be influenced by the primed goal. This could tilt him/her slightly in the direction of saying "yes" to something s/he would have otherwise said "no" to.

Our conceptualization of the interplay between conscious and subconscious goals is different from dual-process conceptions (e.g., Evans, 2008). Under dual-process theories, each goal draws from an independent pool of cognitive resources (Shiffrin & Schneider, 1977). For example, cruise control would rely on one engine in the car and a driver on another engine in the car and they would provide power separately. If subconscious goals operated through a second mental system, there would not be a negative effect on performance when an incongruent goal was primed. To examine this alternative hypothesis, Stajković et al. (2007) tested the effect of a primed accuracy and a set speed goal on proofreading performance. If both goals draw from the same mental pool, performance will suffer. If each goal draws from an independent mental pool, performance should be both faster and more accurate. Their findings rejected a dual-process hypothesis.

Stajković et al. (2007) defined goal conflict according to Lewin's field theory (1935, p. 123) as "a situation in which oppositely direct, simultaneous acting forces . . . work upon the individual." Like in their 2006 study, the authors primed a goal with the scrambled sentence task. This time, however, they primed one goal for accuracy and set the other for speed. The authors chose speed and accuracy as incongruent goals because of their inherent trade-offs and their ubiquitous presence in human affairs. Accuracy logarithmically relates to the speed with which a task is completed. At high speed, correct responses occur at levels no greater than chance (i.e., they are random). As people reduce speed, their accuracy increases (Wickelgren, 1977). Beersma et al. (2003) evidenced this trade-off and concluded, "most complex tasks require some degree of both speed and accuracy, but there are trade-offs that make meeting both task requirements difficult." Effectively dealing with this trade-off requires cognitive processing power to assure that inaccuracy does not exceed the pre-set tolerable industry, company, normative, or legal standard. Figure 5.5 presents the sentences used to prime a subconscious accuracy goal.

Next, the authors set a conscious goal for speed. To measure performance, Stajković et al. (2007) developed a proofreading task that described the history of Sears. They embedded word-choice, grammatical, and spelling errors throughout the text. In the *no goal* group, the instructions stated the technical requirements of the task: "circle the spelling, grammar, and word choice errors you find in the following three pages of text." In the *conscious goal* group, the instructions set a specific speed goal (pilot tested to be at the 90th percentile of difficulty) by stating: "Your goal for this task is speed. Specifically, you are to complete proofing of at least 35 lines of this text. Try to go fast." Participants were given five minutes to read the text and circle as many errors as they could find. Figure 5.6 presents the full text of this proofreading task.

The dependent variable was the number of correct errors circled. This measure represents an efficiency of proofreading performance because it includes both speed and accuracy; the more typos a participant circled, the faster they performed, but only correctly identified errors counted. The authors did not use a speed-only measure, as it would capture only the conscious goal dimension of the task. In other words, a speed-only measure would label a participant who worked quickly but made many mistakes as a "high performer." We analyzed the data with a two-way factorial ANOVA using contrast coded predictors and a model comparison approach. The benefit of this approach over traditional ANOVA is that it provides an integrated approach to statistical inference, but the underlying algebra is equivalent (Judd, McClelland, & Ryan, 2009, p. 167). Specifically, whereas traditional ANOVA focuses on population

1. was	Bob	visits	yesterday	married
2. was	mirror	always	right	she
3. around	quality	the	improved	we
4. melts	water	when	butter	heated
5. precise	required	are	butter	measurements
6. pet	soccer	the	gently	dog
7. must	car	we	be	careful
8. involved	I	planning	meticulous	it
9. wood	eating	pie	she	likes
10. correct	crown	be	you	may
11. on	sleeping	turn	the	lamp
12. he	thorough	is	try	very
13. draw	circle	perfect	a	sunshine
14. an	aspirin	Suzie	clock	took
15. me	the	details	give	spicy
16. a	trees	fly	kite	go
17. is	exam	we	error-free	this
18. the	bubbly	exact	thing	same
19. sang	sweetly	robin	the	scratching
20. clock	boiling	my	accurate	is

Figure 5.5 Scrambled sentences to prime accuracy.

1. Sears, Roebuck and Co. have been a dominant force in the retail inbustry for many years,
2. actually over a century, and has continaully shown a dominance in the way that there
3. business is run. However, in 1992 Saers suffered an extreme financial lost and was faced
4. with the posibility of a deteriorating business if changes were not make in many areas of
5. the large retrailer. Some of these changes would include an new Chief Executive Officer,
6. Arthur C. Martinez. Under his leathership Sears, Roebuck and Co. would seen an extreme
7. turnaround not only financially but also internally thorough the stors. Sears, Roebuck
8. and Co. was able to previal and once againe is starting to show dominance in the retail
9. industry, found now to be number two in the retrail industry. Sears, Roebucke, and Co.
10. has had a remarkable success, has suffered bed times, and has found successful once again.
11. Sears, Roebuck and Co. have over a century fool of history and incredible achievements.
12. In 1886, a Chicago jewlery company shipped an order of gold watches to a Minneapolise
13. jewelry store. When the jewelry store refused delivary a station agent by a name of
14. Richard Sears decided to purchase the shippment and try to sell them too other station
15. agents. This proved too be successful for Richard Sears, and in 1886, he begun a company
16. known as R.W. Sears Watch Company in Minneapolis. A year later in 1887, Sears moved
17. his new faund business in Chicago, and placed in advertisement at the newspaper for a
18. watchmaker. The ad recieved a response from a Indian man by the name of Alvah C.
19. Roebuck. Saers hired Reobuck and in 1893 the corporate name of the frim became Sears,
20. Roebuck and Co. Business tourned out to be very profitable for the company, and in the
21. 1890's the mail order industry for Sears, Roebuck and Co. begun to take of.
22. As of 1895, Sears had introduced a mail ordre catalog that consisted of 532 pages ofering
23. shoes, women's garmets, wagons, fishing tacckle, stoves, furniture, saddles, bicycles, etc.
24. that helped custumers in rural areas receive merchandise who they might not be able to
25. frind at local stores. In 1901, needing more financial support, Sears for the first time offred

Figure 5.6 Proofreading task.

26. common and prefferred stock in the open market and became publicaly owned. In 1906,
27. Sears expanded and oppened an office in the Dallas, Texas. In 1925 the openning of retail
28. stores begun, and by the end of 1927 Sears had twenty-seven stoers in operation, and only
29. one shorty year later in 1928 one hundred ninety two stores was in operation. Once again,
30. the expansion it least doubled itself and Sears in 1929 was operating thee hundred
31. nineteen stores and by 1933 four hundred were placed around the cauntry. This
32. expansion was massive and remrakable. In 1931, Sears noted the the need for car
33. insurance in an environment that was becaming engorged with this convenient firm of
34. transportation. Hence, the beginnings of Allstate Insurence Company which became a
35. fully ovned Sears subsidiary. Between the years of 1940's and 1970's Sears went though
36. many changes and expansions making at one of the leading, if not top, retail contendors.
37. One idea that Sears developped and perfected were the idea of developing the store around
38. the merchandize. What this means is thet a selling floor plan would be developed, where
39. merchandise was to be placed within the store, and than the design of a outer building
40. would be developed. Also, betwen the years of 1940's and the 1970's Saers expanded
41. north, into Canadia and also, south into Mexico. As the 1980's and 1990's roled around
42. Sears fell on hard times, but in the same breathe they worked on many aspectes of their
43. business and have successfuly started to make a strong commeback.

Figure 5.6 (Continued)

parameters with a tight connection to sampling and probability distributions, a model comparison approach focuses on the predicted model, highlighting model fit and parsimony, with a clearer link to the proportional reduction of variance (η_p^2) explained by the independent variables of interest. The following model tested the hypotheses:

$$Performance = b_0 + b_1 * Good + b_2 * Prime + b_3 * Goal * Prime$$

We centered and contrast coded goal as $-.5$ for no conscious goal and $.5$ for conscious goal. Then, we coded primed goals as $-.5$ for no primed

goal, .5 for primed goal. We were most interested in the parameter estimate for the interaction term, b_3. Using centered, contrast coded predictors allowed us to interpret b_3 as the change in performance when
participants in the conscious goal group were primed. Figure 5.7 shows
the full model results. The negative conscious × primed goal interaction
was significant, explaining 5% of the variance ($\eta_p^2 = .05$).

Next, Figure 5.8 shows the slope of the interaction, descriptive statistics, and all data points. We plotted data points on both sides of the X

Model Tested	Proofreading Performance $= b_0 + b_1$*Goal $+ b_2$*Prime $+ b_3$*Goal*Prime			

Source Table Results

Parameter Description	b_j	SE	F^*	p
b_0: Average performance, holding all variables constant.	54.63	1.78	935.66	<.001***
b_1: Average effect of conscious goal, holding primed goal constant.	7.97	3.57	4.98	.028*
b_2: Average effect of primed goal, holding conscious goal constant.	4.64	3.7	1.69	0.197
b_3: Change in the effect of conscious goal on performance when a conflicting primed goal is simultaneously present.	-16.13	7.14	5.1	.026*

Model Result	Proofreading Performance $= 54.63 + 7.97$*Goal $+ 4.64$*Prime $- 16.13$*Goal*Prime

Applying the Model to Predict Performance
Goal (-.5) = No Conscious Goal, Goal (.5) = Conscious Goal
Prime (-.5) = No Primed Goal, Prime (.5) = Primed Goal

Speed Goal, No Primed Goal	$60.33 = 54.63 + 7.97$*(.5)+ 4.64*(-.5) - 16.13*(.5)*(-.5)
No Conscious Goal, Accuracy Primed Goal	$57.00 = 54.63 + 7.97$*(-.5)+ 4.64*(.5) - 16.13*(-.5)*(.5)
Speed Goal, Accuracy Primed Goal	$56.91 = 54.63 + 7.97$*(.5)+ 4.64*(.5) - 16.13*(.5)*(.5)
No Conscious Goal, No Primed Goal	$44.29 = 54.63 + 7.97$*(-.5)+ 4.64*(-.5) - 16.13*(-.5)*(-.5)

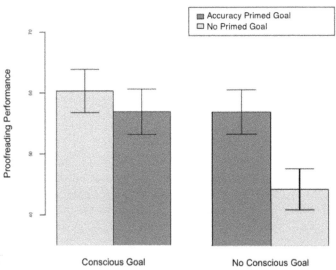

Figure 5.7 Interaction of conscious speed goal and conflicted accuracy primed goal.

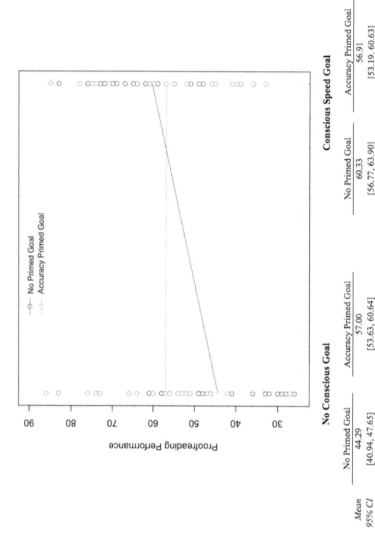

Figure 5.8 This figure plots the proofreading performance means by condition, illustrating the negative interaction between a conscious speed goal and conflicted accuracy primed goal. The circles represent data points from participants in two experimental conditions.

axis, with slopes for each independent variable to illustrate which data points are influencing performance. We tested for outliers using studentized residuals, corrected by Bonferroni equation to account for the number of tests conducted. We found no significant outliers.

Sergent (2018) conducted two more laboratory studies to examine if cognitive load underscores the negative effects of incongruent primed and conscious goals. Sergent (2018) primed participants with either speed or accuracy (or no prime), then assigned either a difficult or do best conscious goal, and finally presented participants with a logical problem-solving task. The instructions informed participants they would perform a reasoning task with a limited set of facts. Based on the information provided, participants recreated a job interview schedule and identified applicants given an offer. In the difficult conscious goal group, Sergent (2018) assigned participants a goal to answer 13 out of 14 questions correctly. Sergent (2018) conducted two versions of the experiment. Figure 5.9 shows the first version in which information cues were relatively straightforward. Figure 5.10 shows the second version in which the information cues were more disconnected, requiring abstract thinking.

Participants primed with a subconscious accuracy goal were 12.63% more accurate in their responses than participants in the control group (version 1). Participants primed with a subconscious speed goal were 9.83% less accurate in their responses compared to the control group (version 1). Participants assigned a difficult conscious goal were 7.44% more accurate in their responses than were participants assigned a do best goal (version 1). Thus, the negative effect of the incongruent primed goal

---

Your supervisor recently interviewed seven job applicants for an open position on your team—Sara, Tom, Victoria, Will, Xenia, Yuri, and Zara—each on a different one of seven consecutive days. Each applicant was interviewed exactly once. Any applicant that was hired was given the job offer during the interview.

Due to a reshuffling of office personnel, the schedule of interviews and job offers has gone missing, and your supervisor has asked you to re-create it. After speaking with several colleagues, you have deduced the following facts:

• Sara was interviewed on the last day and was not given an offer
• Will was interviewed one day before Sara
• Zara was interviewed immediately after Yuri
• Zara was the second applicant to be offered a job
• Xenia and Victoria were interviewed two and three days after Zara, respectively
• Out of Xenia and Victoria, only one received an offer and it was Victoria
• Tom was interviewed on Day 3 and was given an offer
• Exactly two applicants were given offers after Tom was interviewed

Who was interviewed on which days, and who received offers?

Figure 5.9 Sergent (2018) Version 1.

Your supervisor recently interviewed seven job applicants for an open position on your team—Sara, Tom, Victoria, Will, Xenia, Yuri, and Zara—each on a different one of seven consecutive days. Each applicant was interviewed exactly once. Any applicant that was hired was given the job offer during the interview.

Due to a reshuffling of office personnel, the schedule of interviews and job offers has gone missing, and your supervisor has asked you to re-create it. After speaking with several colleagues, you have deduced the following facts:

- Tom was interviewed on day three
- The person interviewed on day four was not offered a job
- Sara was interviewed after Will was interviewed
- Both Xenia and Victoria were interviewed after Zara was interviewed
- No applicants were given offers after Will was interviewed
- Exactly two applicants were given offers after Tom was interviewed
- Zara was the second applicant to be offered a job
- Xenia was not offered a job, but Tom was offered a job

Who was interviewed on which days, and who received offers?

Figure 5.10 Sergent (2018) Version 2.

eliminated the positive effect of the difficult conscious goal. Moreover, the congruent primed and conscious goals positively interacted to boost performance. As Sergent (2018) hypothesized, participants assigned with a difficult conscious goal exerted more mental effort, but those primed with a subconscious goal did not. This supports the hypothesis that priming subconscious goals enhances performance without consuming attentional resources.

Findings on the more complex task (version 2) were similar. Participants assigned a difficult conscious goal were 10.89% more accurate in their responses compared to those assigned a do best goal. Participants primed with a subconscious *speed* goal were 11.21% less accurate than those in the control group. Again, these results demonstrate the possibility for incongruent primed goals to offset the positive effect of conscious goals on performance. Sergent (2018) further found that mental efficiency mediated the positive effect of the primed subconscious accuracy goal on performance. This means that priming a congruent goal boosted performance by helping participants to more effectively allocate resources to maximize their efficiency on the task.

Other Moderators and Mediators of Primed Goal Effects

Building on the two laboratory studies of Stajković et al. (2006, 2007), Latham, Stajković, and Locke (2010) proposed a systematic program of research on primed goals in OB. Empirical research to date has documented the following results. Chen and Latham (2014) differentiated between primed learning and primed performance goals. The authors replicated the finding from Winters and Latham (1996) that established differential effects of consciously set performance versus consciously set learning goals on task performance. Instead of setting goals consciously, the authors primed these two types of goals. They primed the learning goal with a picture of Rodin's *The Thinker* (similar to Image 5.1) and the performance goal with a picture of an athlete crossing a finish line (similar to the Image 5.2).

The original pattern of results with conscious learning and performance goals was replicated, but the primed learning goal only improved performance when new knowledge was needed for successful completion of the task. This shows that primed learning and primed performance goals influence behavior similarly to setting these two types of goals.

Ganegoda, Latham, and Folger (2016) examined the effect of conscious and primed fairness goals on negotiation tactics and compared the effects of performance goals and behavioral goals for fairness. Priming a fairness goal resulted in identical effects to setting a fairness goal on negation tactics. Justice saliency mediated the primed goal effect and the effect of the assigned behavioral goal. These findings substantiated similarities between primed goals and conceptual predicates of goal-setting theory.

Image 5.1 Rodin's *The Thinker* to prime a learning goal.

Image 5.2 Marathon runner crossing the finish line to prime achievement.

Given the similarities between outcome effects of primed and conscious goals, research next evaluated possible mechanisms underlying the
effects. Latham, Brcic, and Steinhauer (2017) tested choice and effort,
two mediators in goal theory. In their first experiment, the prime was
similar to one of these three photos in Image 5.3:

Participants primed with the 400 lb. photo exerted more physical effort
when pressing on a digital weight scale than those primed with the other
two photos. This finding is particularly interesting because the photo

Image 5.3 Priming varying levels of goal difficulty.

showed lifting up weights and the experiment tested an effect of pressing down, indicating that the mind automatically switched the effects in the needed direction.

In their second experiment, participants primed with the 400 lb. photo self-set more difficult goals for a subsequent task than those primed with the other photos. The pattern of performance on the subsequent task indicated that priming difficult goals increased performance. Together, these findings suggest that priming difficult goals leads to higher self-set goals and better performance, another finding consistent with goal theory.

Stajković, Latham, Sergent, and Peterson (2018) conducted a laboratory experiment to test motivation as a possible mechanism of the primed goal effect. Like conscious goals, primed goals were conceptualized to have motivational properties. Up to this point, though, the only study assessing motivation was Latham and Piccolo (2012); the authors found that need for achievement was heightened after goal priming, but need for achievement was not tested as a mediator. Stajković et al. (2018) found that priming a subconscious achievement goal increased participants' motivation for the task. Motivation fully mediated the relationship between the primed goal and its performance effect.

Next, Itzchakov and Latham (2018) conducted three experiments to examine the mediating effect of feedback and self-set goals on the relationship between primed goals and performance. Findings indicated that providing feedback amplified the positive performance effect of a primed effectiveness goal. In Experiments 2 and 3, the authors asked participants to self-set a goal before the performance task. Participants primed with an effectiveness goal set a higher conscious goal than those in the control group. The self-set goal mediated the effect of a primed goal on performance when feedback was provided.

In summary, these experiments in OB support a causal relationship between a primed goal and performance. Though application is important to OB research, only five experiments on primed goals have been conducted in the field, which we describe next.

Primed Goals in OB Field Experiments

With call center employees working on a fundraising task for a university, Shantz and Latham (2009) conducted a conceptual replication of the Stajković et al. (2006) experiments. Instead of word-search matrix and scrambled sentences to prime achievement, Shantz and Latham (2009) used a photo of an athlete crossing a finish line (Image 5.2). Their field study revealed impressive effects.

Performance means reported by the authors in their Table 5.1 showed that compared to average performance of 12.27 in the no prime–do best condition, priming a goal increased performance 36.02%, difficult goal alone performed at 17.20, an increase of 40.17%, and both primed goal and difficult goal performed at 20.67, an increase in performance of 68.45%. Said differently, adding a difficult goal to a primed goal increased primed goal effectiveness by 32.43% (36.02 + 32.43 = 68.45) and adding a primed goal to a difficult goal increased conscious goal effectiveness by 28.28% (40.17 + 28.28 = 68.45).

Shantz and Latham (2011) conducted two more studies in call centers with primed and conscious goals and concluded that the two goals work better than either one alone. Latham and Piccolo (2012) replicated these effects over a week. They also added a third condition to prime a more specific goal with a photo of sales agents performing their jobs. Participants primed with the specific goal raised more money compared with those primed with the other two photos.

Next, Itzchakov and Latham (2018) conducted a field study in a customer service department in Israel. The authors manipulated the primed goal by changing employees' desktop background photos. Employees primed with an effectiveness goal received a picture of a businessman crossing a finish line, pumping his fist in the air with excitement. Those primed with an ineffectiveness goal, which is rather unique, received an image of a businessman sitting at his desk, leaning forward in frustration with his hands on his head. The control group received a photo of a tree. Employees primed with the effectiveness goal performed significantly better than they had on their previous shift. Similar to their laboratory findings, these authors found that feedback amplified the primed effectiveness goal effect on performance and led to setting more difficult goals for the future.

Each of the four field studies described used a photo to prime a goal. Although words were used effectively to prime goals in the laboratory, those lab experiments administered the words with contrived tasks, as in sentence unscrambling or word-search puzzles.

Stajković, Latham, Sergent, and Peterson (2018) conducted a fifth OB field experiment in a customer service organization to examine if a subconscious achievement goal could be primed with words embedded in typical communication in a real business organization. In particular, these authors conducted their study in a company where the CEO often sent a weekly motivational email to employees on Monday mornings. His emails generally included comments on company accomplishments and congratulatory notes to employees. Given this precedent, the authors primed an achievement goal by asking the CEO to include prime words in his email to half of the employees (see Chapter 4 for emails). The other half of the employees received an email similar in content but with no achievement words embedded in it. This manipulation captured the effects of a primed subconscious achievement goal on job performance within the existing communication channels and social dynamics of the company. It also represents the first time an actual company

CEO primed goals to improve employees' job performance without their awareness of it.

This study revealed that employees primed with an achievement goal performed 15% more effectively and 35% more efficiently than those in the control group over a five-day workweek. Both measures were automatically tracked. These findings showed the notable outcome utility of priming goals in a business organization at little to no financial cost.

Summary

Research in OB continues to show similarities in effects, mediating processes, and boundary conditions between deliberately-set and primed-subconscious goals. Ostensibly, examining the interplay of two goals operating at two levels of cognitive processing is more theoretically gripping and practically fruitful than studying their isolated effects.

The research we reviewed in this chapter suggests that when a conscious goal and a primed subconscious goal aim at the same desired end, they enhance performance beyond their independent effects. In contrast, when a conscious goal is incongruent with a primed subconscious goal, the two goals compete for mental resources from the same cognitive pool. Consequently, incongruence of the two goals increases cognitive load and impairs performance. Thus, understanding what cues in the workplace have a potential to prime subconscious goals and how they interact with conscious goals can facilitate employee performance beyond understanding the influence of each goal individually.

References

Aarts, H., Custers, R., & Marien, H. (2009). Priming and authorship ascription: When nonconscious goals turn into conscious experiences of self-agency. *Journal of personality and social Psychology, 96*(5), 967–979.

Aarts, H., & Dijksterhuis, A. (2000). Habits as knowledge structures: Automaticity in goal-directed behavior. *Journal of Personality and Social Psychology, 78*, 53–63.

Bargh, J. A. (2005). Bypassing the will: Toward demystifying the nonconscious control of social behavior. *The New Unconscious, 12*, 37–58.

Bargh, J. (2017). *Before you know it: The unconscious reasons we do what we do.* New York, NY: Simon and Schuster.

Bargh, J. A., & Chartrand, T. L. (2000). The mind in the middle. In H. T. Reis & C. M. Judd (Eds.), *Handbook of research methods in social and personality psychology* (pp. 253–285). New York, NY: Cambridge University Press.

Bargh, J. A., Gollwitzer, P. M., Lee-Chai, A., Barndollar, K., & Trötschel, R. (2001). The automated will: Nonconscious activation and pursuit of behavioral goals. *Journal of Personality and Social Psychology, 81*, 1014–1027.

Bargh, J. A., Raymond, P., Pryor, J. B., & Strack, F. (1995). Attractiveness of the underling: An automatic power → sex association and its consequences for sexual harassment and aggression. *Journal of Personality and Social Psychology, 68*(5), 768–781.

Baumeister, R. F., Heatherton, T. F., & Tice, D. M. (1994). Losing Control: How and Why People Fail at Self-Regulation. San Diego, CA: Academic Press,.

Beersma, B., Hollenbeck, J. R., Humphrey, S. E., Moon, H., Conlon, D. E., & Ilgen, D. R. (2003). Cooperation, competition, and team performance: Toward a contingency approach. *Academy of Management Journal, 46*, 572–590.

Bipp, T., & Kleingeld, A. (2011). Goal-setting in practice: The effects of personality and perceptions of the goal-setting process on job satisfaction and goal commitment. *Personnel Review, 40*(3), 306–323.

Carver, C. S., & Scheier, M. F. (1998). *On the self-regulation of behavior.* New York, NY: Cambridge University Press.

Chartrand, T. L., & Bargh, J. A. (1996). Automatic activation of impression formation and memorization goals: Nonconscious goal priming reproduces effects of explicit task instructions. *Journal of Personality and Social Psychology, 71*(3), 464–478.

Chartrand, T. L., & Bargh, J. A. (2002). Nonconscious motivations: Their activation, operation, and consequences. In A. Tesser, D. A. Stapel, & J. V. Wood (Eds.), *Self and motivation: Emerging psychological perspectives* (pp. 13–41). Washington, DC: American Psychological Association.

Chen, X., & Latham, G. P. (2014). The effect of priming learning vs. performance goals on a complex task. *Organizational Behavior and Human Decision Processes, 125*, 88–97.

Chen, S., Lee-Chai, A. Y., & Bargh, J. A. (2001). Relationship orientation as a moderator of the effects of social power. *Journal of Personality and Social Psychology, 80*(2), 173–187.

Custers, R., & Aarts, H. (2007). In search of the nonconscious sources of goal pursuit: Accessibility and positive affective valence of the goal state. *Journal of Experimental Social Psychology, 43*(2), 312–318.

Dijksterhuis, A. (2014). Welcome back theory! *Perspectives on Psychological Science, 9*(1), 72–75.

Evans, J. S. B. (2008). Dual-processing accounts of reasoning, judgment, and social cognition. *Annual Review of Psychology, 59,* 255–278.

Fishbach, A., Dhar, R., & Zhang, Y. (2006). Subgoals as substitutes or complements: The role of goal accessibility. *Journal of Personality and Social Psychology, 91*(2), 232–242.

Fishbach, A., Friedman, R. S., & Kruglanski, A. W. (2003). Leading us not into temptation: Momentary allurements elicit overriding goal activation. *Journal of Personality and Social Psychology, 84*, 296–309.

Fitzsimons, G. M., & Bargh, J. A. (2003). Thinking of you: Nonconscious pursuit of interpersonal goals associated with relationship partners. *Journal of Personality and Social Psychology, 84*(1), 148–164.

Ganegoda, D. B., Latham, G. P., & Folger, R. (2016). The effect of a consciously set and a primed goal on fair behavior. *Human Resource Management, 55,* 789–807.

Hassin, R. R., Bargh, J. A., & Zimmerman, S. (2009). Automatic and flexible: The case of nonconscious goal pursuit. *Social Cognition, 27*(1), 20–36.

Itzchakov, G., & Latham, G. P. (2018, December 12). The moderating effect of performance feedback and the mediating effect of self-set goals on the primed goal-performance relationship. *Applied Psychology, 0*(0), 1–36.

Kanfer, R., Ackerman, P. L., Murtha, T. C., Dugdale, B., & Nelson, L. (1994). Goal setting, conditions of practice, and task performance: A resource allocation perspective. *Journal of Applied Psychology, 79*, 826–835.

Kanfer, R., & Kanfer, F. H. (1991). Goals self-regulation: Applications or theory to work settings'. In M. L. Maehr & P. R. Pintrich (Eds.), *Advances in motivation and achievement* (pp. 287–326), Greenwich, CT: JAI Press.

Kay, A. C., Wheeler, S. C., Bargh, J. A., & Ross, L. (2004). Material priming: The influence of mundane physical objects on situational construal and competitive behavioral choice. *Organizational Behavior and Human Decision Processes, 95*(1), 83–96.

Kruglanksi, A. W., Shah, J. Y., Fishbach, A., Friedman, R., Chun, W. Y., & Sleeth-Keppler, D. (2002). A theory of goal systems. In M. P. Zanna (Ed.), *Advances in Experimental Social Psychology* (Vol. 34, pp. 331–378). San Diego, CA: Academic Press.

Kukla, A. (1972). Foundations of an attributional theory of performance. *Psychological Review, 79*, 454–470.

Latham, G. P., Brcic, J., & Steinhauer, A. (2017). Toward an integration of goal setting theory and the automaticity model. *Applied Psychology, 66*, 25–48.

Latham, G. P., & Piccolo, R. F. (2012). The effect of context-specific versus non-specific subconscious goals on employee performance. *Human Resource Management, 51*, 511–523.

Latham, G. P., Stajković, A. D., & Locke, E. A. (2010). The relevance and viability of subconscious goals in the workplace. *Journal of Management, 36*, 234–255.

Lewin, K. (1935). *A dynamic theory of personality*. New York, NY: McGraw-Hill.

Locke, E. A. (2015). Theory building, replication, and behavioral priming: Where do we need to go from here? *Perspectives on Psychological Science, 10*, 408–414.

Locke, E. A., & Latham, G. P. (2004). What should we do about motivation theory? Six recommendations for the twenty-first century. *Academy of Management Review, 29*, 388–403.

Marien, H., Custers, R., Hassin, R. R., & Aarts, H. (2012). Unconscious goal activation and the hijacking of the executive function. *Journal of Personality and Social Psychology, 103*, 399–415.

Paas, F. G., van Merriënboer, J. J., & Adam, J. J. (1994). Measurement of cognitive load in instructional research. *Perceptual and Motor Skills, 79*, 419–430.

Posner, M. I., & Petersen, S. E. (1990). The attention system of the human brain. *Annual Review of Neuroscience, 13*(1), 25–42.

Schwarz, N., Strack, F., Hilton, D., & Naderer, G. (1991). Base rates, representativeness, and the logic of conversation: The contextual relevance of "irrelevant" information. *Social Cognition, 9*(1), 67–84.

Sergent, K. (2018). *Positive and negative interaction effects of assigned conscious and primed subconscious goals on performance and a mediating role of cognitive load (ProQuest Dissertations)*.

Shah, J. Y., & Kruglanski, A. W. (2002). Priming against your will: How accessible alternatives affect goal pursuit. *Journal of Experimental Social Psychology, 38*(4), 368–383.

Shantz, A., & Latham, G. P. (2009). An exploratory field experiment of the effect of subconscious and conscious goals on employee performance. *Organizational Behavior and Human Decision Processes, 109*, 9–17.

Shantz, A., & Latham, G. (2011). The effect of primed goals on employee performance: Implications for human resource management. *Human Resource Management, 50*(2), 289–299.

Sheeran, P., Aarts, H., Custers, R., Rivis, A., Webb, T. L., & Cooke, R. (2005). The goal-dependent automaticity of drinking habits. *British Journal of Social Psychology, 44*(1), 47–63.

Sheeran, P., Webb, T. L., & Gollwitzer, P. M. (2005). The interplay between goal intentions and implementation intentions. *Personality and Social Psychology Bulletin, 31*(1), 87–98.

Shiffrin, R. M., & Schneider, W. (1977). Controlled and automatic human information processing: II. Perceptual learning, automatic attending and a general theory. *Psychological Review, 84*(2), 127–190.

Smeesters, D., Warlop, L., Van Avermaet, E., Corneille, O., & Yzerbyt, V. (2003). Do not prime hawks with doves: The interplay of construct activation and consistency of social value orientation on cooperative behavior. *Journal of Personality and Social Psychology, 84*(5), 972–987.

Stajković, A. D., Latham, G. P., Sergent, K., & Peterson, S. (2018). Prime and performance: Can a CEO motivate employees without their awareness? *Journal of Business and Psychology, 0*(0), 1–12.

Stajković, A. D., & Locke, E. A. (2004). Goal priming: A new approach to goal research. Master tutorial. *Society for Industrial and Organizational Psychology*. Chicago, IL.

Stajković, A. D., Locke, E. A., & Blair, E. S. (2006). A first examination of the relationships between primed subconscious goals, assigned conscious goals, and task performance. *Journal of Applied Psychology, 91*, 1172–1180.

Stajković, A. D., Locke, E. A., & Blair, E. S. (2007). *What happens to performance when conscious and subconscious goals are in conflict*. Presented at the Academy of Management, Human Resources, and Managerial and Organizational Cognition Divisions, Philadelphia, PA.

van Merriënboer, J. J., & Sweller, J. (2005). Cognitive load theory and complex learning: Recent developments and future directions. *Educational Psychology Review, 17*, 147–177.

Vuilleumier, P. (2005). How brains beware: Neural mechanisms of emotional attention. *Trends in Cognitive Sciences, 9*(12), 585–594.

Webb, T. L., & Sheeran, P. (2003). Can implementation intentions help to overcome ego-depletion? *Journal of Experimental Social Psychology, 39*, 279–286.

Wickelgren, W. A. (1977). Speed-accuracy tradeoff and information processing dynamics. *Acta Psychologica, 41*(1), 67–85.

Winters, D., & Latham, G. P. (1996). The effect of learning versus outcome goals on a simple versus a complex task. *Group & Organization Management, 21*, 236–250.

6 Organizational Behavior Research on Priming Goals Guided by the Goal Contagion Model

Star-crossed lovers, doomed by the depths of the Atlantic Ocean, found themselves aboard the RMS *Titanic* in 1912. We know the story. Soon after they share a passionate moment, with Rose wearing nothing but the *Heart of the Ocean*, an iceberg scrapes the *Titanic* and the ship begins to sink. The passionate love story ends abruptly as the couple fights to stay above the rising ocean water. In the final scene, the lovers cling to a door panel, but its buoyancy is only strong enough to keep one person afloat. Holding her hand, Jack tells Rose she will die an old woman. Slowly, Jack fades away into the murky depths of the icy Atlantic. Rose is rescued and lives to an old age, still wearing the *Heart of the Ocean*.

Millions of viewers around the world watched this ending scene and were struck with evocative emotional reactions. Why? Because humans are vulnerable to experiencing emotions, as well as complex behaviors, that they witness in others; people "catch" feelings from others around them, directly or vicariously. In extreme cases, people can exhibit physical symptoms that they observe in someone else, despite not being exposed to the same physical stimuli (i.e., toxins causing mass psychogenic illness). The relatively recent discovery of mirror neurons has provided scientific evidence that the human brain does indeed experience the emotional and cognitive states of others through contagion.

Contagion epitomizes adaptive biological, physiological, and psychological processes. At a biological level, humans have neurons that fire when watching a person perform an act. This helps our brains to understand what others are doing and to empathize with them (Wang, 2006). Professor Paul Ekman devoted his career to studying the universalism of human emotions. The cumulative body of knowledge he built suggests that expressions of seven emotions (fear, surprise, anger, disgust, contempt, sadness, happiness) transcend cultural boundaries. The expression of these basic emotions has been documented to unfold in the same manner even in the remotest corners of the globe (Ekman & Friesen, 1971).

At a physiological level, contagion is expressed through mimicry of motor acts. People tend to adopt the postures, gestures, and mannerisms of others without intent or awareness; in the literature, this is referred to as a "chameleon effect" (Chartrand & Bargh, 1999). From an evolutionary perspective, automatic mimicry has functional value. It was critical to adaptive self-regulation before the advent of language because it enabled us to signal to others when predators or prey were nearby. It also signaled to others what we thought, where mimicking someone was a good sign, unless it turned into mocking them (Lakin, Jefferis, Cheng, & Chartrand, 2003).

At a psychological level, contagion refers to automatic adoption and striving toward goals people infer others to be pursuing. That is, people automatically infer goals they think underlie the behaviors of others. In this chapter, we focus on goal contagion by describing an experimental study that showed the power of goal contagion and its behavioral and cognitive priming effects on performance of an auditing task.

Public Auditing: A Profession Between a Rock and a Hard Place

Despite multifaceted regulations from both government and professional organizations, public accounting scandals still take place. Why? Is the profit motive simply too strong for public auditors to resist ingratiating themselves with their clients? This would be consistent with what economists call rational profit-driven behavior in the marketplace. But, if auditors know they should preserve the public trust, why do they favor their clients to their own professional peril? Maybe auditing attracts people more susceptible to moral transgressions than other professions, or auditors are particularly skilled at camouflaging their vice by a goal ascribing to public virtue. These explanations, however, are doubtful considering that public auditing has long been considered the "watchdog of capitalism."

Dating back to the onset of the Industrial Revolution, when expansion of business highlighted the need for oversight mechanisms to detect financial fraud, public auditing emerged as investors increasingly relied on financial reports of corporations. Following the stock market crash of 1929, public audits became an obligatory process in the United States. Over the years, regulators have continued to develop and refine auditing standards. In particular, the U.S. Congress passed the Sarbanes-Oxley Act of 2002 (SOX) which created the Public Company Accounting Oversight Board (PCAOB). This act delegated authority to the PCAOB to establish both audit and professional accounting standards. Since 2002, the PCAOB has enacted a plethora of new standards to improve the accuracy of financial reporting.

Despite numerous attempts to attenuate contrary motives between serving the public or the client, whether one confers court cases (e.g., *Taylor, Bean & Whitaker Plan Trust v. Pricewaterhouse Coopers LLP*, 2018), research (e.g., Ball, 2009; Hail, Tahoun, & Wang, 2018; Low, Davey, & Hooper, 2008), popular press (e.g., Henning, 2018), or government reports (e.g., Ceresney, 2013; SEC, 2016), the conclusion appears consistent: regulations have failed in the 15 intervening years since SOX 2002 to resolve the question of how to prevent auditors from favoring the client at the expense of the public. A skeptic may conclude that extant theories in accounting are not being used or are ineffective, or the problem is so contemptuous that it cannot be fully solved due to the structure of it.

No man can serve two masters.

(Matthew 6:24)

The inherently opposing interests in the auditing profession have put auditors, their clients, and regulators between a rock and a hard place, embittering some of the relationships among these parties. Based on priming research in organizational behavior, it appears a person can serve two masters, but without awareness of doing so, and consequently engage in behaviors inexplicable to oneself. We suggest that the burgeoning complexity of the business world has surpassed extant theorizing in auditing, such that theories are insufficiently developed to address the contemporary mores in this profession.

Specifically, goal contagion in public auditing leaves auditors susceptible to primes that activate subconscious client goals (Sergent & Stajković, 2018). A primed subconscious goal to favor the client can undermine auditors' conscious goal to protect the public. In this scenario, neither are regulations impotent nor are auditors morally feeble and economically corrupt; regulations do not resolve the issue at hand, and auditors are unaware of the conflict. When two conscious goals are in conflict, auditors can seek clarification. When one goal is operating subconsciously without awareness, however, the auditor is unable to detect the conflict and deliberately remedy it. Extensive regulations were passed to "force a restructuring of the accounting profession and radically alter independence requirements for accounting firms that audit SEC registrants" (AICPA, 2002). But, if auditors are unaware of the underlying goal conflict from deep within, then regulations are incapable of fixing it.

Auditing lends itself to an examination of a conflict between primed and conscious goals because of the inherent trade-offs in this profession. Briefly, all public companies are required to undergo an audit of their financial statements to ensure fair and objective reporting. Otherwise, financial markets are vulnerable to rampant false information. The public auditors are employees of third-party audit firms. So far, so good. Where the rubber hits the road is that the audit firm is paid by the client—not by the government mandating the audit or a professional regulating body such as the American Institute of Certified Public Accountants (AICPA). The clients, especially if they swim in murky financial waters, are treasure-ships for the plundering, and auditors, of course, know it.

For context, according to the Audit Analytics database, in fiscal year 2017 J.P. Morgan Chase paid PwC $67.4M in audit fees and $32M in non-audit fees; Microsoft paid Deloitte $43.5M in audit fees and $14.9M in non-audit fees; Amazon paid Ernst & Young $17.7M in audit fees and $2.2M in non-audit fees; and Citigroup paid KPMG $64.7M in audit fees and $33.1M in non-audit fees. This disconnect between normative and financial mandates—the public goal of the profession and the revenue generation from clients—creates a fertile ground for a conflict of interest to percolate. The questions becomes how to uphold the public interest while simultaneously fostering strong client relationships to ensure continued business in the future.

Although we focus on auditing in this chapter, goal trade-offs are germane to other occupations as well. Consider, for example, the trade-offs in law enforcement between protecting the public and protecting oneself, within attorneys between seeking a death penalty for an offender in the courtroom while adhering to personal religious values that might go against the death penalty, in medicine between the medical interest of the patient and cutting costs for the hospital, in academia between quality and quantity of publications, in entrepreneurship between securing investors and protecting novel ideas, in government between representing the people and serving your own interests, and for hourly employees between increasing efficiency and padding wages by slowing down.

Tension Between Public Goals and Client Goals

The persistence of scandals in auditing has sparked a spirited debate on whether auditors can uphold their goal to protect the public amidst a growing climate of client-centeredness. Said differently, is there a solution given the self-evident schism in this profession? An underlying assumption of regulations is that auditors consciously pursue client goals at the expense of public goals. Many assume that auditors involved in scandals are corrupt, and that if they wanted to, they could remedy their unscrupulous actions. Alternatively, scandals can result from incompetence, but few believe that excuse given the expertise and licensure requirements in the profession. This leaves malicious intent as the assumed underlying motive. This assumption ignores the possibility that inherent goal conflict in auditing has pushed some of the professionals into subterranean psychological space.

On one hand, auditors claim "independence is such a crucial part of who accountants are, what they stand for, and is one of those motherhood things that just would never be forfeited" (Gendron, Suddaby, & Lam, 2006, p. 172). On the other hand, the profession is experiencing a "profound crisis marked by the emergence of a new era whose consequences remain to be seen and studied" (Dirsmith, Covaleski, & Samual, 2015, p. 174). In the last five years, unfortunately, public accounting firms have managed to show that even dark regions of financial machinations still yet have darker corners.

Consider the following examples. Ernst & Young settled with Lehman Brothers. They agreed to pay $99M in damages to investors and $10M to the state of New York following a lawsuit alleging that they helped Lehman deceive investors by removing debt from the balance sheet (Freifeld, 2015). KPMG lost many audit clients following an accusation it missed conspicuous signs of tax evasion of the wealthy Gupta family in South Africa (Skoulding, 2018). In 2007, PwC paid $225M to Tyco shareholders for "failing to notice" that the company overstated its income by $5.8 billion (Bukhari, 2017). The Financial Reporting Council (FRC) filed formal complaints against Deloitte for failing to challenge Autonomy's accounting and disclosure of purchases and sales (Chapman, 2018). The FRC alleged that Deloitte's auditing conduct fell "significantly short of the standards reasonably to be expected of a member or member firm" of the accounting professional body. Somewhat alarming for unbridled market competition enthusiasts, these four global audit firms conduct 97% of U.S. public audits and all audits of the UK's top 100 corporations.

Following these financial scandals, most audit firms rebranded to present themselves as all-encompassing "professional services" by providing consulting services. These services range from regulation compliance to IT, to mergers and acquisitions, to corporate strategy. This emerging entrepreneurial spirit is partly justified by the potential for earning extra revenue by helping clients handle wrenching changes in contemporary organizations. For this reason, auditors are now viewed as mediators between clients and the outside world; they are expected to guide clients through difficult situations. This has resulted in a "modern accounting industry [that is . . .] more like a business than a [duty-bound] profession" (Macey & Sale, 2003, p. 1167). Auditing is now practiced as one product in a suite of services sold by professional service firms. This transformation of audit professionals into self-seeking knowledge workers has caused scholars to speculate on the "death of the professions" (Krause, 1994, p. 3; Brint, 1994, p. 17), and practitioners to state that "commercialization is out of control" (Gendron & Spira, 2010, p. 296). For example, Ernst & Young changed its pre-2008 motto: "Quality in everything we do" to "Building a better working world." Whose working world is better—the public's or clients'?

Tension between public and client goals continues to resonate among regulators and professional standard-setters, because public accounting firms are toying with chicanery. For example, the six largest auditing firms paid out $5.66 billion to settle 362 allegations related to audit and non-audit services, with 65% of these related to public company audits (Reinstein, Pacini, & Green, 2017). Despite auditors espousing autonomy and independence in the service of a public goal that transcends commercial interests, the evidence indicates they continue to veer off course. These detours come with a hefty price tag, reflected in tangible litigation costs and intangible depredations of lost public trust.

Public accounting firms propagate their commitment to public goals, but research suggests commercialism has altered the goals within the profession. This tension is delicate; for over a century the professions of medicine, law, and public accounting gained social status and authority by offering an expert service to society. Accordingly, they adhered to a "service ideal" in assisting clients. The sociology of the professions' literature has suggested a widespread transformation of professional identity from that of the objective expert to an organization-based knowledge worker (Abbott, 1988; Reed, 1996).

If this transformation is indeed taking place, it raises concern at the SEC, who stated that it granted the profession monopoly status in order to serve the public interest. Several scholars have argued the profession is "losing its soul" in the pursuit of "monetizing" its practices. We ground our theory in more earthly possibilities where nobody has lost their soul. Instead, we contend the actors are simply unaware of the problem because the goal conflict operates automatically below awareness.

Subconscious Goal Contagion in the Accounting Profession

Commercialism of the accounting profession "exists as an inherently contradictory, and *often suppressed*, element of the institutional logic of professionalism" (Suddaby, Gendron, & Lam. 2009, p. 414). Therefore, client goals are increasingly ingrained in auditors' subconscious. Critics have brought attention to this by questioning the motives of college graduates who work at big four accounting firms (see Brooks, 2018):

> Few graduate employees at the big four arrive with a passion for rooting out financial irregularity and making capitalism safe. They are motivated by good income prospects for moderate performers, plus maybe a vague interest in the world of business.

With this in mind, Cooper and Robson (2006, p. 433) reported that in hundreds of interviews, none of the auditors stated that their focus was on protecting the public; instead, auditors spoke in terms of service to their valued clients. Many claim newly qualified accountants at major audit firms "generally slip into 'technocratism,' applying standards lawfully but to the advantage of clients, not breaking the rules but not making a stand for truth and objectivity either" (Brooks, 2018). This has caused a perception in the profession that career progression requires auditors to "fit in" above all else.

For this reason, new auditors are likely to observe their senior colleagues acquiesce to client goals. Through this observation, auditors are susceptible to "catching" the client goal via goal contagion. As described in Chapter 4, observation of others gradually creates a subconscious association between the observed action and inferred goal. Applying goal contagion to auditing, when an auditor encounters a client cue, it primes a subconscious goal to favor the client. This goal causes the auditor automatically to pursue client goals, even if ever so slightly. For example, a client prime in the morning can detour judgement in minimal ways. Yet, over the course of the audit, skewed judgements accumulate. In the end, an auditor could conclude a report is "materially accurate" even if, in reality, it has material errors. We call this the subconscious carryover effect, where experiences accumulate over time in the subconscious, reach the tipping point of how much we can keep bottled up before imploding, and eventually bleed into the present (Bargh, 2017).

Because the human mind perpetually segues from one situation to the next, the vestiges of previous experience only gradually dissipate. Accordingly, for example, cues can prime client goals during an audit in several ways. Public audits are often completed at the client site. This facilitates communication between auditors and clients. But, it also exposes auditors to repeated client primes throughout the day, e.g., signs on the building, branded posters in hallways, and seeing the clients' faces (Shah, 2003a, 2003b). Client-branded stationary, such as notepads, pens, or notes, can also prime client goals (e.g., Kay, Wheeler, Bargh, & Ross, 2004), as can emails from clients with branded signature lines. Thus, auditors encounter client-related goal primes as part of their normal, daily work routine.

Piggybacking on the aforementioned arguments is the criticism of the nature of the professional goal to protect the public. Broad qualitative goals such as to "protect the public interest" are unrelated to any specific auditing task, leaving concern for their effectiveness. In particular, in goal theory, qualitative broad goals are ineffective because when people are asked to "do their best," they have no external, numeric referent. This causes individuals to generate a wide range of idiosyncratic performance levels with varied levels of what is acceptable and what is unacceptable (Locke & Latham, 2002). Theoretically, an assigned broad goal should be ineffective, especially when juxtaposed with a conflicting primed goal to favor the client.

Experimental Evidence

Sergent, Covaleski, and Stajković (2019) tested the hypothesis that priming a client goal undermines a professional goal to protect the public in an experiment with 426 accounting students. Participants had completed a financial accounting course and were knowledgeable on auditing the accuracy and completeness of financial statements. The authors used an audit task that focused on finding mistakes and making a judgement. Historically, when auditors made errors during assessment of financial statements, incompetence was assumed (Kadous, 2000). Goal contagion theory, though, introduces a possibility that a primed client goal can sabotage even a competent and public goal–orientated auditor.

Following Stajković et al. (2006, 2007), a scrambled sentences task was used to prime a subconscious goal to favor the client. Participants were randomly assigned to one of three primed goal conditions: primed client goal, primed public goal, or no prime goal. In the primed client goal group, participants unscrambled the sentences shown in Figure 6.1; in the primed public goal group they unscrambled the sentences in Figure 6.2.

1. cooperated	Josh	boiling	them	with
2. they	supportive	push	always	are
3. loyalty	her	runs	deep	shampoo
4. a	ocean	fly	kite	go
5. they	coffee	an	formed	alliance
6. was	client	the	friendly	rhyme
7. consider	a	laughed	it	favor
8. understanding	was	pills	manager	the
9. company	she	the	raining	appreciated
10. melts	water	when	butter	heated
11. strong	barking	their	relationship	is
12. customer	the	first	comes	and
13. hoot	woman	assisted	the	George
14. apple	business	a	Mary	runs
15. song	was	milks	the	empowering

Figure 6.1 Scrambled sentences used to prime a client goal.

1. protected	Josh	boiling	kids	his
2. they	social	refrigerator	are	people
3. serve	soldiers	country	their	shampoo
4. a	ocean	fly	kite	go
5. they	coffee	a	formed	government
6. she	support	gave	moral	rhyme
7. laughed	property	was	communal	it
8. civil	neighbor	is	my	pills
9. tree	from	humanity	save	war
10. melts	water	when	butter	heated
11. we	our	barking	did	duty
12. should	first	quality	come	and
13. hoot	woman	assured	the	George
14. apple	public	in	Mary	runs
15. song	was	milks	the	patriotic

Figure 6.2 Scrambled sentences used to prime a public goal.

Did you notice the pattern in these sentences? In Figure 6.1, if you look back you will see the words *cooperated, supportive, loyalty, alliance, client, favor, manager, company, relationship, customer, assisted, business,* and *empowering.* Similarly, in Figure 6.2 you will notice the words *protected, social, serve, government, moral, communal, civil, humanity, duty, quality, assured, public,* and *patriotic.* Although participants do not consciously register the connection among these words during the task, their subconscious picks up the underlying theme. Subconscious recognition of the theme activates the inferred client goal, i.e., to help the client. The automatic behavior that ensues supports the goal, without awareness that a goal was primed and is being actively pursued.

After unscrambling the sentences, the authors gave participants instructions for the audit task that was developed by a certified public accountant (CPA). In this task, participants had to agree the cash balance to a summary schedule, bank reconciliations and confirmation, deposit slips, and outstanding checks. Embedded errors included over-reporting deposits in transit, under-reporting outstanding checks, counterfeit checks, fraudulent account numbers and bank statements, and accelerated recognition of inventory payments. Thus, all errors were advantageous to the client.

For participants assigned a professional goal, the instructions stated: "In this task, you will act as an auditor to protect the public interest by testing accuracy of amounts, dates, and account numbers provided by the client to supporting documents." Participants were given a post-experimental awareness questionnaire that consisted of six validated questions (see Bargh & Chartrand, 2000, p. 85). Participants who indicated an awareness of the prime were removed from data analysis.

The assigned professional goal to protect the public caused participants to find significantly more errors than those in the no conscious goal group. This finding illustrates that assigning even a broad, professional goal has a positive effect on performance. Likewise, priming participants with a subconscious public goal also improved their audit performance compared to a control (no primed goal) group. This finding shows that embedding public-related cues in the audit environment could help auditors to continually strive to uphold the public interest, even if they are unaware of the subconscious goal.

But what happened when participants were primed with a subconscious client goal? As hypothesized, priming participants with a subconscious client goal caused them to find significantly fewer errors on the audit task compared to the control group. Yet, when asked if the previous task affected them in any way, participants all said "no." This demonstrates that a conflicted primed goal can sabotage task performance without awareness.

In addition to main effects, the authors found a significant interaction. When participants were both assigned a professional goal and primed with a subconscious public goal, audit performance improved beyond the simple sum of the individual effects. This positive interaction finding replicates the effects from Stajković, Locke, and Blaire (2006) and Sergent (2018). The implication for audit professionals is that combining both an assigned public goal and priming a subconscious public goal will lead to the best performance outcomes. When, however, the assigned public goal was combined with a primed subconscious client goal, the primed client goal overrode the positive effects of the conscious goal. In other words, the primed client goal was strong enough to "pull down" the positive effects of the assigned goal. This interaction is illustrated in Figure 6.3.

In addition to having participants circle errors, the audit task required participants to indicate whether the cash balance was accurate or inaccurate. Based on the errors found, the correct decision would have been to conclude the cash balance was inaccurate. The authors tested how the goal manipulations affected the probability of participants making the correct decision.

The probability of reaching a correct audit decision increased by a factor of 2.63 when participants were assigned a conscious professional goal compared to when no conscious goal was assigned. In addition, the primed subconscious goal significantly impacted the probability of reaching the correct decision. Specifically, the probability of making a correct judgement increased from 95% when only a conscious goal was assigned to 98% when a public subconscious goal was also primed. Markedly, this probability dropped to 87% when a conscious public goal was paired with a primed subconscious client goal. Taken together, this study demonstrates the power of conflicted subconscious goals to undermine the positive effects of conscious goals without awareness.

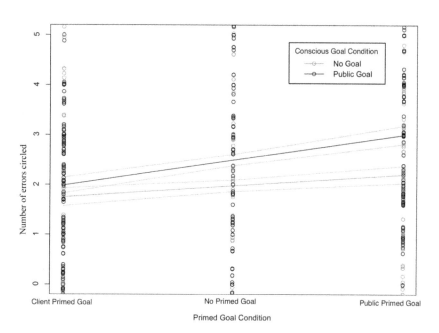

Figure 6.3 This figure depicts the interaction between the conscious and primed subconscious goal. The error bars represent the 95% confidence intervals. This graph was generated using "plot" package in R, and data were plotted with the "jitter" to visually remove overlaps.

Summary

Conflicted forces shape practice in the auditing profession. Regulators continue to propose structural reforms, but greater attention is needed on the nexus of market forces and psychological dynamics. The realities of this profession are nuanced. Goals to favor the client reside in the subconscious and can be inadvertently primed to sabotage auditors' conscious intent. Because this conflict goes unnoticed, the findings reviewed in this chapter provide an impetus for rectifying the slippery slope many scholars claim the auditing profession is on. Whether we should hold individual auditors responsible for actions that unfold without their awareness is unclear. But, one implication is evident: regulations that emphasize standards to protect the public are inadequate to change behaviors if auditors are unaware of subconscious causes of those behaviors. On the upside, these results show that assigning a professional goal and priming a public goal together enhance performance beyond either goal alone. Further study of goal-related causes and consequences in auditing can offer theory-driven solutions for the practical reduction of scandals in the auditing profession

References

Abbott, A. (1988). *The systems of professions: An essay on the division of expert labor*. Chicago: University of Chicago Press.

AICPA. (2002, January 1). Members vote down bylaws amendment. *CPA Letter*.

Ball, R. (2009). Market and political/regulatory perspectives on the recent accounting scandals. *Journal of Accounting Research*, 47(2), 277–323.

Bargh, J. A., & Chartrand, T. L. (2000). The mind in the middle. In H. T. Reis & C. M. Judd (Eds.), *Handbook of Research Methods in Social and Personality Psychology* (pp. 253–285). New York, NY: Cambridge University Press.

Brint, S. (1994). *In an age of expert*. Princeton NJ: Princeton University Press.

Brooks, R. (2018, May 29). The financial scandal no one is talking about. *The Guardian*.

Bukhari, J. (2017, February 28). 5 PwC scandals far worse than Oscar envelopegate mix up. *Fortune*. Retrieved from www.theguardian.com/news/2018/may/29/the-financial-scandal-no-one-is-talking-about-big-four-accountancy-firms

Ceresney, A. (2013, September 19). Financial reporting and accounting fraud. *U.S. Securities and Exchange Commission Speech*. Retrieved from www.sec.gov/news/speech/spch091913ac

Chapman, B. (2018, May 31). Accountancy watchdog brings action against Deloitte over multibillion dollar Autonomy scandal. *Independent*. Retrieved from www.independent.co.uk/news/business/news/deloitte-financial-reporting-council-disciplinary-action-autonomy-scandal-audit-a8377071.html

Chartrand, T. L., & Bargh, J. A. (1999). The chameleon effect: The perception–behavior link and social interaction. *Journal of Personality and Social Psychology*, 76(6), 893–910.

Cooper, D., & Robson, K. (2006). Accounting, professions and regulation: Locating the sites of professionalization. *Accounting, Organizations and Society*, 31, 415–444.

Dirsmith, M., Covaleski, M. A., & Samual, S. (2015). On being professional in the 21st century: An empirically-informed essay. *Auditing: A Journal of Practice and Theory, 34*, 167–200.

Ekman, P., & Friesen, W. V. (1971). Constants across cultures in the face and emotion. *Journal of Personality and Social Psychology, 17*(2), 124–129.

Freifeld, K. (2015, April 15). Ernst & Young settles with N.Y. for $10 million over Lehman auditing. Thompson Reuters, Business News. Retrieved from www.reuters.com/article/us-ernst-lehman-bros/ernst-young-settles-with-n-y-for-10-million-over-lehman-auditing-idUSKBN0N61SM20150415

Gendron, Y., & Spira, L. (2010). Identity narratives under threat: A study of former members of Arthur Andersen. *Accounting, Organizations and Society, 35*, 275–300.

Gendron, Y., Suddaby, R., & Lam, H. (2006). An examination of the ethical commitment of professional accountants to auditor independence. *Journal of Business Ethics, 64*, 169–193.

Hail, L., Tahoun, A., & Wang, C. (2018). Corporate scandals and regulation. *Journal of Accounting Research, 56*(2), 617–671.

Henning, P. J. (2018, November 30). G.E., Tesla, and Snap are under accounting investigation. Here's what they should worry about. *The New York Times.* Retrieved from www.nytimes.com/2018/11/30/business/dealbook/general-electric-tesla-snap-accounting-investigation.html

Kadous, K. (2000). The effects of audit quality and consequence severity on juror evaluations of auditor responsibility for plaintiff losses. *The Accounting Review, 75*, 327–341.

Kay, A. C., Wheeler, S. C., Bargh, J. A., & Ross, L. (2004). Material priming: The influence of mundane physical objects on situational construal and competitive behavioral choice. *Organizational Behavior and Human Decision Processes, 95*(1), 83–96.

Krause, E. (1994). *Death of the guilds: Professions, states and the advance of capitalism, 1930 to the present.* New Haven: Yale University Press.

Lakin, J. L., Jefferis, V. E., Cheng, C. M., & Chartrand, T. L. (2003). The chameleon effect as social glue: Evidence for the evolutionary significance of nonconscious mimicry. *Journal of Nonverbal Behavior, 27*(3), 145–162.

Locke, E. A., & Latham, G. P. (2002). Building a practically useful theory of goal setting and task motivation: A 35-year odyssey. *American Psychologist, 57*, 705–717.

Low, M., Davey, H., & Hooper, K. (2008). Accounting scandals, ethical dilemmas and educational challenges. *Critical Perspectives on Accounting, 19*(2), 222–254.

Macey, J., & Sale, H. A. (2003). Observations on the role of commodification, independence, and governance in the accounting industry. *Villanova Law Review, 48*, 1167.

Reed, M. (1996). Expert power and control in late modernity. *Organization Studies 17*, 573–598.

Reinstein, A., Pacini, C. J., & Green, B. P. (2017). Examining the current legal environment facing the public accounting profession: Recommendations for a consistent US policy. *Journal of Accounting, Auditing & Finance,* 0148558X16680717.

SEC (2016). SEC Announces Financial Fraud Cases, 2016-74. Retrieved from https://www.sec.gov/news/pressrelease/2016-74.html

Sergent, K., Covaleski, M., & Stajković, A. D. (2019). How a subconscious goal to favor the client can inadvertently sabotage a conscious audit goal to protect the public: A new perspective on an old debate. Unpublished manuscript.

Sergent, K., & Stajković, A. D. (2018). Prime and punishment: When subconscious goals sabotage conscious goals. *Academy of Management Proceedings*, *1*, doi.org/10.5465/AMBPP.2018.15413abstract

Shah, J. (2003a). Automatic for the people: How representations of significant others implicitly affect goal pursuit. *Journal of Personality and Social Psychology*, *84*, 661–681.

Shah, J. (2003b). The motivational looking glass: How significant others implicitly affect goal appraisals. *Journal of Personality and Social Psychology*, *85*, 424–439.

Skoulding, L. (2018, July 25). KPMG South Africa hit hard as more clients sever ties following audit scandals. *Accountancy Age*, Retrieved from www.account ancyage.com/2018/07/25/kpmg-south-africa-hit-hard-as-more-clients-sever-ties-following-audit-scandals/

Stajković, A. D., Locke, E. A., & Blair, E. S. (2006). A first examination of the relationships between primed subconscious goals, assigned conscious goals, and task performance. *Journal of Applied Psychology*, *91*, 1172–1180.

Stajković, A. D., Locke, E. A., & Blair, E. S. (2007). *What happens to performance when conscious and subconscious goals are in conflict.* Presented at the Academy of Management, Human Resources, and Managerial and Organizational Cognition Divisions, Philadelphia, PA.

Suddaby, R., Gendron, Y., & Lam, H. (2009). The organizational context of professionalism in accounting. *Accounting, Organizations and Society*, *34*, 409–442.

Taylor, Bean & Whitaker Plan Trust v. Pricewaterhouse Coopers LLP. (2018). Reuters. 11th Judicial Circuit for Miami-Dade County, Florida, Case No. 2:11-cv-746-BJR.

Wang, S. (2006, February 1). Contagious Behavior. *Observer*. Retrieved from www.psychologicalscience.org/observer/contagious-behavior

7 Organizational Behavior Research on Priming Self-Efficacy as a Means to a Goal

This chapter presents the latest empirical research on priming self-efficacy as a means to a goal. Guided by the model of means-goal priming, in this research, subconscious self-efficacy triggers a goal representation, which then automatically initiates previously formed goal-behavior associations. In the means-goal model of priming, a goal *per se* is not primed, its associated mean is. Self-efficacy is one of the most empirically supported predictors (i.e., means) of goal attainment (Bandura, 2013; Bandura & Cervone, 1983).

Conceptually rethinking the architecture of self-efficacy by testing it as a primed means to a goal adds breadth and utility to theory. Practically speaking, surrounding employees with cues that prime self-efficacy brings goals into focus automatically, stoking the "keep your eye on the ball" notion. In contrast, environments devoid of self-efficacy primes can create an "out of sight, out of mind" problem. We next review social cognitive theory to explicate the operations of self-efficacy, followed by new conceptual development connecting self-efficacy as a means to a goal that can be primed.

Social Cognitive Theory

In conceptions of human agency presented in social cognitive theory, self-referent thought mediates the relationship between knowledge and behavior (Bandura, 1986). Skill and will do not necessarily produce expected outcomes. Instead, intermediary self-referent cognitive processes translate experience and knowledge into behaviors. See Stajković and Sergent (2019) for more details on social cognitive theory as the conceptual foundation of perceived self-efficacy. For this chapter, we turn to explanations of perceived self-efficacy.

Perceived Self-Efficacy as a Self-Referent Thought

Self-efficacy is a malleable belief formed by a personal appraisal of how well one can execute action to handle any given prospect. This self-referent thought is central in the transitive phase between experience and behavior. Even if people have what it takes to succeed, they will forsake cherished outcomes if they doubt they can do it. The notion that people who are riddled by doubt have little incentive has weathered the test of time:

> [F]or he who doubts is like a wave of the sea that is driven and tossed by the wind.
>
> (The New Testament of the Bible, James 1:6)

Those with high self-efficacy are more likely to initiate effort and sustain persistence in the transgressions of life and work. This can-do belief has transformative power.

Some people question their efficacy to invest effort. For example, Michelangelo initially refused Pope Julius II's offer to paint the ceiling of the Sistine Chapel, though he reconsidered and, obviously, succeeded. To reverse the correlates, some question their efficacy notwithstanding their experience. Despite having a successful, if not legendary, experience as Prime Minister during WWII, 1940–1945, Winston Churchill wrangled with the decision of whether to run for office again in 1951. Other stories of self-efficacy often epitomize perseverance after failure. The adaptive self-regulatory influence of self-efficacy transcends time, cultures, and occupations, as exemplified in the following stories.

Beethoven's childhood music teacher declared him a hopeless composer. Jane Austen faced criticism from Ralph Waldo Emerson, who remarked, "Miss Austen's novels . . . seem sterile in artistic invention, imprisoned . . . without genius, or wit." Charles Dickens' famous novel *A Christmas Carol* was rejected by his publisher; he financed the publication himself despite his dire financial situation. Abraham Lincoln had two business ventures fail, lost eight elections, and had a nervous breakdown before becoming the 16th president of the United States. George Orwell's famous book *Animal Farm* was rejected by publishers, including one who told him it was "impossible to sell animal stories in the U.S.A." Walt Disney was turned down by hundreds of banks to develop Disneyland and was fired from his newspaper job for "lacking ideas." Jimmy Page brought a small guitar he received for Christmas to school and asked if anyone would teach him to play. A good Samaritan taught him a few chords that are now the most represented chords in the sermonic music of Led Zeppelin. George Lucas spent four years racking up rejections for *Star Wars*. Steven Spielberg was rejected twice from USC's School of Cinematic Arts. As a child, Prince's father told him that he lacked talent and would never amount to much in music. Michael Jordan was cut from his high school basketball team.

Oprah Winfrey was fired from one her first jobs as a television reporter because the producers thought she was "unfit for TV." Lisa Kudrow, famous for her role as Phoebe on *Friends*, landed that career-changing role after she was fired from another popular sitcom. Vera Wang, a fashion designer, entered the industry only after her dreams of being a figure skater were crushed when she did not make the 1986 Olympic team. J. K. Rowling was living on welfare and received a dozen rejections before her Harry Potter series changed the lives of kids around the world. Madonna, one of the highest-grossing solo artists ever, was rejected several times before landing a record deal. A rejection letter from Millennium Records in 1981 stated, "The only thing missing from this project is the material." Anna Wintour, the legendary *Vogue* editor-in-chief, was fired from her junior editor position at *Harper's Bazaar*.

We can deduce several conclusions from these stories about self-efficacy as a self-referent thought. First, if these individuals had accepted failure, history would look different. Second, "material" was present in each example, but external forces rejected it; these individuals were not "empty suits," a derogatory phrase used to describe confident people without backing. Despite social rejections, people in the above examples believed in the enabling power of their *can-do belief*. Reverse the correlates and ask yourself if these people could have endured if they ruminated and focused on their failures? Viola Davis, an award-winning actor, summarized the underlying message of self-efficacy:

> "Nobody tells you about failure . . . People always talk about winning, vision boards, getting what you want. People also don't talk about fear. It's always keeping fear at bay. Squelching it. Throwing it away . . . So, now I get it at this age, I get it. That life literally is what you make out of it"—*Vulture*, 2014.
>
> (quoted in Sincrich, 2017)

These stories are underwritten by the adage, *if you believe you achieve, if you doubt you go without*. Skill and will are necessary but insufficient to reach your goal. You must also believe that you can actualize your potential. Doubt is a psychological bondage that keeps you at bay; self-efficacy is a psychological mechanism that unlocks your potential.

Dimensions and Measurement of Self-Efficacy

Self-efficacy varies among three dimensions. First is magnitude. This is the level of goal difficulty a person believes s/he can reach. Second is strength. This refers to certainty of your belief for a magnitude of achievement, e.g., I believe I can reach a goal of 5 out of 10 with 100% certainty, but for a goal of 9 out of 10 my certainty is 20%. Third is generality. Some goals rely on specific efficacy beliefs, e.g., earn a *5/5* performance ranking. Other goals depend on domain-related self-efficacy, such as having a goal to be promoted. For more details on the generality dimension, see the research by Stajković (2006) and Stajković, Lee, Greenwald, and Raffiee (2015) on core confidence.

Figure 7.1 presents the scale to measure self-efficacy along these dimensions. To use and interpret this scale, you must first decide on the goal and respective levels. Second, the certainty percentages assume non-ordinal data, i.e., the differences between the levels are unequal. To illustrate, imagine stacking bricks. Your effort to stack the third brick is approximately equal to your effort to stack the twelfth brick. In contrast, if you are running a marathon, your effort to complete mile 2 will be unequal to your effort on mile 20. Third, if an employee believes that accomplishing a goal at level is impossible, it could warrant a 0% certainty. Finally, self-efficacy can be measured as a magnitude (sum of magnitude levels), certainty (sum of positive certainties), or composite (sum of certainty ratings for a given magnitude level).

Antecedents of Self-Efficacy

In social cognitive theory, self-efficacy has four antecedents. Self-efficacy is malleable—people can both develop it and lose it. Here, we describe how it can be enhanced.

Enacted Mastery

This is personal experience of enacting mastery of the task, i.e., past performance. This antecedent has the strongest relationship with performance. It reflects direct experience with the task, and its evaluation is straightforward. The more we practice a specific task, the higher our

Magnitude:			Certainty:
Pertains to some specific goal and its specific level:			0%–100%
I believe I can	achieve this goal	at level 1	____e.g., 100%
I believe I can	. . .	at level 2	____e.g., 92%
I believe I can	. . .	at level 3	____e.g., 80%
I believe I can	. . .	at level 4	____e.g., 70%
I believe I can	. . .	at level 5	____e.g., 65%
I believe I can	. . .	at level 6	____e.g., 60%
I believe I can	. . .	at level 7	____e.g., 45%
I believe I can	. . .	at level 8	____e.g., 30%
I believe I can	. . .	at level 9	____e.g., 10%
I believe I can	. . .	at level 10	____e.g., 2%

Figure 7.1 Scale used to measure perceived self-efficacy beliefs.

self-efficacy for it will be. When Bandura began his pioneering work on self-efficacy, he worked with patients suffering from agoraphobia—fear of open spaces. Bandura believed psychological maladjustment persisted because of a perceived inability to conquer it. To enact mastery, Bandura encouraged patients to take a small step outside. This provoked anxiety and worry, but it revealed that perceived fears were unwarranted. Gradually, the distance was increased to raise self-efficacy, one step at a time.

Vicarious Learning

In the absence of direct experience, humans can learn from others. Instructors can couple vicarious learning with enacted mastery through guided modeling. For example, a trained model enacts and explains the behaviors. Then, a trainee repeats the steps. PIGS feedback follows. Incremental self-efficacy building through vicarious modeling can be conducted with an array of performance tasks (e.g., sales and sports), learning undertakings (e.g., teaching and presentations), and social pursuits (e.g., networking and socializing).

Verbal Persuasion

Imagine your manager is assigning duties for an upcoming project. You raise your hand to volunteer. Your manager turns and responds, "Ah . . . no, not you Randy, let's have someone else do that." How would you feel? Being on the receiving end of a public expression conferring lack of confidence is unpleasant, and chances are it will lower your self-efficacy. Verbal (i.e., social) persuasion is an expression of confidence or doubt from others about your ability to reach a goal. For it to impact efficacy, the source should be knowledgeable about your performance (not a mother who provides unconditional praise) and trustworthy (feedback from untrusted people is dismissed or devalued). Social persuasion often comes from forces outside your control. One example is "social engineering," such as propaganda insinuating that "you can have it all, and if you don't, someone else is to blame." Social propaganda may be accurate in your particular case, but it might potentially be setting many other people up to fail by boosting unrealistic efficacy.

Physiological Strain and Psychological Arousal

Visualize yourself on a 14-hour flight from Chicago to Beijing. You are traveling to meet potential customers. The flight lands Friday afternoon, and your schedule begins that evening with socializing. Your weekly schedule is packed, but this is a normal business routine for you. Your self-efficacy for this trip is high. Except, Thursday morning before the flight you suddenly come down with a nasty cold. Would this affect your self-efficacy assessment for this demanding business trip? Probably. Similar reasoning pertains to psychological arousal. If people are excited, assessment of self-efficacy can become inflated. In contrast, stress, anxiety, and worry often lower the appraisal of self-efficacy. A simple recommendation is to wait until you return to a more typical physiological and psychological condition and then appraise your self-efficacy.

What Self-Efficacy Is Not

Self-efficacy is not performance expectancy. Expectancy of promotion can be low because of budget-cutting, restructuring, or new hires, or because your boss simply dislikes you. Nonetheless, your self-efficacy for the work leading to a promotion can be high; you believe you can execute tasks to the level of others who earned a promotion. In academia, for example, the rejection rate in top-tier journals hovers around 90%. This means that 10% of articles submitted by roughly equally qualified and educated individuals will be accepted. Yet, many scholars still believe they can conduct and write high-quality research, despite a low publication expectancy.

Self-efficacy is not self-esteem. Self-esteem is defined as "the overall evaluation of personal worth that people make and maintain with regard to themselves" (Gardner & Pierce, 1998, p. 49). Self-worth and self-efficacy are not necessarily correlated. An employee with high self-esteem is one who perceives himself to be of high personal worth. A perception of self-worth is good, but it does not necessarily translate into high efficacy for a specific task. In contrast, a criminal defense lawyer might have high self-efficacy for winning courtroom cases, but s/he may have low self-worth for having freed many defendants with prior criminal records.

Self-Efficacy Effectiveness

Converging evidence from varied sources and methods has verified a positive link between self-efficacy and a host of outcomes (Bandura, 2018). For instance, from infancy through lifespan, self-efficacy helps to account for such diverse phenomena as cognitive functioning and coping in education (Brown et al., 2008; Stajković, Bandura, Locke, Lee, & Sergent, 2018), performance in innumerable occupational roles (Brown, Lent, Telander, & Tramayne, 2011; Stajković & Luthans, 1998), development of career and vocational trajectories (Brown & Lent, 2016, 2017), pro-social behaviors in adolescents and adults (Caprara, Alessandri, Di Giunta, Panerai, & Eisenberg, 2009; Caprara, Barbaranelli, Pastorelli, & Cervone, 2004), coaching and competitive strivings in sport (Feltz & Hill, 2018; Park et al., 2018), behavioral adaptation to advanced information technology (Bandura, 2002), moral (mis)conduct (Bandura, 2016), global interdependencies and cultural influences (Bandura, 1995), and initiation and sustainability of disease-prevention and health-promotion behaviors (Sheeran et al., 2016). These effects span the far regions of the world (see Smith, 2002).

Taken together, perceived self-efficacy has been where the human action is. According to Google Scholar, perceived self-efficacy has been studied in about 1,130,000 reports over the last 20 years. There were published on average 154 articles *per day* on it. As borne out by data, perceived self-efficacy is one of the focal concepts in psychology and organizational behavior literatures.

Perceived Self-Efficacy as a Means to a Goal

Perceived self-efficacy is a cognitive means to goal attainment because it facilitates analytic and decisional process regarding performance (Bandura, 1999). In analytic mode, perceived self-efficacy impacts quality of thinking pertaining to new challenges, the level of effort to exert, and how long to sustain persistence. In decisional mode, perceived self-efficacy governs how costs and benefits of options stack up.

Before people initiate effort toward the goal, they tend to weigh, evaluate, and integrate information about their perceived capability to accomplish the goal. Those with low self-efficacy construct a self-debilitation chain of reflections and behaviors. They perceive difficult goals as threatening. This lowers their commitment toward the goal, if not causes them to evade the goal all together. The result is stifled career choices. People who did not think that they could do something gave up prematurely or did not act at all and had their professional choices restricted as a result. This is often followed with self-reflective ruminations over perceived deficiencies. This leads to visualizing an unpleasant future to come, instead of figuring out ways to achieve the goal. There is a way to romanticize a psychological issue, but a cogent conclusion is this: Unless people believe they can mobilize their motivational, cognitive, and behavioral resources to do what it takes to reach the goal, they will probably put forth lackluster effort, cease the pursuit altogether, or settle for mediocre solutions. Hence, low perceived self-efficacy has implications for organizations because it takes on one of managers' archetypal queries: Why some employees fail to reach a goal when they know what to do and have the capacity to do it?

In contrast, employees with high perceived self-efficacy approach difficult goals as challenges to be mastered. Consequently, they are more committed to the goal. When setbacks ensue, high self-efficacy accelerates recovery. Attributions of failure are made to rectifiable internal causes, e.g., "I can apply more effort," or "I will develop new skills." Thus, in addition to skill, will, and contingent consequences, high self-efficacy is an enabler of goal attainment and pursuit. Taken together, ascertaining one's self-efficacy involves a generative stream of analytic and decisional thought configured into an integrated personal can-do belief system.

> Most courses of action are initially organized in thought. People's beliefs in their efficacy shape the types of anticipatory scenarios they construct and rehearse. Those who have high sense of efficacy visualize success scenarios that provide positive guides and supports for performance. Those who doubt their efficacy visualize failure scenarios and dwell on the many things that can go wrong.
>
> (Bandura, 1995, p. 6)

Cognitive assessment of perceived self-efficacy relies on conscious deliberations. However, as discussed throughout this book, employees' conscious resources are in short supply, and doubling down on perceived self-efficacy requires more, not less, attention involvement. Because the current workplace requires unprecedented makeover to close emerging social, psychological, and performance gaps across domains of organizational functioning (Gallup, 2017), many employees fear they can handle it all (Lord, Diefendorff, Schmidt, & Hall, 2010). Their concerns are typically linked to perceived doubt and not to the objective difficulty of executing work demands (Bandura, 2013). Doubt zaps attentional resources. Doubt breeds anxiety, and anxiety impairs efficient functioning of the goal-directed attentional system (Eysenck & Calvo, 1992). Anxious individuals worry about threats to their current goal (Eysenck, Santos, Derakshan, & Calvo, 2007), which puts pressure on attentional resources to respond to threatening stimuli. Increased pressure on attentional resources caused by doubt and anxiety exasperates cognitive overload.

A theory challenge is to disentangle the conflict between increased doubt in today's workplace morphing into cognitive overload and the fact that human attentional capacity changes at an evolutionary horse and a buggy pace. Managers need to find ways to align these confluences, because mounting doubt in light of straining job adjustments will lead to withdrawal of effort, if not total disengagement. Because appraisal of self-efficacy relies on conscious contemplations, increasing external pressure like, "you can do this, c'mon," would elevate employee cognitive load. Hence, we propose a new approach to mobilizing the benefits of self-efficacy at work—its cognitive automation as a means to a goal.

Primed Self-Efficacy as a Means to a Goal

Subtle Influences on Perceived Self-Efficacy

Research has examined whether perception of self-efficacy is malleable to anchoring bias. For example, Cervone and Peake (1986) found that when participants were exposed to a random high number, compared with a random low number, those in the high number group rated their perceived self-efficacy higher than those in the low number group. Similarly, when participants were asked to measure self-efficacy in ascending order of challenge (e.g., "how strongly do you believe you can accomplish 5," "how strongly do you believe you can accomplish 8"), compared with descending order, those in the ascending order group rated their self-efficacy higher than those in the descending group.

Similarly, Bouffard-Bouchard (1990) arbitrarily manipulated self-efficacy by suggesting that students in the experiment were of higher or lower standing compared with a fabricated group. When students were made to believe they were of higher standing, their perceived self-efficacy increased. This caused them to set higher goals, use more efficient problem-solving strategies, and perform better than those of equal ability whose perceived self-efficacy was superficially lowered. Even though it was arbitrarily influenced, raised self-efficacy fostered perseverance (Jacobs, Prentice-Dunn, & Rogers, 1984), elevated physical stamina (Weinberg, Gould, Yukelson, & Jackson, 1981), and improved decision-making quality (Wood & Bandura, 1989).

Cognitive Automation of Self-Efficacy as a Means to a Goal

Although research on illusory (in)competence showed that subtle cues impact (in)efficaciousness and subsequent outcomes, job performance is neither based on arbitrary information nor can such information be manipulated like in those experiments. Instead, job performance relies on well-established knowledge structures, generally characterized by knowing the functions that are instrumental to performance. Functional means-to-goal links are formed by (a) education and training (e.g., medical school to medical practice), (b) enacted personal experiences where a certain mean was often facilitative to a goal (e.g., networking to career advancement), and (c) vicarious perception that a means facilitates an outcome (e.g., MBA degree to fast career promotions). A goal system is defined as a mental structure of facilitative links among means and goals (Shah & Kruglanski, 2003). Unlike direct priming of goals, which relies on associations formed through repetition and/or conditioning, priming a goal with its associated means relies on a functional relationship between the mean and the goal.

> The longer participants pursued a goal through a given means, the higher the likelihood that these attainment behaviors primed the goal they were pursuing.
>
> (Shah & Kruglanski, 2003, p. 1120)

Because perceived self-efficacy is a means to a goal, can its subconscious counterpart be primed to activate associated goals automatically?

To be clear, in this proposed model of priming, enhancing perceived self-efficacy by priming arbitrary stimuli is not involved. Instead, a theory assumption is that an association between self-efficacy and a goal exists in memory already, and that priming self-efficacy can activate this linked goal. Likewise, we differentiate priming self-efficacy based on a functional, rather than a semantic, relation to goals. Whereas functional relations are formed by a link between a goal and means that serve the goal, semantic associations rely on shared meaning. Although concepts have different meanings in different contexts, people generally recognize semantic associations; these relationships remain stable. For example, when Chartrand and colleagues (2008) primed participants with the word "dog," they automatically displayed more loyal behaviors. This is because "dog" and "loyal" are semantically related (also *nurse—hospital, grass—green*).

Fitzsimons and Bargh (2003) conducted an experiment to examine if participants primed with their relationship partner automatically straightened up before their date arrived. The assumption was that participants had internalized a link from appearance to an impression goal. Similarly, when participants were primed with mother, they performed better on an achievement task. This is because mothers help kids with school homework. Based on this research, we propose that once a facilitative cognitive association between self-efficacy and goals is formed, people subconsciously store the link so they do not have to restate it every time they encounter a similar situation. As long as self-efficacy functionally precedes a goal in the goal system hierarchy, priming self-efficacy will lead to "bottom-up" activation of the goal it supports.

Whether primed conscious or subconscious self-efficacy will guide self-regulation will depend on whether an individual is acquiring novel behavior or executing a well-established behavior (Bandura, 1986; Carroll & Bandura, 1990). During acquisition phases of a behavioral repertoire, individuals need perceived self-efficacy to help analyze if they can execute the demands and to decide on strategies to translate early feedback to proficient action (Carroll & Bandura, 1987). Once an individual forms a facilitative means to a goal and achieves related behavioral proficiency, perceived self-efficacy beliefs stabilize. These beliefs are internalized and subconsciously stored. When the person encounters a self-efficacy cue, it primes the related goal into action with no need for attentional processing. If automated behavior fails to produce desired results or significant changes in task demands occur, consciousness is re-engaged to identify the problem and devise better ways of handling it. At this point, the individual will reappraise self-efficacy through deliberate reflection. After s/he crystallizes the updated self-efficacy-behavior link, it becomes the habitual way of executing behavior. The individual then re-encodes and stores the updated belief in his/her subconscious, and control of action reverts to subconscious regulation (see Evans, 2008; Evans & Stanovich, 2013).

Empirical Evidence

Guided by these conceptions, Stajković, Bandura, Sergent, and Greenwald (2019) conducted seven experiments to test the following complementary research questions: (1) Can self-efficacy be primed to operate without awareness? (2) If it can, does primed self-efficacy have convergent and incremental predictive validity with perceived self-efficacy? (3) Do the two levels of efficacy operate within a dual cognitive system such that each independently contributes to behavior? (4) Can self-efficacy be routinized and primed to influence task-specific behavior without awareness? In all seven experiments, the authors relied on the ideomotor response activation. This presumes that participants have previously established a link in memory between self-efficacy and related behavior.

In Experiment 1, the authors verified the ideomotor premise by testing if participants act automatically on primed self-efficacy without appraising it consciously. Participants were 86 evening MBA students from a university in the Upper Midwest who were randomly assigned to one of two groups. Students assigned to the primed self-efficacy group received sentences with embedded prime words shown in Figure 7.2. Participants assigned to the control group unscrambled neutral sentences.

After unscrambling the sentences, all participants performed a brainstorming task. They had two minutes to list as many uses as possible for a brick. Non-uses (e.g., smash it) were excluded, and duplicate uses such as "to build a house" or "to build" were counted as a single use. To ensure that the sentences did not bias conscious perceptions of efficacy, participants were probed with six awareness questions to test for knowledge of the embedded words. If responses indicated an awareness of the self-efficacy theme, their data was removed before analyses. Students primed with self-efficacy brainstormed more uses than did students in the control group.

In a second experiment, the authors randomly assigned 45 evening MBA students from a Southwest university to the same two groups. Instead of brainstorming, they were presented with a geometric tracing task (see Chapter 2). The authors were interested in whether priming self-efficacy would cause the participants to spend more time trying to solve the puzzle. Unbeknownst to participants, the puzzle was unsolvable. On average, students primed with self-efficacy spent three minutes longer working on the puzzle.

The next experiment had two purposes. It tested how priming self-efficacy impacts performance, but also verified the priming task was affecting subconscious, not conscious, beliefs. Although an awareness

For the next task, you will be provided with several word sets. Each word set contains five words. Your task is to make a grammatically correct sentence using **FOUR** of the five words in each set. In doing so:

a) You cannot change the tense of the verbs (e.g., "flew" to "fly"), and
b) The sentence must make sense without any punctuation except an end period.

An example:
flew   eagle   the   water   around   (set of five words)
The eagle flew around.   (correct **four**-word sentence)

1. glass	can	do	I	well
2. my	strong	is	self-belief	twists
3. melts	water	when	butter	heated
4. control	I	performance	my	wall
5. spicy	wind	likes	he	food
6. have	I	high	object	self-efficacy
7. a	what	worse	smile	great
8. I've	faith	myself	sweeten	in
9. on	sleeping	turn	the	lamp
10. am	personally	printer	I	optimistic
11. self-assured	very	I	deals	am
12. somewhat	type	prepared	was	I
13. trust	I	ability	pyramid	my
14. do	I	things	rabbit	well
15. an	aspirin	he	clock	took
16. believe	in	I	antenna	myself
17. strong	have	capability	clean	I
18. tiger	very	self-confident	I	am
19. sang	sweetly	robin	the	scratching
20. her	likes	swear	car	she

Figure 7.2 Scrambled sentences to prime self-efficacy.

check was used in the first two studies, in this experiment implicit doubt was measured. The premise examined was that if subconscious self-efficacy was activated, then primed participants should display less implicit doubt. To further mitigate the possibility that self-efficacy was operating consciously, trait optimism, knowledge, and cognitive ability were measured. The performance task was solving 24 anagrams, and participants had one minute to solve as many as possible. Figure 7.3 presents an example of the task.

After two practice rounds of anagrams, participants unscrambled the sentences. Next, implicit doubt was assessed. As described in Chapter 3, projective measures tap into subconscious constructs. The authors adapted McClelland's thematic apperception test, which asks participants to write stories about pictures. The text of the stories was used to analyze implicit motives. All participants were given the following instructions:

> This is a test of your creative imagination. A picture will be printed at the top of each page. Please spend about twenty seconds looking at the picture and then about three minutes to make up a story about it. Notice there is one page for each picture. The same four questions

```
acrot _____
                          evah _____
bene _____
                          dunre _____
socle _____
                          ouatb _____
doro _____
                          eehr _____
talnp _____
                          enm_____
ebtu _____
                          yoatd _____
libl _____
                          seur _____
eterh _____
                          imdn _____
inef _____
                          lmsal _____
wenk _____
                          lewl _____
nsee _____
                          dugteb _____
stmhno _____
                          reubmn _____
```

Figure 7.3 Word anagram task.

will be asked. They will guide your thinking and enable you to cover all the elements of a plot:

1. What is happening, who are the persons?
2. What has led up to this situation? That is, what has happened in the past?
3. What is being thought? What is wanted? By whom?
4. What will happen? What will be done?

Participants had four minutes to write a story for each photo (with four photos total). The text was analyzed using a software that looks for patterns. The authors were interested in stories reflective of high or low doubt. Examples of responses scored high on implicit doubt are as follows:

> "You'll never be good enough." "You call yourself an artist?" "Why don't you do something with your life?" Zoey was drowning in thoughts of all the remarks she had heard over the last 4 years. Everybody doubted her. Nobody believed in her.
> Think stupid think.
> She wants to go out and be her own thing, but she isn't confidence.

Juxtapose the responses above with the following story excerpts observed:

> Gaby has a goal and missing out on a few hangout nights is worth it for being about to receive a full academic scholarship.

Tanya will go to bed like she does every night and dream of a better life.

She is trying do better in school.

As can be gleaned from these examples, students who unscrambled sentences with prime self-efficacy words used fewer doubt words (e.g., worry, anxious, fearful, doubtful) in their stories. After the picture story task, participants performed more rounds of the anagram task. Consistent with the first experiment, students primed with self-efficacy solved more anagrams than did students in the control group. Moreover, when past performance, GPA, ACT, trait optimism, and implicit nAch were added as predictors, primed self-efficacy continued to predict performance. This speaks to the predictive power of primed subconscious self-efficacy beliefs.

Up to this point, perceived self-efficacy was unmeasured. In the next experiment, participants consciously appraised their perceived self-efficacy from 0% to 100% that they could meet 10 increasingly difficult performance levels (see Figure 7.1). The authors analyzed if participants primed with self-efficacy exhibited higher scores of perceived self-efficacy. There was no significant statistical relationship. Thus, it seems primed self-efficacy operates subconsciously without affecting conscious beliefs. After participants rated perceived self-efficacy, they performed the brainstorming task. Both primed and perceived self-efficacy improved brainstorming performance. These effects held after controlling for prior performance.

Together, primed self-efficacy affected performance without awareness, and both primed and perceived self-efficacy operated independently. But, could subconscious self-efficacy be more important when a person is experiencing repeated success? It seems more likely that the subconscious takes over when habitual behavior produces a desired outcome. In contrast, could perceived self-efficacy be more important when a person is experiencing failure? It seems plausible that conscious self-efficacy re-engages to adjust behavior and improve performance. To examine these questions, 122 evening and executive MBA students at a Midwest university were randomly assigned to the two self-efficacy groups. In addition, they were randomly assigned to a success or a failure group.

After completing the first few tasks and self-efficacy scale, students in the success group were asked to "Think of two times in which you succeeded in an intellectual pursuit, succeeding to achieve a level that would be consistent with your personal standards of accomplishment." Students in the failure group received the same prompt, except the words "succeeded" and "succeeding" were replaced with "failed" and "failing." After the prompt, participants wrote a short description of their experiences. Next, they performed several rounds of word anagrams. Consistent with prior findings, students primed with self-efficacy solved more anagrams. Likewise, students with higher perceived self-efficacy performed better than did those with low self-efficacy. Again, primed self-efficacy was unrelated to perceived self-efficacy, supporting the dual-process conception. The hypothesized interactions, however, were unsupported. This suggests that both primed and perceived self-efficacy are equally valuable contributors to performance under success and failure conditions.

In the first six experiments, a general concept of self-efficacy (e.g., "I can do it") was primed. But, social cognitive theory treats the efficacy belief system as a differentiated set of beliefs linked to specific tasks, not as an omnibus trait (Bandura, 1997). Think, for example, about Broadway stars. They differ in their perceived efficacy to fulfill the acting, musical, dance, and emotive aspects of their craft and to fuse them together into a theatrical performance. Thus, the authors conducted an experiment to test if subconscious self-efficacy can be routinized to produce automatic, task-specific behavior. To do this, 97 evening MBA students at a Midwest university were randomly assigned to one of three groups. Two of the three groups were identical to the prior experiments. The third group was primed with the self-efficacy words and with math words (e.g., count, addition). After students unscrambled sentences and rated their perceived efficacy, they performed a simple addition task. This assumes MBA students have routinized addition at the subconscious level. Participants had one minute to solve as many three-digit addition problems as possible. Figure 7.4 presents an example of this task.

811 + 804 = _____

397 + 821 = _____

181 + 192 = _____

983 + 379 = _____

375 + 893 = _____

345 + 833 = _____

171 + 710 = _____

980 + 886 = _____

937 + 858 = _____

706 + 295 = _____

120 + 377 = _____

953 + 552 = _____

581 + 100 = _____

356 + 446 = _____

739 + 830 = _____

849 + 631 = _____

744 + 865 = _____

462 + 117 = _____

836 + 724 = _____

117 + 883 = _____

328 + 672 = _____

364 + 676 = _____

464 + 601 = _____

690 + 468 = _____

Figure 7.4 Math addition task.

Consistent with the hypothesis, students primed with math self-efficacy solved more problems than did students primed with general self-efficacy. The results from the prior experiments were also replicated; students primed with general self-efficacy outperformed students in the control group. Again, perceived self-efficacy improved performance, but its effect was independent of primed self-efficacy. These findings suggest that self-efficacy can be primed to autogenerate task-specific behavior without awareness. Notably, priming a more specific self-efficacy produced a stronger performance effect for that specific task.

Though intriguing, these experiments were conducted in a lab with students. To expand the generality of findings, a field experiment in a business organization was conducted. Participants were employees of a customer call center in the U.S. Their job involved answering phone calls to address questions and give solutions to customer inquiries and complaints. On Monday morning of the experimental week, the CEO sent two emails. He sent the first one to employees randomly assigned to the primed self-efficacy group:

> As we enter our busiest quarter, I want to offer some words of inspiration to counteract the upcoming service challenges. Although your job is challenging, I hope you **trust your ability** to **do things well. If you believe in yourself** and in your **capability** you can **control your** performance. Your **self-belief** and **can-do** attitude make a difference to the customer. If you have **faith in yourself** and are **self-assured** that you can resolve customer issues successfully, then it can happen. Think **optimistically** and be **self-confident** about your work. If nothing else, having high **self-efficacy** about work should improve your day.

His second email was sent to employees randomly assigned to the control group:

> As we enter our busiest quarter, I want to take a moment out of your day to remind you that it is you who play the largest role in determining our company's successful call handling performance. Whether or not customer issues are resolved to their satisfaction is up to you. Your call handling ability represents the most important competency for you to develop as you continue your career with this company. As you live by our company motto—have fun, make money, grow your career—know that you play an important role in the performance of our company.

Job performance was assessed with two measures. *Average Call Handling Time* (ACHT) is the time in seconds an employee handles a customer call. This measure captures speed but does not indicate if they resolved the customer's issue. *Average Call Resolution Time* (ACRT) is the percentage of time employees resolve the customer's issue in one call. Performance was measured on Monday and on average over for the week.

On Monday, employees in the primed self-efficacy group had lower call handling time than those in the control group by 32.98 seconds. Employees primed with self-efficacy resolved, on average, 2.46% more calls the first time compared with other employees. Did these results hold over the entire week? Surprisingly, yes. Analyzing average performance over the week, employees primed with self-efficacy had an average call handling time that was 38.25 seconds less than that of employees in the control group. Moreover, employees primed with self-efficacy resolved 7.93% more calls the first time compared to other employees. One caveat is that employees could not be probed for awareness. Thus, the authors could not unambiguously conclude that these effects occurred subconsciously, though the performance differences caused by the altered text in the email was tangible and sizeable.

Finally, the single effect sizes from the seven experiments were meta-analyzed. The average effect size between subconscious self-efficacy and behavior was $d = .43$, $p <.01$, 95% CI [0.27, 0.58], and single effect sizes were homogeneous, $Q_t(\mathrm{df} = k{-}1 = 6) = 8.41$, $p = .21$. The homogeneity test offers empirical assurance that manipulations of the subconscious self-efficacy across the seven experiments were consistent. The average effect size of $d = .43$ for primed self-efficacy, albeit from this small meta-analysis, is similar to meta-analytically derived average effect of perceived self-efficacy on performance, $G(r_+) = .38$, supporting the contention that subconscious self-efficacy results in similar outcomes as conscious, perceived self-efficacy.

Summary

Perceived self-efficacy relies on a budget of limited attention resources. If one rushes to attentional processing, the budget will be exhausted. We examined primed self-efficacy as an unsung hero in social cognitive theory. Primed and perceived self-efficacy in tandem offered a more complete theoretical representation of how self-efficacy influences behavior. The challenges of modern life place a premium on people's efficacy for personal renewal to sustain daily trials and to shape their future. Unless people can gauge optimal allocation of attentional resources to the perceptions of self-efficacy for any task and context, primed self-efficacy comes to the rescue.

References

Bandura, A. (1986). *Social foundations of thought and action.* Englewood Cliffs, NJ: Prentice-Hall, Inc.

Bandura, A. (Ed.). (1995). *Self-efficacy in changing societies.* New York, NY: Cambridge University Press.

Bandura, A. (1997). *Self-efficacy: The exercise of control.* New York, NY: Freeman.

Bandura, A. (1999). Social cognitive theory: An agentic perspective. *Asian Journal of Social Psychology, 2*(1), 21–41.

Bandura, A. (2002). Growing primacy of human agency in adaptation and change in the electronic era. *European Psychologist, 7,* 2–16.

Bandura, A. (2013). The role of self-efficacy in goal-based motivation. In *New developments in goal setting and task performance* (pp. 171–181). New York, NY: Routledge.

Bandura, A. (2016). *Moral disengagement: How people do harm and live with themselves.* New York, NY: Worth Publishers.

Bandura, A. (2018). Toward a psychology of human agency: Pathways and reflections. *Perspectives on Psychological Science, 13,* 130–136.

Bandura, A., & Cervone, D. (1983). Self-evaluative and self-efficacy mechanisms governing the motivational effects of goal systems. *Journal of Personality and Social Psychology, 45,* 1017–1028.

Bouffard-Bouchard, T. (1990). Influence of self-efficacy on performance in a cognitive task. *The Journal of Social Psychology, 130,* 353–363.

Brown, S. D., & Lent, R. W. (2016). Vocational psychology: Agency, equity, and well-being. *Annual Review of Psychology, 67,* 541–566.

Brown, S. D., & Lent, R. W. (2017). Social cognitive career theory in a diverse word. *Journal of Career Assessment, 25,* 173–180.

Brown, S. D., Lent, R. W., Telander, K., & Tramayne, S. (2011). Social cognitive career theory, conscientiousness, and work performance: A meta-analytic path analysis. *Journal of Vocational Behavior, 79,* 81–90.

Brown, S. D., Tramayne, S., Hoxha, D., Telander, K., Fan, X., & Lent, R. W. (2008). Social cognitive predictors of college students' academic performance and persistence: A meta-analytic path analysis. *Journal of Vocational Behavior, 72,* 298–308.

Caprara, G. V., Alessandri, G., Di Giunta, L., Panerai, L., & Eisenberg, N. (2009). The contribution of agreeableness and self-efficacy beliefs to prosociality. *European Journal of Personality, 24,* 36–55.

Caprara, G. V., Barbaranelli, C., Pastorelli, C., & Cervone, D. (2004). The contribution of self-efficacy beliefs to psychosocial outcomes in adolescence: Predicting beyond global dispositional tendencies. *Personality and Individual Differences, 37,* 751–763.

Carroll, W. R., & Bandura, A. (1987). Translating cognition into action: The role of visual guidance in observational learning. *Journal of Motor Behavior, 19,* 385–398.

Carroll, W. R., & Bandura, A. (1990). Representational guidance of action production in observational learning: A causal analysis. *Journal of Motor Behavior, 22,* 85–97.

Cervone, D., & Peake, P. K. (1986). Anchoring, efficacy, and action: The influence of judgmental heuristics on self-efficacy judgments and behavior. *Journal of Personality and Social Psychology, 50,* 492–501.

Chartrand, T. L., Fitzsimons, G. M., & Fitzsimons, G. J. (2008). Automatic effects of anthropomorphized objects on behavior. *Social Cognition, 26*(2), 198–209.

Evans, J. S. (2008). Dual-processing accounts of reasoning, judgment, and social cognition. *Annual Review of Psychology, 59,* 255–278.

Evans, J. S. B., & Stanovich, K. E. (2013). Dual-process theories of higher cognition: Advancing the debate. *Perspectives on Psychological Science, 8,* 223–241.

Eysenck, M. W., & Calvo, M. G. (1992). Anxiety and performance: The processing efficiency theory. *Cognition & Emotion*, 6(6), 409–434.

Eysenck, M. W., Derakshan, N., Santos, R., & Calvo, M. G. (2007). Anxiety and cognitive performance: Attentional control theory. *Emotion*, 7(2), 336–353.

Feltz, D., & Hill, C. (2018). Understanding group motivation gains in exercise and sport contexts. *Journal of Sport and Exercise Psychology*, 40, s5.

Fitzsimons, G. M., & Bargh, J. A. (2003). Thinking of you: Nonconscious pursuit of interpersonal goals associated with relationship partners. *Journal of Personality and Social Psychology*, 84, 148–164.

Gallup. (2017). *State of the global workplace.* Washington, DC: Gallup, Inc.

Gardner, D. G., & Pierce, J. L. (1998). Self-esteem and self-efficacy within the organizational context: An empirical examination. *Group & Organization Management*, 23, 48–70.

Jacobs, B., Prentice-Dunn, S., & Rogers, R. (1984). Understanding persistence: An interface of control theory and self-efficacy theory. *Basic and Applied Social Psychology*, 5, 333–347.

Lord, R. G., Diefendorff, J. M., Schmidt, A. M., & Hall, R. J. (2010). Self-regulation at work. *Annual Review of Psychology*, 61, 543–568.

Park, S. E., Myers, N., Ahn, S., Lee, S., Sullivan, P., & Feltz, D. (2018). Proposed sources of coaching efficacy: A meta-analysis. *Journal of Sport and Exercise Psychology*, 40, 261–276.

Shah, J. Y., & Kruglanski, A. W. (2003). When opportunity knocks: Bottom-up priming of goals by means and its effects on self-regulation. *Journal of Personality and Social Psychology*, 84, 1109–1122.

Sheeran, P., Maki, A., Montanaro, E., Avishai-Yitshak, A., Bryan, A., Klein, W. M., & Rothman, A. J. (2016). The impact of changing attitudes, norms, and self-efficacy on health-related intentions and behavior: A meta-analysis. *Health Psychology*, 35, 1178–1188.

Sincrich, J. (2017, February 1). 19 Successful women get real about the times they failed. *Women's Health*. Retrieved from www.womenshealthmag.com/life/a19945222/how-to-be-successful-after-failure/

Smith, D. (2002). The theory heard 'round the world. Albert Bandura's social cognitive theory is the foundation of television and radio shows in the developing world that have changed lives of millions by fostering health behaviors. *Monitor on Psychology*, APA, 33, 30. See also: Confidence man: Psychology pioneer Albert Bandura puts his theories to work helping people to believe in themselves and change their world. *Stanford Magazine*, September/October 2006.

Stajković, A. D. (2006). Development of a core confidence-higher order construct. *Journal of Applied Psychology*, 91(6), 1208–1224.

Stajković, A. D., Bandura, A., Locke, E. A., Lee, D., & Sergent, K. (2018). Test of three conceptual models of influence of the big five personality traits and self-efficacy on academic performance: A meta-analytic path-analysis. *Personality and Individual Differences*, 120, 238–245.

Stajković, A. D., Bandura, A., Sergent, K., & Greenwald, J. M. (2019). *The role of dual-process self-efficacy in adaptive functioning.* Unpublished manuscript.

Stajković, A. D., Lee, D., Greenwald, J. M., & Raffiee, J. (2015). The role of trait core confidence higher-order construct in self-regulation of performance and attitudes: Evidence from four studies. *Organizational Behavior and Human Decision Processes*, 128, 29–48.

Stajković, A. D., & Luthans, F. (1998). Self-efficacy and work-related performance: A meta- analysis. *Psychological Bulletin, 124,* 240–261.

Stajković, A. D., & Sergent, K. (2019). *Social cognitive theory.* Forthcoming chapter in Oxford Classic Bibliographies in Management. New York, NY: Oxford University Press.

Weinberg, R. S., Gould, D., Yukelson, D., & Jackson, A. (1981). The effect of preexisting and manipulated self-efficacy on a competitive muscular endurance task. *Journal of Sport Psychology, 3,* 345–354.

Wood, R., & Bandura, A. (1989). Social cognitive theory of organizational management. *Academy of Management Review, 14,* 361–384.

8 Organizational Behavior Research on Priming Goals Guided by History of Reinforcement

Narendra is a hardworking manager who has been at his job for three years. He likes his job, but his new boss is pushing him to work longer hours. Narendra is a salaried employee unpaid for overtime. In the past, his manager offered to buy pizza to entice him to work longer. Last week, Narendra was assigned a goal to finish a shipment that had been delayed because of a bug in the software. He has already worked late every night for a week. The project is due today, and Narendra is on track to meet his goal, but it will require an exhausting 12-hour day. Around 4 p.m. today, however, Narendra's wife surprised him with tickets for the big game this evening. Will Narendra stay to achieve his goal or abandon the goal and go to the game with his wife?

People face goals that compete for attentional resources, physical energy, and time. The choices we make are often influenced by contingent reinforcement. In this example, Narendra's decision will depend on whether the pleasure he derives from the game trumps the value of the reinforcer attached to reaching his goal on time. If a history of reinforcement implies that pizza will be a reinforcer, then Narendra will probably abandon the goal in favor of the game. Instead, if his manager made a sizable cash bonus contingent on completing the project on time, Narendra may stay. The choice depends, though, on the history of reinforcement Narendra has built over time.

The effect of contingently applied positive reinforcement on behavior is one of the most agreed-upon findings in the science of organizational behavior (SOB). In his seminal book on motivation, Vroom (1964, p. 13) stated,

> [W]ithout a doubt the law of effect or principle of reinforcement must be included among the most substantiated findings of experimental psychology and is at the same time among the most useful findings for an applied psychology concerned with control of human behavior.

Similarly, in his classic work in social psychology, Bandura (1986, p. 228) concluded,

> [H]uman behavior cannot be fully understood without considering the regulatory influence of response consequences.

A reinforcer is a contingent consequence that increases frequency of a desired behavior. Three reinforcers commonly used in organizations are money, feedback, and social recognition (Luthans & Stajković, 2009).

Since Skinner (1938) formulated the principles of operant conditioning, research in OB has accumulated support for the effects of contingently and consciously applied positive reinforcement (Stajković & Luthans, 1997, 2001, 2003). This research, though, has not considered the possibility of priming goals based on history of reinforcement. Grounded in the principles of the auto-motive model, we posit that reinforcers used to reinforce goal attainment in the past can become associated in memory with related goals and behaviors. In this way, supraliminal priming of reinforcement can trigger a mental representation of a goal, leading automatically to behavior. Consider the opening example. If Narendra was positively reinforced with money for achieving this goal in the past, then priming money will potentially influence his choice to stay. Priming money does not involve issuing money. Instead, it involves presenting the concept of money outside of the subject's awareness. If priming money, social recognition, or feedback alters employee behavior in ways consistent with administering these reinforcers, organizations will never be the same.

Money

In the story of organizations, money plays a central character. Many employees deal with money daily, and the notion of profit hovers in the workplace. People earn money at work and then dispense it on mortgages, rent, insurance, schooling, daycare, food, gas, coffee, and nearly everything needed to survive and prosper. On its face, money has been a pervasive component of human affairs since antiquity. Across the social sciences, research supports money as a key predictor of human thought and action, but with varied implications. For instance, money as a valued exchange medium is at the center of both *The Communist Manifesto* of Marx and Engels (1848) and neoclassical economics (Veblen, 1990), but for contrasting reasons. In social psychology, money as a semiotic meaning-maker figures into research on happiness, satisfaction with life, and subjective well-being (Diener & Seligman, 2004; Diener, Tay, & Oishi, 2013) but also into research on anxiety, depression, and clinical practice (Seligman, 2007).

Because many working adults earn money from employment, compensation research has focused on examining how money affects work outcomes. Short of a few skeptical views (e.g., Deci, 1972), research has shown consistent support for pay for performance as a reliable predictor of outcomes across organizations, employees, methods of implementation, and national cultures. Despite the accumulated body of money research incrementally built over decades, social psychologists have questioned its relevance. For example, in their chapter on "Money at Work," Furhnahm and Argyle (1998, pp. 204–2019) stated:

> It comes as a surprise to many people to be told, or find out for themselves, that most psychology books that deal with work (occupational, organizational, and industrial psychology) are unlikely to refer to money at all. . . . Money per se is usually seen as one of many rewards at work, and in itself not particularly important.

Others have labeled money research as "dustbowl of pure empiricism" and "stacking up of bricks," arguably, implying this research lacks prospective thinking (Bijleveld & Aarts, 2015, p. 28).

An interest in thought-provoking effects of primed money emerged in social psychology (Vohs, Mead, & Goode, 2006, 2008). To prime money is to trigger its mental representation, which then activates automatically thoughts and behaviors associated with money. Imagine, for instance, that your supervisor assigned to you a goal to review and interpret two years of cash flow statements to predict future trends of a potential acquisition target. You sit and ponder how to approach this task. On the wall in front of you hangs one of these two posters:

Would your goal-directed behavior differ depending on which poster was on the wall? Vohs et al. (2006) found the answer to be yes. When money was primed, such as with a poster on the wall, participants were more likely to prefer solitary activities, lack desire to work with others, separate themselves from others, and abstain from seeking help. This is because money primed a goal to be self-sufficient. Extrapolating this to the work scenario, the money poster might increase the likelihood of you reserving an empty conference room, putting headphones in, and resisting seeking help. Yet, these behaviors automatically unfold without you knowing a subconscious "self-sufficiency" goal primed by the money poster caused them. Extending this inquiry, Zhou, Vohs, and Baumeister (2009) asked participants to count either 80 $100 bills or 80 pieces of paper. After participants finished, the authors presented them with the following scale:

The scale consists of words that describe different feelings and emotions. Indicate to what extent you feel the following emotions at the present moment:

(1) Not at all   (2) A little   (3) Moderately   (4) Quite a bit   (5) Extremely

Respected___	Unwanted___	Unappreciated___	Significant___
Devalued___	Valued___	Rejected___	Accepted___

Figure 8.1 Southampton Social Self-esteem Scale.

This scale is called the Southampton Social Self-esteem Scale (Sedikides, 2008). It measures social distress. What did Zhou and colleagues find? Priming money activated a self-sufficiency goal and aroused related emotions. In turn, participants primed with money reported less distress. Though notable, that effect was purely perceptual. It did not address whether priming money actually reduced distress or caused participants to simply conceal it more. In a follow-up experiment, Zhou and colleagues asked participants to immerse their fingers in hot water (50 °C) for 30 seconds, and again at a moderately hot temperature (43 °C) for 60 seconds. Then, participants reported experienced pain on a nine-point scale. Pain should reflect changes in water temperature; it should be unrelated to the priming money task. Yet, participants who counted money versus paper reported significantly less pain. To determine if touching money caused these effects, Zhou et al. (2009) conducted a second set of experiments. Instead of counting money, participants listed either their expenditures for the last 30 days or described the weather conditions over the last 30 days. The findings were consistent.

Priming money is not without negative side effects. In an experiment with 66 working adults, Pfeffer and DeVoe (2009) asked participants to calculate either their own hourly wage or to calculate the average hourly wage in the U.S. Then, participants responded to the following statements on a scale from 1 (strongly disagree) to 9 (strongly agree):

1. I am willing to volunteer for an organization I care about without financial compensation for me
2. Even for an organization I care about, I am unwilling to work without getting paid
3. I'm unlikely to undertake any type of work without being paid
4. Volunteering is a worthwhile use of my time even if I do not get paid
5. Without some financial compensation, it is not worth doing volunteer work

Participants who calculated their own hourly wage compared with others were less willing to volunteer, as shown by their responses to these statements.

Molinsky, Grant, and Margolis (2012) conducted a study with working professionals. They randomly assigned 50 professional managers to either unscramble sentences with money words or unscramble neutral sentences. Next, participants thought about delivering negative feedback to a colleague who was not pulling her weight on the team. The study protocol informed participants that this colleague was competent, but sometimes failed to show up at morning meetings because she does not own a car. Participants imagined they would meet with this person tomorrow and wrote down what they would say. The experimenters enlisted two independent coders to read responses and rate them from 1 (not at all compassionate) to 7 (extremely compassionate). What did they find? When managers were primed with money, they exhibited significantly *less* compassion in their responses compared with the other managers who had not been primed.

In a second study with undergraduates at a private university, the same authors gave participants one of the following two lists and asked them to use the words to write a story:

List 1	*List 2*
economic rational	book
logical	car
fiscally responsible	chair
efficient	computer
profitable	desk
self-interested	pen
cost-benefit analysis	street
businesslike	table
professional	trashcan

Figure 8.2 List sorting manipulation to prime money.

After participants wrote a story, they read a memo informing them the school was facing financial hardships. The memo stated the school needed to revoke a $3,000 scholarship from three honor students. It stated that the students "do not yet know that they are losing their scholarships and may not be able to write honors theses as a result." Participants were instructed to draft a letter delivering the bad news to students. Independent raters coded letters on a 1–7 compassion scale. In addition, participants completed an empathy scale and indicated the extent to which they viewed expression of emotion as unprofessional. Participants primed with money expressed less compassion, reported less empathy, and perceived an expression of emotion as more unprofessional than students in the control group. These findings imply that priming money affects both behaviors associated with money goals, as well as associated emotions.

Now, imagine that you finished eating lunch at a cash-only restaurant. You have $10 left in your pocket. You pass a donation jar (one of the three jars shown here). The jar is collecting money for a charity that provides long-term aid to children and mothers in developing countries. Will your willingness to donate some amount of money depend on the design of the jar?

Transparent-empty   Transparent-full   Opaque

Ekici and Shiri (2018) conducted this experiment with 186 participants using similar photos to the above (e.g., an empty box, half-full box, opaque box). One might think the transparent-full jar prompted the most donations, i.e., if others donated, I should too. Interestingly, Ekici and Shiri (2018) found that willingness to donate was significantly higher when participants saw the opaque jar compared to the other two transparent jars. Why? The authors asserted that a "dark side" of a self-sufficiency goal is a decreased responsiveness to the needs of others. This can cause people to "prefer individualism over communality" (p. 139).

In a follow-up field study, the authors placed a donation box for UNICEF in a public library. On Monday, the box was opaque; on Tuesday, it was transparent-empty; and on Wednesday, it was transparent-full. A research assistant approached patrons in the library and asked if they were willing to take part in a campaign. Then, the researcher left the room. After the patron left, the researcher returned to count the donation. Consistent with the first study, the opaque box caused people to donate more money than the other two designs. The dollar value of donations did not differ between the transparent-empty and transparent-full boxes. Moreover, people who were approached when the opaque box was in the library were more willing to volunteer than people approached in the presence of the transparent boxes. These findings suggest that priming money triggers a goal to make money, which decreases people's willingness to give money away.

Because money priming unfolds without awareness, the downstream consequence is an inability to pinpoint the conflict between heightened motivation and self-sufficiency and drop in cooperation and ethical conduct. Extrapolating this to organizations suggests priming money can compromise employee behaviors. By studying money priming, scholars and practitioners will gain a theoretical understanding of inconsistencies caused by exposure to money. Empirically, though, money priming effects in social psychology have failed to replicate, have been suspected of duplicitous analyses, and some have even been retracted (Chatterjee, Rose, & Sinha, 2013). Therefore, organizations should use caution before implementing money primes to increase motivation or self-sufficiency.

Social Recognition and Feedback

One of our students, like so many other employees, did her job; she was not unhappy, but she was not bubbling over with zest and energy either. After 20 years with her employer, her business was subdivided into two different companies. She now worked for a new organization, and a new manager supervised her work. Midway through the semester, the change in her demeanor was palpable; she was radiating enthusiasm and losing weight. When we asked what sparked the change, she said, "Well, nothing really . . . I am just so happily engaged in my job I am eating healthier and exercising more." The answer was clear. Since she started working for a new manager, her motivation had increased, and she regained a sense of purpose in her work and personal life. When we asked her about the change in leadership, she told us that her new manager appreciates her and tells her regularly how she is doing in her job, exclaiming, "He trusts me, believes in me, and he tells me that."

Social recognition is a powerful currency in human affairs. In organizations, social recognition is defined as "contingently informal genuine acknowledgement, approval, and appreciation for work well done to another individual and/or group" (Luthans & Stajković, 2009, p. 240). Social recognition has a wide appeal because it requires virtually no financial resources. Few ever get too much of it, as noted by an employee in Wagner and Harter's (2006, p. 54) study:

> For me, receiving praise and recognition kind of sets off a little explosion inside. It's kind of like, "oh, that was good, but you know what? I can do better." It helps give you drive to want to continue achieving.

Theoretically, the effectiveness of social recognition depends on three dimensions: (1) outcome utility, (2) informative content (i.e., feedback), and (3) forethought as a psychological mechanism (Stajković & Luthans, 2001, 2003). Outcome utility refers to the connection between the recognition and its expected benefits, such as a promotion or raise. The greater the outcome utility, the more effective social recognition is at changing behavior. Informative content refers to the feedback value of the recognition. Showing employees how much you value their work with social recognition is inutile with non-contingent standardized phrases (e.g., good job!). Consider these stories submitted to the *Government Executive* mini-blog (Rutzick, 2007):

> I started my own way of rewarding my colleagues . . . I pass out miniature figurines of pigs with wings . . . People seem to enjoy them because of the recognition of doing something special. And they make great conversation starters so that people can brag a little about what they've accomplished.
> —Jeffrey K. Bower, Defense Logistics Agency

> One day, the director came to my office and handed me a "Catch Me Doing Something Right" lapel pin. Of course, eventually everyone received at least one. I never figured out how that was supposed to motivate us. We all agreed that except for the day we received the pin, we must have been doing something wrong. It was a really bad idea that he obviously heard about in one of his many business meetings.
> —Anonymous

As illustrated, indiscriminate recognition becomes an "empty reward," rendering it ineffective. Too often, managers mistakenly assume that gimmicks, such as pins, plaques, employee of the month, or gift cards will reinforce desired behaviors similar to the manager in the first example. The problem with this approach is that it lacks informative content (e.g., "I know you stayed late last week to finish preparing the management report for the committee meeting today. It was a great success"). The more informative the recognition is, the greater the likelihood of increasing motivation for subsequent behaviors. Finally, forethought is a cognitive mechanism that permits perceiving future desired outcomes in the present. Without it, people cannot mentally operationalize recognition as a reinforcer (Stajković & Luthans, 2001). In the second example above, the employee was unable to connect the reinforcer with the desired behavior, preventing her from exercising forethought.

Why are feedback and recognition powerful reinforcers in the workplace? Because one major determinant of self-construal is how we believe others will regard our actions (Sullivan, 1953). During goal pursuit, we analyze our progress through both our own lens and the lens we believe others hold. Because self-appraisal occurs frequently during goal striving, the informative content we glean from others becomes associated in memory with a goal. In this way, people form associations between people (cues), behaviors (that are reinforced), and goals. When the person is encountered, the goal is primed. Although OB research has yet to examine primed goals related to feedback and social reinforcement, findings from social psychology shed light into this possibility.

For example, imagine we asked you to generate two goals to pursue this year and to articulate an action plan to achieve them. Then, we inserted the faces in the image shown here as a faded backdrop (for this example, pretend this person is your mentor at work):

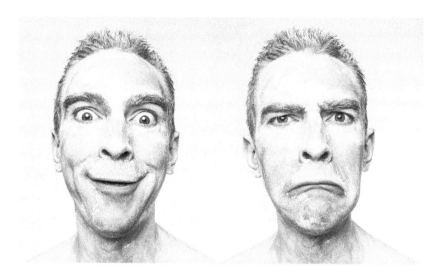

Next, imagine we asked you to answer these questions:

1.   How good do you feel your goals are, overall?
2.   How important are these goals?
3.   How effective is your action plan likely to be?
4.   How much do you like your goals?
5.   Assign a grade from 0%–100% to your goals and action plan.

Would your ratings depend on which photo was used as a backdrop? Baldwin, Carrell, and Lopez (1990) conducted a similar study with graduate psychology students who were asked to generate research ideas. Students subliminally primed with an approval face of their advisor (i.e., positive feedback) rated their ideas higher compared with those primed with the disapproving face (i.e., negative feedback). The implication is that implied feedback, either positive or negative, primes goal-to-behavior reactions in the same way that providing feedback face-to-face does.

Now, visualize yourself sitting alone in the waiting area of an airport. A researcher approaches you and asks if you will complete a short questionnaire. You agree, and the experimenter asks you to read one of the following two scenarios:

1.   Think of a good friend whom you know quite well and with whom you do not work. Write down the initials of whom you are thinking. Provide a vivid description of the person's appearance, the length of time you have known the person, their age, hobbies, and career objectives.

2.   Think of a co-worker whom you know quite well, with whom you have a positive relationship, and who is approximately equal in terms of status at work (i.e., not a supervisor nor a subordinate) but who is not a friend outside of work. [same questions as in (1) followed]

Fitzsimons and Bargh (2003) found that participants who read the first scenario were more likely to volunteer for a second study compared with those primed with a co-worker goal. At the end of the study, the researchers asked participants if they felt the first task influenced their willingness to volunteer; no participants reported such a belief. This demonstrates that priming goals associated with prior interpersonal relationships influence thoughts and intentions without conscious awareness.

In another study on interpersonal goal priming, Shah (2003) informed participants they will complete an anagram task that relies on verbal fluency. The instructions claimed "individuals with a high degree of verbal fluency could find 80% of all the possible solutions" (p. 670). Forthwith, participants provided the name of someone who would most want them to have verbal fluency (positive social recognition) and the name of someone who would least want them to have it (negative recognition). To disguise the prime, the experimenters asked participants to give a host of other names in various unrelated ways.

During the performance task, the name of either the person in support or opposition of verbal fluency was subliminally primed (50 milliseconds backward masked). Then, participants rated their commitment to doing well and the perceived difficulty of the task. Priming positive recognition increased goal commitment compared to a control group and priming negative recognition decreased goal commitment compared to a control group. The same pattern was found with performance. People primed with positive reinforcement performed better and persisted longer than participants in the control condition, and those primed with negative recognition performed worse and persisted less than those participants in the control group.

Taken together, feedback and social recognition can prime goals to impact automatically subsequent behavior. Yet, research on these effects in OB is virtually nonexistent. We call for future research to examine the impact of goal priming guided by history of reinforcement as it relates to work relationships. Extrapolating the findings reviewed in this section, seeing the face or reading the name of co-workers, supervisors, or even customers can prime goals that were reinforced with recognition or feedback by this person in the past, for better or worse.

Summary

Thorndike's law of effect, published over a century ago (1898), continues to be empirically supported across disciplines, and notably so in SOB.

Simply, a desired behavior followed by a desired consequence is likely to be repeated. Studies in social psychology on subconscious effects of reinforcers extrapolated to organizations suggest that employees automatically adopt and pursue goals when primed by a history of reinforcement. Research indicates that money, social recognition, and feedback are each capable of becoming subconsciously associated with goals they reinforce and related behaviors. In this way, when a reinforcer is used as a prime, employees act in accordance with how they would if the reinforcer was consciously applied. Given the lack of evidence, though, on the effectiveness of these primes in business settings, future research is needed to better understand antecedents and consequences of priming reinforcers for subconsciously modifying work behavior.

References

Baldwin, M. W., Carrell, S. E., & Lopez, D. F. (1990). Priming relationship schemas: My advisor and the Pope are watching me from the back of my mind. *Journal of Experimental Social Psychology, 26*(5), 435–454.

Bandura, A. (1986). *Social foundations of thought and action.* Englewood Cliffs, NJ: Prentice.

Bijleveld, E., & Aarts, H. (2015). *The psychological science of money.* New York, NY: Springer.

Chatterjee, P., Rose, R. L., & Sinha, J. (2013). Retracted article: Why money meanings matter in decisions to donate time and money. *Marketing Letters, 24*(2), 109–118.

Deci, E. L. (1972). The effects of contingent and noncontingent rewards and controls on intrinsic motivation. *Organizational Behavior and Human Performance, 8*(2), 217–229.

Diener, E., & Seligman, M. E. (2004). Beyond money: Toward an economy of well-being. *Psychological Science in the Public Interest, 5*(1), 1–31.

Diener, E., Tay, L., & Oishi, S. (2013). Rising income and the subjective well-being of nations. *Journal of Personality and Social Psychology, 104,* 267.

Ekici, A., & Shiri, A. (2018). The message in the box: How exposure to money affects charitable giving. *Marketing Letters, 29*(2), 137–149.

Fitzsimons, G. M., & Bargh, J. A. (2003). Thinking of you: Nonconscious pursuit of interpersonal goals associated with relationship partners. *Journal of Personality and Social Psychology, 84*(1), 148.

Furhnahm, A., & Argyle, M. (1998). *The psychology of money.* New York, NY: Routledge.

Luthans, F., & Stajković, A. D. (2009). Provide recognition for performance improvement. In E. A. Locke (Ed.), *Handbook of principles of organizational behavior* (pp. 239–253). Oxford: Blackwell Publishing.

Marx, K., & Engels, F. (1848). *The Communist Manifesto.* Selected Works by Karl Marx and Frederick Engels. New York, NY: International Publishers.

Molinsky, A. L., Grant, A. M., & Margolis, J. D. (2012). The bedside manner of homo economicus: How and why priming an economic schema reduces compassion. *Organizational Behavior and Human Decision Processes, 119,* 27–37.

Pfeffer, J., & DeVoe, S. E. (2009). Economic evaluation: The effect of money and economics on attitudes about volunteering. *Journal of Economic Psychology*, *30*, 500–508.

Rutzick, K. (2007, February 23). Best and worst rewards: Share you stories. *Government Executive*. Retrieved from www.govexec.com/pay-benefits/2007/02/best-and-worst-rewards-share-your-stories/23793/

Sedikides, C. (2008). *The Southampton state self-esteem scale*. Un-published manuscript. Southampton, England: University of Southampton.

Seligman, M. E. (2007). *The optimistic child: A proven program to safeguard children against depression and build lifelong resilience*. New York, NY: Houghton Mifflin Harcourt.

Shah, J. (2003). Automatic for the people: How representations of significant others implicitly affect goal pursuit. *Journal of Personality and Social Psychology*, *84*(4), 661–681.

Skinner, B. F. (1938). *The Behavior of organisms: An experimental analysis*. New York, NY: Appleton-Century.

Stajković, A. D., & Luthans, F. (1997). A meta-analysis of the effects of organizational behavior modification on task performance, 1975–95. *Academy of Management Journal*, *40*(5), 1122–1149.

Stajković, A. D., & Luthans, F. (2001). Differential effects of incentive motivators on work performance. *Academy of Management Journal*, *44*(3), 580–590.

Stajković, A. D., & Luthans, F. (2003). Behavioral management and task performance in organizations: Conceptual background, meta-analysis, and test of alternative models. *Personnel Psychology*, *56*(1), 155–194.

Sullivan, H. S. (1953). *The interpersonal theory of psychiatry*. New York, NY: Norton.

Thorndike, E. L. (1898). Animal intelligence: An experimental study of the associative processes in animals. *The Psychological Review: Monograph Supplements*, *2*(4), i.

Veblen, T. (1990). *Imperial Germany and the industrial revolution*. Transaction Publishers.

Vohs, K. D., Mead, N. L., & Goode, M. R. (2006). The psychological consequences of money. *Science*, *314*(5802), 1154–1156.

Vohs, K. D., Mead, N. L., & Goode, M. R. (2008). Merely activating the concept of money changes personal and interpersonal behavior. *Current Directions in Psychological Science*, *17*, 208–212.

Vroom, V. H. (1964). *Work motivation*. New York, NY: Wiley.

Wagner, R., & Harter, J. K. (2006). *12: The elements of great managing* (Vol. 978, No. 1–59992). New York, NY: Gallup Press.

Zhou, X., Vohs, K. D., & Baumeister, R. F. (2009). The symbolic power of money: Reminders of money alter social distress and physical pain. *Psychological Science*, *20*(6), 700–706.

9 Limitations, Methods, and Future Research

At this point, we hope to have established that cognitive automation via primed goals can bring value to organizations as a new alternative for optimizing employee performance. Amid promise, this path of potential progress is still only partly paved, with the remaining twists and turns needing clarifications. In this chapter, we address several limitations of the conceptual framework we propose and of priming technique in general. We then suggest how to address them in future research. This chapter is mostly about the nitty-gritty of conducting priming research.

Limitations and Clarifications

Legacy of Freud

Some topics set off alarm bells when introduced. For example, as soon as we introduce cognitive automation at professional presentations, an audience member inevitably asks us to clarify the extent to which Freud's legacy is included in our conceptual framework.

On the upside, Freud's analysis of subconscious is still the most comprehensive, though Jung's writing is, arguably, more comprehensible. Freud's ideas about the existence and relevance of the subconscious were pioneering and many of this theories have received empirical support (Westen, 1998). On the downside, by vehemently insisting that all people, not only those with brain lesions and injuries, harbor subconscious deviousness, Freud ostensibly "polluted" the subconscious, especially in the minds of those outside of the psychological sciences.

Briefly, Freud derived many of his claims from case studies of his patients with brain impairments; those points were not met with as much support as his general views about the subconscious as foundational mental activity, which are beyond reproach. So, the broad sandbox in which we play in this book was put together by Freud and refined by Jung, and the specifics on the priming technique and priming goals are of more recent ideations.

Conceptual Framework We Propose Is Platform-Dependent

The gravity of our conceptual framework is the guiding role of goals in human pursuits. The conceptualizations we presented were mostly under the aegis of goal-setting theory. But, self-regulation at work can also be influenced by other variables (Kanfer & Chen, 2016; Lord, Diefendorff, Natemeyer & Hersey, 2011; Zedeck, 2010). Given that stored memories, knowledge, and motives are plentiful, future research can examine if other variables are amiable to cognitive automation in organizations and what kinds of outcomes we can expect from those forms of cognitive automation. Given our goal theory platform, whether the same conceptualizations and connections would generalize to other variables is unclear, at least for now. For example, people encounter primes via internet, TV, radio, magazine, and newspapers, and they may ignore virtually all of them. The fruitful questions for future theory development and research are, "Which primes other than goals 'take' and which do not?" and "How much influence, on their own and combined with their conscious counterparts, do they have?"

Cognitive Automation: When Virtue Brings Vice

As mentioned in Chapter 4, faux-pas can occur when people automatically infer goals underlying the behavior of others. As with other recent advents in life (e.g., social media), cognitive automation can result in logic-chopping consequences. In such cases, awareness of the existence of psychological mechanisms such as cognitive automation can help get us out. We next offer several vivid examples of unintended cognitive automation.

An example with an immediate life-threatening consequence is pilots handling the plane when it stalls. A stall happens for multiple reasons (e.g., miscalculations of the weight of the plane, altitude, and speed), but pilots practice repeatedly in a simulator two ways to get out of a stall. Pilots are trained to push the flying joystick forward, as this shifts the nose of the plane down (to decrease altitude) and to increase speed to boost the throttle. Physics should take care of the rest assuming there is enough altitude left. Unfortunately, many pilots do the opposite. They pull the flying column backward, as this is an instinctual reaction if you want to fly up. Tragically, pulling up increases the drag and reduces the speed, usually plunging the plane. Pilots spend many training hours to consciously override the natural goal automaticity link of *go up, pull up*. Yet, stall crashes in aviation mostly occur because pilots mishandle the joystick/nose of the plane in the direction of this automaticity despite hours of training to do just the opposite.[1] Basically, when the pressure of the situation exhausts attentional resources, cognitive automaticity takes over.

Here is a lighter example. Imagine you are speaking with a colleague who abruptly excuses him/herself and leaves. You think you must have said something to upset him/her, so you ponder what it could be. Then, your colleague returns exuding cheer. It puzzles you. What happened? The person needed to go to the bathroom. S/he tried not to interrupt the parley, but could not hold it any longer. Hence, the abrupt dash. It turns out, your automatic goal inference was incorrect, causing wasteful attentional rumination. A similar example we mentioned earlier involved an employee coming early to a board meeting. The inferred goal can be a rational one to arrive on time. It can also be a menacing one to gain favors with executives. Making the wrong automatic goal inference introduces error into the world of "truth," which can snowball into greater and more costly errors thereafter.

Here is a personal example. The day we were writing these lines, both of us got upset stomachs that evening. We automatically blamed the restaurant where we ate lunch. Despite nothing bothering us at lunchtime, we concocted a host of attributes to infer the restaurant food standards were subpar. We both concurred, not questioning our "logical" conclusion. The next day, we came to the office, and it reeked. Immediately, we checked the small office fridge and noted the temperature at 20 °C versus where it should be at 3 °C. The broken fridge had caused leftovers to go bad. If we had enough attentional resources the evening before, we would have likely checked the fridge as the logical source of the problem. Instead, we readily adopted the incorrect automated response—blame the restaurant.

Although these examples reflect undesired effects of cognitive automation, we should not throw the baby out with the bathwater. We ought to be aware of the negative side effects and foster the positive ones, as with other consequential aspects of life. Food is good, unless overindulged. Alcohol has anti-inflammatory properties, but excess drinking impairs health. Travel is exciting, lest it is exhausting. Fire is useful, unless handled carelessly. Cars are convenient, unless we abuse the driving privilege and hurt someone.

Method Issues

Priming research has challenges, especially when it comes to using consistent and comparable methods. In that light, we scrutinize six components of priming subconscious goals and suggest how these issues can be tackled more rigorously in future research.

Supraliminal and Subliminal Priming

Goals can be primed either supraliminally or subliminally. Supraliminal priming occurs when the prime is visible, but a person is unaware of its influence on behavior. For example, supraliminal priming includes embedding word primes into scrambled sentences (Srull & Wyer, 1979) and word-search puzzles (Bargh, Gollwitzer, Lee-Chai, Barndollar, & Tröetschel, 2001) and using Scrabble tiles (Bargh et al., 2001). Because the prime is in plain sight, people can recognize, evaluate, and report it. For this reason, some scholars claim (incorrectly) that supraliminal primes do not operate outside of a person's awareness. According to the critics, if stimuli enter one's perception system, s/he cannot be unaware of the stimuli. To further demonstrate this view, consider the following reviewer comment in response to a money priming study (not conducted by us):

> [T]he authors seem to assume that in scrambled sentence manipulations, people can be "unaware" of the money-related construct. Is this really true? After all, after de-scrambling a sentence, people should clearly have conscious access aware of the content of the sentence. One could well take the position that people are only "unaware" of some stimulus, if they cannot report this stimulus' identity.

The discord boils down to the definition of *awareness*. To simplify, optical visibility does not equal cognitive awareness. For instance, have you ever put your sunglasses on, and then forgot you were wearing them? Momentarily, you lost awareness of the glasses, despite seeing them in front of your eyes. Just because supraliminal primes are visible in a sensory manner, "it does not necessarily imply that they were consciously *seen*" (Kouider, Dehaene, Jobert, & Bihan, 2006, p. 2020). This is the crux of supraliminal priming: the prime is visible, but the person is unaware of its influence on their thought and action. The goal priming materials we have provided illustrate supraliminal primes.

Subliminal priming is a transitory presentation of the prime (e.g., on a computer screen), followed by an immediate masking of its presentation. Primes must enter the subconscious threshold of vision but not cross into the conscious threshold for subliminal perception to befall us (Cheesman & Merikle, 1984). Finding this subliminal "sweet spot" is more easily described than empirically determined because thresholds vary across individuals (Bargh, 2005). If research succeeds in finding it, subliminal priming undoubtedly occurs without awareness.

Subliminal priming has sparked controversy (Hardaway, 1990), and has, on occasion, been labeled cult science (Bargh, 2005; Greenwald, Spangenberg, Pratkanis, & Eskenazi, 1991). For example, in the 1950s James Vicary claimed to boost concession sales by subliminally flashing "Eat Popcorn" and "Drink Coke" during a movie, which infuriated the public. By Vicary's admission, this was a hoax. He apologized. The cynics were unmoved.

Neuroscientists Kouider and colleagues (2006) examined which method generates stronger effects. They measured brain activity following exposure to supraliminal and subliminal primes. Using functional magnetic resonance imaging (fMRI), they found supraliminal primes to elicit greater brain activity than subliminal primes. Heightened brain activity led to faster responses, suggesting that supraliminal primes generate stronger behavioral effects. Together, supraliminal priming appears a more ecologically valid priming technique and is a more impactful method of priming goals.

Types of Primes

The studies we reviewed in prior chapters used supraliminal priming by words and photos to trigger goals. In other disciplines, aromas released into the air have primed goals, as have statues, magazines, and various other art forms. Do these primes differ in their capacity to trigger subconscious goals and in strength of their effects?

In neuroscience research, patients with visual agnosia can sometimes make better semantic judgements when concepts are presented as words compared with pictures; yet, other patients do just the opposite (Vandenberghe, Price, Wise, Josephs, & Frackowiak, 1996). To investigate the effects of word versus photo primes in semantic networks, Carr, McCauley, Sperber, and Parmelee (1982) primed participants with words or photos and measured response time latency. They concluded that semantic representation is more easily activated by photos than by words, i.e., *a picture speaks a thousand words*. Yet, the authors also found that when they used photos as primes, the information retrieval process was slower and put more demands on attentional capacity. This suggests that priming with photos may not be as advantageous for reducing cognitive load as priming with words. To our knowledge, though, empirical research on these differences is limited to semantic networks. Theory in linguistic anthropology invokes spirited debate concerning the power of words versus photos (McCarthy, 2017).

Juxtaposing neuroscience and linguistic anthropology, we arrive at the following polemic. Words, a linguistic stimulus, trigger a motive by activating the center for language in the cerebral cortex. Photos, a visual stimulus, trigger a motive by activating the brain's visual center in the occipital lobe (Sweeney, 2009). Words generate priming power linguistically (reading and processing prime words) and visually (seeing the words). Photos involve only visual activation because language is uninvolved. Cognitive process behind prime words is tridimensional: conceptual cues, linguistic cues, visual cues. A photo is two-dimensional: conceptual cues, visual cues. Because words activate an additional cognitive process, perhaps they generate more mental "action," resulting in greater priming power. For example, parents and educational systems encourage kids to read books, not caricature-based comic strips (though kids may prefer the opposite). Yet, several anthropology scholars vehemently argue, at the bewilderment of others, that language is an unnecessary evolutionary add-on that mind still tries to circumvent (see

McCarthy, 2017) because processing it can be taxing. Future research should examine if word and photo priming interventions produce synergistic effects, compared to either intervention alone.

The Number and Ratio of Cues and Their Prime-ability

The number and ratio of prime cues to neutral cues has been inconsistently applied across priming goal studies. This irregularity muddles our knowledge of sufficient and necessary prime ratio strength. On one hand, if primes are too strong, the goal will cross into consciousness, and the priming manipulation loses its purpose. On the other hand, if primes are too weak, the goal may not be activated. When we first conducted priming research, this was one of the questions on which we sought early guidance. Consider the variation in priming ratios of published studies at that time:

1. Chartrand and Bargh (1996): Study 1 used a ratio of 53% (participants were asked to unscramble 15 sentences, 8 of which contained a prime word).
2. Bargh, Chen, and Burrows (1996): Study 2 used a ratio of 73% (participants were asked to unscramble 30 sentences, 22 of which contained a prime word).
3. Bargh et al. (2001): Study 1 used a ratio of 54% (7 prime words out of 13 total words in a 10 × 10 word-search matrix).
4. Chen, Lee-Chai, and Bargh (2001): Study 1 used a ratio of 60% (participants were asked to unscramble 10 sentences, 6 of which contained a prime word).

The average ratio in these four experiments was 60%. As Stajković, Locke, and Blair (2006) were preparing priming protocols for their experiments, they emailed John Bargh about the 60% average ratio derived from his studies (as shown above) and asked, "Does this look about right?" The answer was,

> The ratio varies based on the distinctiveness and salience of the primes as embedded . . . I'm surprised that the average is 60% (but will take your word for it at present) as my memory is that the ratio is more like 33% (9–12 out of 30, for the most part, at least in scrambled sentences version).

Then, Stajković et al. (2006) emailed Tanya Chartrand asking the same question. The answer was,

> I will say that I oftentimes use a higher ratio than 60% now (usually more like 90% prime words).

A related procedural point is how to treat responses on a priming task that are accurate but incomplete, e.g., a participant unscrambled most of the sentences but not all. Should researchers exclude partial responses and include only "clean manipulations"? Should they include partial responses but weight their impact? Similarly, what if participants did not follow the instructions but nonetheless completed the task by reaching a stated outcome? For example, in word-search puzzle, despite instructions to search for words horizontally, vertically, and diagonally, some participants go their own curvilinear ways to create and circle a prime word. Thus, participants read the prime word as intended, but not in the instructed way. Does cutting corners save attention resources, which helps on the next task? Or, are participants equally primed and, thus, any observed effects are "clean"?

A related conceptual point is determining if priming effects are continuous in strength, such that a higher prime–no prime ratio generates stronger effects, or if they are dichotomous, such that after a trigger level is reached, any increases in the prime-to-neutral stimuli ratio have no additional significant effects. If priming is dichotomous, then handling omissions of prime words is key to avoid method variance, i.e., variance created by differences in methods/procedures. Extant research seems to indicate a dichotomous nature of priming effects, given the "Once activated, the goals" language used to describe priming manipulations (e.g., Chartrand & Bargh, 2002). If priming is indeed a "tripwire," then we need to figure out if all constructs respond to the same strength of manipulations. This leads us to the next section, in which we discuss if constructs are equally prime-able.

Certain subconscious goals may be more easily primed than others because of evolution. That is, if certain goals were critical for human survival, then they are probably ingrained deep in the human psyche. This could make people more susceptible to those goal primes. To reverse the correlates, if humans have pursued a goal over long evolutionary time, it could create a ceiling effect. In that scenario, it would be more challenging to prime ingrained goals. Relatedly, the centrality of goals in human affairs has evolved. For example, it was more critical for our early ancestors to run away fast (speed) from a lion than to assess methodically the marginal calorie cost of each next step and, thus, the escape path of least energy exertion (accuracy). The relative importance of goals from an evolutionary perspective may influence which goal primes "take" and which do not; but, it may not, given the emergence of sophisticated human activities based on accuracy, such as medicine/surgery, fine arts, and space shuttle flights, to name a few.

Duration of Priming Effects

Goals lose motivational power when the goal is attained. New goals are needed for new pursuits. Accordingly, after a primed goal is achieved, its effects on behavior dissipate (see Bargh et al., 2001, Experiment 4). In laboratory experiments, duration of priming is usually measured within a few minutes. Moreover, experiments include what Bargh (2017) calls a "stop the world button." Experimenters build in controls that allow participants to pause, ask questions, and take time to deliberate alternatives. These attributes impinge on ecological validity, i.e., does this generalize to life? In our field studies (Stajković et al., 2018, 2019), we primed employees on Monday morning, and found performance increases throughout the week. In the following week, though, employee performance normalized. It seems the weekend reset participants' goal-directedness. By Friday, primed employees likely felt they had attained their weekly goal. To our knowledge, an average effect over one week of goal priming effects is the longest duration documented in a business organization. We call for future research to conduct longitudinal designs to offer more insight into duration effects of goal priming. For instance, if an organization hangs a money photo in the hallway to prime a self-sufficiency goal, how long will the money poster impact employee behavior, if at all? When will the money priming effects wear off?

Moderating Effects of Individual Differences

Moderators, or boundary conditions, are variables that change the strength or sign of a relationship. For example, goals affect performance, but when people harbor doubt, the relationship between goals and performance weakens. In the literature, we use the term "individual differences" to represent characteristics endogenous to an individual (e.g., height, personality, IQ) that create variance in outcomes. We next discuss three individual differences that potentially moderate the link between primed goals and performance.

First, goal importance moderates the strength of priming effects (Weingarten et al., 2016). When a person values a goal, it becomes more accessible in memory, making it easier to prime. For example, "the more individuals are concerned about watching their weight, the faster they should be able to activate the goal of dieting in response to the presentation of fattening food" (Fishbach, Friedman, & Kruglanski, 2003, p. 298). Similarly, people respond to primed reward cues (a penny vs. a pound) in the same way they respond to physically receiving those rewards (see Pessiglione et al., 2007). Because perception of goal importance varies by the individual, it can moderate priming effects.

Second, gender and attractiveness (i.e., "beauty premium") influence priming effects. For example, while performing cognitive tasks, men get distracted when they interact with women but not when they interact with other men (see Bargh, 2017); this occurs frequently without awareness. Hundhammer and Mussweiler (2012) found that both supraliminal and subliminal gender primes strengthened gender-based self-perceptions by eliciting greater submissiveness in women's behavior and greater assertiveness in men's behavior. When study participants were "physiologically aroused" (Hansen & Krygowski, 1994, p. 27), subliminal exposure to sexual stimuli fostered formulation of behavioral strategies to become closer to a partner of another sex in an experiment, despite participants reporting no awareness of the prime or its influence on their actions. Gender and "beauty premium" could confound effects of priming interventions.

Finally, to our knowledge, no study has directly examined comparability of primed goals across cultures. For example, if English language prime words were used in a U.S. study and replicated with equivalent French prime words in France, are the prime interventions comparable? During a study debriefing, an Austrian student commented that to prime achievement for him, the word would need to be in German to trigger associations in his subconscious. This anecdotal evidence casts doubt on the validity of arbitrary comparisons across languages and cultures without empirical research with equivalent not only literal but also functional word translations.

Awareness Assessment

Priming is intriguing because people can be affected by factors they fail to register consciously. In this line of inquiry, documenting that participants process a prime-outcome effect without awareness is a means to an end (Bargh, 1992). Without a rigorous awareness assessment, researchers have no way of knowing and validating whether a study examined conscious or subconscious processes. This ambiguity tarnishes conclusions.

In theory, effects unfold if a cue from the environment primes a goal in the subconscious that then triggers goal-behavior associations into automatic action without awareness. In research, whether this theory assertion is empirically valid depends on the examination of two questions: (a) Were participants probed for awareness with a sensitive-enough awareness measure? and (b) Did the probe detect awareness of the relationship between the manipulated prime and the measured outcome?

One source of confusion in this literature has been the definition of priming effects. Priming is a process in which "environmental stimuli may affect subsequent responses by activating mental constructs without *conscious realization*" (Weingarten et al., 2016, p. 474, emphasis added). Yet, we still find "priming studies" that explicitly instructed participants to think, feel, or behave in a certain way. For example, if we asked you to "imagine having ample access to money" and "imagine never having to worry about paying the bills," would such instructions bring money-related thoughts into your consciousness? Probably. Yet, several researchers have defined this identical instruction as a "priming" manipulation

(Caruso, Shapira, & Landy, 2017). When we confronted these authors about their loose definition of priming, the authors responded,

> At a basic level, priming involves observing how exposure to one stimulus influences response to a subsequent stimulus. One can be conscious or unconscious about the initial exposure (i.e., the presentation of the prime) and/or its effect.

If priming was defined as a mechanism that increases probability of a behavioral response—either conscious or subconscious—then nearly every experimental manipulation qualifies as priming. We cannot vacillate among these points, for the validity of priming effects hinges on the rigorous empirical verification that participants were unaware of the cause-effect processes initiated by the primed construct.

Awareness tests are challenging, as not all methods and measures are equally reliable and because they require demonstrating *absence* of awareness (De Houwer, Tanaka, Moors, & Tibboel, 2018). That is, if you want to know what consciousness does, ask consciousness. But, if you want to know if the conscious is absent, you need to assess it via indirect methods. Consequently, "over the past 30 years . . . psychologists have used increasingly refined methods to assess awareness in studies of priming" (Doyen, Klein, Simons, & Cleeremans, 2014, p. 18). Awareness instruments should not only probe for knowledge of the prime-outcome link, but also they should be sufficiently sensitive and uncontaminated by experimental demands.

For example, an awareness test is insensitive if it misses finding specific conscious knowledge, despite a participant having such knowledge (De Houwer et al., 2018). Consider, for example, that you read instructions printed on a faint photo of money. You notice the photo during the task, complete the task, and then answer over 50 follow-up survey questions about different constructs. At the end of the lengthy survey, you are asked, "What was this study about?" (see Caruso et al., 2017, supplemental material).

Given the ambiguous wording of the question and its position after many unrelated questions, how likely is it that you interpret this question as a probe for your knowledge of the photo from the first task? If intervening items for unrelated studies are introduced between priming and awareness questions coupled with time lapse between the priming task and awareness assessment, participants may be prone to forget about the prime—even if they were previously aware of it. Instead, researchers ought to replace broad questions with specific questions such as, "Did you notice a photo in the first task, and, if so, what was it?"

Stringent awareness assessment criteria have been discussed at length in the literature (Bargh & Chartrand, 2000), but inconsistent application is still widespread. For example, two "many-labs" preregistered replication efforts reported no priming effects, yet neither study tested awareness (McCarthy et al., 2018; Verschuere et al., 2018). What are we to believe—the say-so of studies claiming to assess subconscious effects without empirically verifying unawareness? This is not to say conclusively that these replication studies examined conscious processes, but only that we have no way of empirically verifying plausible alternative explanations. If we apply the definition given to us by Caruso et al. (2017) of priming, then hundreds of goal priming studies in social psychology are but a redundant redoing of thousands of conscious goal studies. As Kahneman (2012) noted in his letter of criticism to social psychologists: "I am skeptical about replications by investigators new to priming research, who may not be attuned to the subtlety of the conditions under which priming effects are observed" (p. 1).

In contrast, a recent preregistered replication that assessed awareness found that nearly one in five participants (19.9%) responded "yes" when asked if they thought the prime affected their performance, and 62.7% of participants responded "yes" when asked if they noticed a link between the prime and measured performance (O'Donnell et al., 2018). Despite reporting no effects in their main analyses, after excluding these aware participants, the priming effect became statistically significant.

Strong Statements, Inadequate Evidence

To demonstrate the consequences of inadequate awareness assessment, consider problems in a recent money priming study. For context on money priming, Vohs, Mead, and Goode (2006) reported money priming effects across nine experiments. Caruso, Vohs, Baxter, and Waytz (2013) likewise reported strong money priming effects. Forthwith, a many-labs replication attempt with 6,333 participants failed to find a money priming effect (Klein et al., 2014). Rohrer, Pashler, and Harris (2015) then conducted a high-powered replication and found no effects. Reflecting on these failed replications, Vadillo, Hardwicke, and Shanks (2016) suggested earlier money priming effects were the result of p-hacking. Given the controversy (c.f., Vohs, 2015), Caruso et al. (2017, p. 1148) claimed to provide "a systematic exploration of manipulations, moderators, and mechanisms of priming effects."

To investigate the controversy, we reviewed the money priming literature and examined 121 money priming experiments to understand how they assessed participants' awareness. Only 33 studies (27.3%) mentioned, even remotely, testing for awareness. Perhaps more surprising was that out of 24,317 participants, only 23 people (.09%) were excluded as being aware. Given this miniscule percentage of aware participants in money priming studies, we outline how future research can improve the methods, using Caruso et al. (2017) to illustrate how *not to* conduct a priming study.

Theory should always guide empirics, especially in priming research, because activation of subconscious mechanisms occurs below awareness. For this reason, priming research demands added sifting and winnowing, both theoretically and empirically.

First, much ink has been spilled in the literature to provide theoretical gruel to the uncertainty expressed by priming critics regarding what is being primed, e.g., associative semantics, procedures, goals, or traits (see Förster, Liberman, & Friedman, 2009). Caruso et al. (2017) claim to "systematically evaluate the effects of different manipulations of the *same construct*" [emphasis added]. An assertion this definitive, i.e., "same construct," requires theoretical support. Without theory, it becomes nearly impossible to understand what construct a money prime activates. The authors assert that money primes "activation of the concept of money," "one's sense of wealth, agency, and self-sufficiency," "self-sufficient behavior," "communal tendencies," and "the idea of having ample money rather than little money" (p. 1149). Insufficient connections among variables left the arguments too distal to be convincing. In correspondence with us, E. Caruso stated, "the lack of clarity was largely beside the point of our paper. We did not claim nor aim to distinguish between these constructs" (Sept. 23, 2017). Juxtapose his response with the article's promise to "make our theories richer, more accurate, and more reliable" (p. 1158) and their claim to have examined "the same construct."

To empirically test if Caruso et al. (2017) examined the "same construct," we conducted a meta-analytic within-group homogeneity test of the 177 money priming effects reported. We found a significant within-group heterogeneity of individual effects sizes, Q (176) = 306.68, $p < .01$. This result held after controlling for dependent variable, Q (145) = 187.43, $p < .01$. This heterogeneity indicated that money priming effects (or lack thereof) cannot be unambiguously attributed to the same population parameter. Heterogeneity of the single effect sizes implies that more than one construct was primed. This muddles interpretation of the reported results.

Failure to theoretically separate conscious and subconscious activation of money increased ambiguity in an already convoluted study. For instance, manipulations used to prime money included asking people to imagine having abundant access to money, choosing the size for new dollar bills, embedding a faint background photo of money, and embedding money-related words in scrambled sentences. With the first two manipulations, conscious thoughts of money were required; this is what Bargh (2016) described as explicit instructions. Therefore, even if all four priming manipulations caused identical effects, the ensuing psychological state of participants could be different. Conscious (money) thoughts compared to subconscious (money) activation demand more attentional resources to generate the same effect (DeShon, Brown, & Greenis, 1996).

Moreover, effects of "thinking about money" can be controlled in practice by avoiding thoughts of money, but deliberate avoidance is impossible with subconscious money primes.

There is also a cause for concern empirically. In two of the three studies, Caruso et al. (2017) included intervening, unrelated items in the questionnaires after priming money, but before awareness assessment. For example, in one study participants watched a violent video and then answered questions about it. The video was unrelated to the money priming study; the authors published those results in a separate report. Yet, the experiment assessed awareness of the money prime after people watched the lurid video. The video, therefore, contaminated awareness probing for the money priming study and increased the likelihood of inaccurate responses. For example, consider this participant's response to the question, "What was this study about?"

> This was a VERY violent video and you should have SPECIFICALLY stated that this video contains violence and gave us the option to continue instead of bringing it up suddenly like that.

In this example, the participant's response was not focused on the money priming study. Therefore, we have no way of determining whether this person was aware of the money prime. For this reason, we used a text analysis software to read all responses in the Caruso et al. (2017) article. Our aim was to test the money priming effects reported in the article, but with only participant data that we could assuredly classify as "unaware" of the prime. The software flagged responses for awareness consistent with the following definition:

> By *genuine awareness* we mean any answer in the debriefing which is "in the ballpark" as to what could have affected responses. In our research, we take a conservative stance and err on the side of over-exclusion if there is any doubt.
>
> (Bargh & Chartrand, 2000, p. 259)

Specifically, the text analysis software (Linguistic Inquiry and Word Count (LIWC)) flagged responses that included words such as *priming*, *sentences*, *imagine*, *money*, *rich*, *bills*, *finance*, *economic*, and *wealth*. LIWC results flagged 206 (11.9%) participants as potentially aware (already excluding the 19 identified by the original authors). We next used the LIWC to assess responses for experimental demand effects. It flagged responses focused on manipulations unrelated to the money priming study. For this, we used words such as *violence*, *birthday*, *group*, *video*, *crime*, *gun*, and *shooting*. LIWC flagged 332 participants that could have been influenced by demand effects. Four raters reviewed all flagged responses. Taken together, the four raters concluded that

110 (6.3%) participants met the awareness criteria specified above, and 85 (4.9%) exhibited demand effects that rendered their assessment of awareness ambiguous.

After eliminating these 195 participants, we reanalyzed the data. We computed Cohen's *d* and its 95% confidence interval using "effsize" package (R version 3.3.3, 2017). We report both the authors' original findings and our revised findings in Table 9.1. This comparative format allows for comparison of the original effects reported in the article and the effects from our re-analysis that used a more stringent awareness exclusion.

In total, we found that 15 money priming effects changed from those reported in the original article. Markedly, all nine counterintuitive (negative) priming effects reported by Caruso et al. (2017) became nonsignificant. Additionally, several money priming effects became significantly positive in accord with hypotheses in the money priming literature (see Vohs, 2015).

Trust But Verify

As Simons (2014, p. 76) noted, "reproducibility is the cornerstone of science"; thus, this section heading, "trust but verify" (p. 76). Unfortunately, because of the lack of reproducibility in the last decade, priming research has faced tempestuous skepticism. We discuss a few possibilities that may have caused low reproducibility of priming results.

One reason is greed, which is not unique to research and science. For instance, after Diedrik Stapel's admission that he fabricated priming results, outrage followed. After his article retraction count skyrocketed (now at 58 publications), pandemonium ensued in social psychology (see Callaway, 2011; Cesario, 2014; Crocker & Cooper, 2011; Kahneman, 2012; Stroebe & Strack, 2014).

For those who do not traffic in the greed–fast professional fame ecosphere, another academic reason for the conundrum is because scads of priming research is atheoretical. Simmons, Nelson, and Simonsohn (2013) reviewed priming studies that lacked a theoretical foundation and presented ridiculous conclusions. For example, Mehta, Zhu, and Cheema (2012) suggested that being exposed to the noise of a moving car 10 meters away increased research creativity compared to working in a low-noise environment. Creativity researchers are good at constructing creative stories for dreadful circumstances, but what is the implication? Move faculty offices closer to noise? If noise increases productivity, then why is there a "quiet rule" in libraries? The force of the arguments in such studies is diminished because it has to fight its way through a far-fetched narrative with little basis in the extant literature. These sorts of publications stunt productive dialogue and spark a purveying spirit of skepticism on priming effectiveness.

Compare such "newsworthy" conclusions with findings that come from the scientific method. Principally, research clinches to theory-driven, rigorously tested, incremental knowledge building. By definition, then, research is a marathon. Rarely can a single study develop all-encompassing conceptual propositions, empirically test hypotheses across sources, and generate cumulative conclusions that push theory forward, guide future research, and meaningfully affect social change. This process is too protracted for some given the relatively short five-year window to "publish or perish," i.e., get tenure or leave.

So, what do a few researchers do? They create a problem that does not exist in the world—only in their minds (also known as Type III error). Then, they try to boil the ocean in one study and hope for a notoriety splash. Social media picks up the tag line, frames it as "tail wags dog," sprinkles correlations into the story, and sensationalizes a shocking new "revelation" in their posts. The more "likes" on Facebook and Twitter, the better.

Most often, these studies lead to conclusions unrelated to behavior of humans on earth. Consider eight experiments reported by Bem (2011). First, he showed participants 48 words. Second, he asked them to write down as many words as they could remember. Third, he provided participants with a random subset of words and asked them to type these words. His results showed that participants were more likely to remember words in the second phase if they practiced typing those words in the third phase. The cause came *after* the effect! Fantastically counterintuitive, this implies a sixth sense exists, bridging the future and the past in reverse, and the participants were not aware of it. Except, no theory of repute in scientific psychology predicts anything remotely close and no study could replicate these findings. Because theory is built fastidiously, incrementally, and cumulatively, scientists are skeptical of the results that come "out of the theoretical blue."

Contributing to Science of Organizational Behavior with Priming Research: What Can We Do?

Our overall recommendation is simple: return to research basics. First, do not use statistical significance as a substitute for intelligence. If findings are reported as statistically significant but are too counterintuitive, e.g., depression of pregnant mothers is good for babies (Sandman, Davis, & Glynn, 2012), interpret them with a healthy dose of skepticism, even if they were published in *Psychological Science*. Unless future research replicates "newsworthy" findings, pay little attention to them for the time being. They may just be the product of statistical significance, which can be meaningless if effects sizes hover a hair above zero. Miniscule effects can be important, for example, in considering the power of negative matter if produced at the Hadron collider, but not for overriding age-long dictums, such as think in advance to formulate a plan B if plan A goes awry, especially if a situation requires a fallback right away. Why do rock climbers wear a harness?

Table 9.1 Re-analysis Using Different Awareness Criterion: Effect Size (Cohen's *d*) and 95% Confidence Intervals Positive Effects Indicate Higher Scores in the Money Priming Condition.

Conditions Compared/Study	Subjective Wealth		General Self-Sufficiency	Number of Solitary Activities	Adjective Ratings			Persistence on Puzzle (Study 3)
	Absolute	Relative			Communion	Agency	Self-Sufficiency	
Background image/control vs. background image/ money								
Caruso et al.								
Study 1 (*n* = 454)	ns	ns	ns	ns	ns	ns	ns	
Study 2 (*n* = 436)	ns	ns	ns	ns	ns	ns	ns	
Re-analysis								
Study 1 (*n* = 445)	ns	ns	ns	ns	ns	ns	0.20 [0.01, 0.38]	
Study 2 (*n* = 407)	ns	ns	ns	0.19 [0.01, 0.39]	ns	ns	ns	
Perceptual estimation/control vs. perceptual estimation/money								
Caruso et al.								
Study 1 (*n* = 456)	-0.27 [-0.45, -0.08]	-0.21 [-0.39, -0.03]	-0.20 [-0.39, -0.02]	ns	ns	ns	ns	
Study 2 (*n* = 425)	-0.26 [-0.45, -0.07]	-0.22 [-0.41, -0.03]	ns	ns	ns	ns	ns	
Study 3 (*n* = 113)	ns	ns	ns	ns	ns	ns	ns	ns
Re-analysis								
Study 1 (*n* = 430)	-0.18 [-0.37, 0.01]	-0.09 [-0.28, 0.10]	-0.12 [-0.31, 0.07]	ns	ns	ns	ns	
Study 2 (*n* = 392)	-0.14 [-0.34, 0.06]	-0.19 [-0.39, 0.01]	ns	ns	ns	ns	ns	
Study 3 (*n* = 110)	ns	ns	ns	ns	ns	ns	ns	ns

Scrambled phrases/control vs. scrambled phrases/money

Caruso et al.

Study 1 (n = 365)	ns	ns	ns	ns	ns	ns	ns
Study 2 (n = 341)	ns	ns	ns	ns	ns	ns	ns
Study 3 (n = 109)	ns	0.54 [0.15, 0.92]	ns	ns	ns	ns	ns

Re-analysis

Study 1 (n = 354)	ns	ns	ns	ns	ns	ns	ns
Study 2 (n = 313)	ns	ns	ns	ns	0.26 [0.03, 0.49]	0.24 [0.02, 0.47]	ns
Study 3 (n = 106)	ns	0.59 [0.19, 0.98]	ns	ns	ns	0.38 [0.01, 0.78]	0.42 [0.03, 0.81]

Imagine life/control vs. imagine life/abundance

Caruso et al.

Study 1 (n = 327)	ns	−0.24 [−0.46, −0.02]	ns	−0.24 [−0.46, −0.02]	ns	ns	ns
Study 2 (n = 342)	ns	−0.25 [−0.46, −0.04]	ns	ns	ns	−0.25 [−0.47, −0.04]	ns
Study 3 (n = 110)	ns	ns	ns	ns	ns	ns	ns

Re-analysis

Study 1 (n = 304)	ns	−0.19 [−0.42, 0.03]	ns	−0.20 [−0.42, 0.03]	ns	ns	ns
Study 2 (n = 319)	ns	−0.20 [−0.42, 0.02]	ns	ns	ns	−0.21 [−0.43, 0.01]	ns
Study 3 (n = 103)	ns	ns	ns	ns	ns	ns	ns

Notes: Boldface type indicates effect sizes for which $p < .05$. An outline indicates the finding changed from what was reported in the focal article. A light shaded background indicates of hypotheses in the focal article, and darker shade indicates a finding is consistent with the hypotheses.

Second, observe the world. If you find something (really) unexplored that is relevant to humans who stand, walk, and talk to each other daily, versus college students who are paid to move their fingers on a keyboard in classroom experiments, give it a try. But, third, ask yourself these questions first: Are you trying to intellectualize something simple? Are you romanticizing brutal events? Are you constructing a lovely story for a hideous occupation? This may be what some journal editors see as attractive new theory development that the rest of the scholarly community did not think of, but most human beings do not think this way. As Jung (1933) warned, "No language exists that cannot be misused" (p. 11).

Fourth, if you decide to study something, then review the extant literature first to guide your study design. Fifth, tighten the links between theory guiding testing and the degree of empirical precision. Sixth, if your results meet the crisis of relevance (e.g., as indicated by citations), move on to other questions, rather than defend to death something just because you wrote it. If someone cares enough about your discoveries, they will try to replicate it. If the replication process (preferably done in many laboratories, across designs and methods, undertaken by many, and excluding your co-authors, advisor, and former doctoral students as journal editors) pans out, priming research will contribute more clearly to cumulative knowledge building in scientific psychology. The process we outline above is a challenge that is managed over time, not solved overnight.

Summary

What is good for academic careers is not necessarily good for knowledge building. Self-promotion in search of academic relevance, aided by atheoretical hypotheses and incredulous methods, can create a chain of doubt. Retractions of priming articles stoked Kahneman's (2012) critique that "field of priming is the poster child for doubts." Copiously insisting on theory guidance, e.g., "Welcome Back Theory" (Dijksterhuis, 2014), inviting greater clarity of statistical reporting (Asendorpf et al., 2013), and even offering self-deprecating sarcasm, e.g., "We Knew the Future All Along" (Bones, 2012), aimed to help. These remedies matter little, however, if scholars continue to conduct priming research of questionable rigor. As John Bargh noted in his response to Kahneman "priming effects are subtle and their design requires high-level skills" (2012, p. 1). We agree and add that self-serving pontification on Twitter and social media's lure for poppycock "discoveries" do not replace the checks and balances of the scientific method.

In the SOB, practical application helps keep Type III error tendencies in check. To clarify, as long as atheoretical speculation is kept in the confined halls of academic corridors, no applied harm is done. However, if professionals apply such ideas at work, where they affect the careers of thousands of employees, our conceptions ought to help us explain and predict things in ways that empirically correspond to actual life of employees.

Note

1 This information is publicly available and is basic physics. Numerous specific examples are presented in the History Channel's Show called "Air Disasters." We have affiliations with neither the channel nor the show.

References

Asendorpf, J. B., Conner, M., De Fruyt, F., De Houwer, J., Denissen, J. J., Fiedler, K., . . . Perugini, M. (2013). Recommendations for increasing replicability in psychology. *European Journal of Personality, 27*(2), 108–119.

Bargh, J. A. (1992). The ecology of automaticity: Toward establishing the conditions needed to produce automatic processing effects. *The American Journal of Psychology*, 181–199.

Bargh, J. A. (2005). Bypassing the will: Toward demystifying the nonconscious control of social behavior. *The New Unconscious, 12*, 37–58.

Bargh, J. A. (2016). Awareness of the prime versus awareness of its influence: Implications for the real-world scope of unconscious higher mental processes. *Current Opinion in Psychology, 12*, 49–52.

Bargh, J. A. (2017). *Before you know it: The unconscious reasons we do what we do.* New York, NY: Simon and Schuster.

Bargh, J. A., & Chartrand, T. L. (2000). The mind in the middle: A practical guide to priming and automaticity research. In H. T. Reis & C. M. Judd (Eds.), *Handbook of research methods in social and personality psychology* (pp. 253–285). Cambridge, UK: Cambridge University Press.

Bargh, J., Chen, M., & Burrows, L. (1996). Automaticity of social behavior: Direct effects of trait construct and stereotype activation on action. *Journal of Personality and Social Psychology, 71*, 230–244.

Bargh, J. A., Gollwitzer, P. M., Lee-Chai, A., Barndollar, K., & Troetschel, R. (2001). The automated will: Nonconscious activation and pursuit of behavioral goals. *Journal of Personality and Social Psychology, 81*, 1014–1027.

Bem, D. J. (2011). Feeling the future: Experimental evidence for anomalous retroactive influences on cognition and affect. *Journal of Personality and Social Psychology, 100*, 407–425.

Bones, A. K. (2012). We knew the future all along: Scientific hypothesizing is much more accurate than other forms of precognition—A satire in one part. *Perspectives on Psychological Science, 7*(3), 307–309.

Callaway, E. (2011). Report finds massive fraud at Dutch universities: Investigation claims dozens of social-psychology papers contain faked data. Nature, *479*, 15.

Carr, T. H., McCauley, C., Sperber, R. D., & Parmelee, C. M. (1982). Words, pictures, and priming: On semantic activation, conscious identification, and the automaticity of information processing. *Journal of Experimental Psychology: Human Perception and Performance, 8*(6), 757–777.

Caruso, E. M., Shapira, O., & Landy, J. F. (2017). Show me the money: A systematic exploration of manipulations, moderators, and mechanisms of priming effects. *Psychological Science, 28*, 1148–1159.

Caruso, E. M., Vohs, K. D., Baxter, B., & Waytz, A. (2013). Mere exposure to money increases endorsement of free-market systems and social inequality. *Journal of Experimental Psychology: General, 142*, 301–306.

Cesario, J. (2014). Priming, replication, and the hardest science. *Perspectives on Psychological Science, 9*(1), 40–48.

Chartrand, T. L., & Bargh, J. A. (1996). Automatic activation of impression formation and memorization goals: Nonconscious goal priming reproduces effects of explicit task instructions. *Journal of Personality and Social Psychology, 71*, 464–478.

Chartrand, T. L., & Bargh, J. A. (2002). Nonconscious motivations: Their activation, operation and consequences. In A. Tesser, D. A. Stapel & J. V. Wood (Eds.), *Self and Motivation: Emerging Psychological Perspectives* (pp. 13–41). Washington, DC: American Psychological Association.

Cheesman, J., & Merikle, P. M. (1984). Priming with and without awareness. *Perception & Psychophysics, 36*(4), 387–395.

Chen, S., Lee-Chai, A. Y., & Bargh, J. A. (2001). Relationship orientation as a moderator of the effects of social power. *Journal of Personality and Social Psychology, 80*(2), 173–187.

Crocker, J., & Cooper, L. (2011, December 2). Editorial: Addressing scientific fraud. *Science, 334*, 1182.

De Houwer, J., Tanaka, A., Moors, A., & Tibboel, H. (2018). Kicking the habit: Why evidence for habits in humans might be overestimated. *Motivation Science, 4*, 50–59.

DeShon, R. P., Brown, K. G., & Greenis, J. L. (1996). Does self-regulation require cognitive resources? Evaluation of resource allocation models of goal setting. *Journal of Applied Psychology, 81*, 595–608.

Dijksterhuis, A. (2014). Welcome back theory! *Perspectives on Psychological Science, 9*(1), 72–75.

Doyen, S., Klein, O., Simons, D. J., & Cleeremans, A. (2014). On the other side of the mirror: Priming in cognitive and social psychology. *Social Cognition, 32*, 12–32.

Fishbach, A., Friedman, R. S., & Kruglanski, A. W. (2003). Leading us not into temptation: Momentary allurements elicit overriding goal activation. *Journal of Personality and Social Psychology, 84*(2), 296–309.

Förster, J., Liberman, N., & Friedman, R. S. (2009). What do we prime? On distinguishing between semantic priming, procedural priming, and goal priming. *Oxford Handbook of Human Action*, 173–192.

Greenwald, A. G., Spangenberg, E. R., Pratkanis, A. R., & Eskenazi, J. (1991). Double-blind tests of subliminal self-help audiotapes. *Psychological Science, 2*(2), 119–122.

Hansen, C. H., & Krygowski, W. (1994). Arousal-augmented priming effects: Rock music videos and sex object schemas. *Communication Research, 21*(1), 24–47.

Hardaway, R. A. (1990). Subliminally activated symbiotic fantasies—Facts and artifacts. *Psychological Bulletin, 107*, 177–195.

Hundhammer, T., & Mussweiler, T. (2012). How sex puts you in gendered shoes: Sexuality-priming leads to gender-based self-perception and behavior. *Journal of Personality and Social Psychology, 103*(1), 176–193.

Jung, C. G. (1933). *Modern man in search of a soul*. Orlando, FL: Harcourt Brace Jovanovich.

Kahneman, D. (2012, 9:21 a.m., Wednesday, September 26). *A proposal to deal with questions about priming effects.*

Kanfer, R., & Chen, G. (2016). Motivation in organizational behavior: History, advances and prospects. *Organizational Behavior and Human Decision Processes, 136*, 6–19.

Klein, R. A., Ratliff, K. A., Vianello, M., Adams Jr, R. B., Bahník, Š., Bernstein, M. J., . . . Cemalcilar, Z. (2014). Investigating variation in replicability: A "many labs" replication project. *Social Psychology, 45*(3), 142–152.

Kouider, S., Dehaene, S., Jobert, A., & Le Bihan, D. (2006). Cerebral bases of subliminal and supraliminal priming during reading. *Cerebral Cortex, 17*(9), 2019–2029.

McCarthy, C. (2017, April 20). The Kekulé problem: Where did language come from? *Nautilus*. Retrieved from http://nautil.us/issue/47/consciousness/the-kekul-problem

McCarthy, R. J., Skowronski, J. J., Verschuere, B., Meijer, E. H., Jim, A., Hoogesteyn, K., . . . Barbosa, F. (2018). Registered replication report on Srull and Wyer (1979). *Advances in Methods and Practices in Psychological Science, 1*(3), 321–336.

Mehta, R., Zhu, R., & Cheema, A. (2012). Is noise always bad? Exploring the effects of ambient noise on creative cognition. *Journal of Consumer Research, 39*(4), 784–799.

Natemeyer, W. E., & Hersey, P. (2011). *Classics of organizational behavior*. Long Grove, IL: Waveland Press.

O'Donnell, M., Nelson, L. D., Ackermann, E., Aczel, B., Akhtar, A., Aldrovandi, S., . . . Balatekin, N. (2018). Registered replication report: Dijksterhuis and van Knippenberg (1998). *Perspectives on Psychological Science, 13*, 268–294.

Pessiglione, M., Schmidt, L., Draganski, B., Kalisch, R., Lau, H., Dolan, R. J., & Frith, C. D. (2007). How the brain translates money into force: A neuroimaging study of subliminal motivation. *Science, 316*(5826), 904–906.

Rohrer, D., Pashler, H., & Harris, C. R. (2015). Do subtle reminders of money change people's political views? *Journal of Experimental Psychology: General, 144*, e73–e85.

Sandman, C., Davis, E., & Glynn, L. (2012). Prescient human fetuses thrive. *Psychological Science, 23*(1), 93–100.

Sergent, K., & Stajković, A. D. (2018). Prime and prejudice. *Applied Psychology, 0*(0), 1–58.

Simmons, J. P., Nelson, L. D., Simonsohn, U. (2013, 17–19 January). *Life after p-hacking. Meeting of the society for personality and social psychology*. New Orleans, LA.

Simons, D. J. (2014). The value of direct replication. *Perspectives on Psychological Science, 9*(1), 76–80.

Stajković, A. D., Bandura, A., Sergent, K., & Greenwald, J. M. (2019). *The role of dual-process self-efficacy in adaptive functioning*. Unpublished manuscript.

Stajković, A. D., Latham, G. P., Sergent, K., & Peterson, S. J. (2018). Prime and performance: Can a CEO motivate employees without their awareness?. *Journal of Business and Psychology*, 1–12.

Stajković, A. D., Locke, E. A., & Blair, E. S. (2006). A first examination of the relationships between primed subconscious goals, assigned conscious goals, and task performance. *Journal of Applied Psychology, 91*, 1172–1180.

Stroebe, W., & Strack, F. (2014). The alleged crisis and the illusion of exact replication. *Perspectives on Psychological Science, 9*(1), 59–71.

Srull, T. K., & Wyer, R. S. (1979). The role of category accessibility in the interpretation of information about persons: Some determinants and implications. *Journal of Personality and Social Psychology, 37*(10), 1660–1672.

Sweeney, M. S. (2009). *Brain*. Washington, DC: National Geographic.

Vadillo, M. A., Hardwicke, T. E., & Shanks, D. R. (2016). Selection bias, vote counting, and money-priming effects: A comment on Rohrer, Pashler, and Harris (2015) and Vohs (2015). *Journal of Experimental Psychology: General, 145*, 655–663.

Vandenberghe, R., Price, C., Wise, R., Josephs, O., & Frackowiak, R. S. J. (1996). Functional anatomy of a common semantic system for words and pictures. *Nature, 383*(6597), 254–256.

Verschuere, B., Meijer, E. H., Jim, A., Hoogesteyn, K., Orthey, R., McCarthy, R. J., . . . Barbosa, F. (2018). Registered replication report on Mazar, Amir, and Ariely (2008). *Advances in Methods and Practices in Psychological Science, 1*(3), 299–317.

Vohs, K. D. (2015). Money priming can change people's thoughts, feelings, motivations, and behaviors: An update on 10 years of experiments. *Journal of Experimental Psychology: General, 144*(4), e86–e93.

Vohs, K. D., Mead, N. L., & Goode, M. R. (2006). The psychological consequences of money. *Science, 314*, 1154–1156.

Weingarten, E., Chen, Q., McAdams, M., Yi, J., Hepler, J., & Albarracín, D. (2016). From primed concepts to action: A meta-analysis of the behavioral effects of incidentally presented words. *Psychological Bulletin, 142*(5), 472–497.

Westen, D. (1998). The scientific legacy of Sigmund Freud: Toward a psychodynamically informed psychological science. *Psychological Bulletin, 124*, 333–371.

Zedeck, S. (2010). *APA handbook of IO psychology*. Washington, DC: American Psychological Association.

10 Application
Is Priming Ready for Prime Time?

Having completed our review of theory, presentation of empirical research in support of theory, and critical analysis of the rudiments of conducting and interpreting priming research, we now reflect on the implications of findings for application in organizations. All things considered, the evidence supports making a tentative conclusion that priming goals is a viable technique for optimizing employee performance and it appears ripe for organizational application.

On the surface, however, it may appear that the conscious mind is the real mind, and the subconscious is its shadow. Given the potential for this misperception, application of primed goals in organizations warrants a detailed discussion.

In the next section, we envision a skeptical manager questioning the applicability of goal priming at work, and we offer answers grounded in our proposed framework of cognitive automation. This "manager" is proverbial, though it embodies conversations we have had with our executive and evening MBA students over the years on the feasibility of goal priming in the workplace.

How Valuable Are Suggestions for Practice Based on Stimuli We Cannot See?

Our stocktaking begins with the following concern: How good are practical suggestions derived from a stimulus that operates below awareness? Is not the prevailing assumption that employees consciously guide their behavior at work? This is a commonsense assumption but, nonetheless, a wrong one (Nisbett & Wilson, 1977; Wilson & Brekke, 1994). In Chapter 9, we reviewed differences between subliminal and supraliminal priming; here, we summarize the pertinent points in a more colloquial way.

As mentioned, research on subliminal influences has focused on stimuli that cannot be seen, and subliminal effects are ephemeral and small (see Greenwald, Klinger, & Schuh, 1995; Loftus & Klinger, 1992). The social psychology research we draw from approaches subconscious influences from a different perspective. Supraliminal primes occur in nature in plain sight, but their influence on outcomes transpires subconsciously. The individual is unaware of the prime's influence, not the prime itself. This perspective is relevant because organizations are context-rich with naturally occurring, visible stimuli, and many of these cues subtly influence employees without them recognizing it. On the whole, the subconscious pertains to processes causing behavior and not to unawareness of the stimuli.

Layering of Influences: Where Do Priming Goals Fit In?

A skeptical manager might next wonder about the layering of influences in the workplace: Where in the arena of work motivation do primed goals fit? What about education, knowledge, culture, and other organizational influences? We see it like this: Graduates approach organizations with an educational "general bag of tricks" to help them maneuver work, i.e., mechanical engineering degree for a bridge-building position. Then, employees who join any given organization go through on-board training and organizational culture fine-tuning to help new employees adapt. Priming, where stimuli from the environment activate subconscious goals, is a mechanism that provides another layer of detailed adjustments to work, social milieu, and the events in the present (Higgins & Bargh, 1987).

Whether a prime enacts automatic behavior in the moment will depend on cue-goal-behavior associations. It is worth reiterating that priming goals is not about enacting simple, routine behaviors. In routine behaviors, people initiate action intentionally, which turns automatic when conscious guidance is unneeded. An example is driving a car. People start driving intentionally, and then cognitive and behavioral automation takes over the routine operations. Sure, priming goals can entail simple operations, but it mostly pertains to complex abstractions where behavior is *not intentionally initiated*. Yet, it unfolds and adapts to deliver intended outcomes, such as job performance (e.g., Stajković et al., 2018).

Why Bother With Primed Goals When We Have Conscious Goals?

Putting another layer of gloss on goal theory is unnecessary, for its research and applied track record speaks for itself. We know conscious goals work. To summarize in one place the pertinent points made previously, we reiterate that priming goals can substitute for some operations of conscious goals. In that process, employees can save attentional resources that would otherwise have been used by conscious goals. The freed attentional resources are now available for other situations that require them. In this way, self-regulation by primed goals circumvents the need for conscious goal regulation.

The benefits of goal priming to organizations are as follows. First, priming goals in organizations carries little cost. The low cost of priming goals, while keeping conscious goal-related trimmings, is an attractive alternative in profit-seeking organizations. A related cost-benefit of priming goals is that it delivers results while allowing business to go on as usual. In contrast, training programs often involve removing employees from their jobs to attend workshops or complete online simulations (Natemeyer & Hersey, 2011; Zedeck, 2010). It can be costly to remove employees from their daily jobs for training. Inviting consulting firms to deliver training is not cheap either. Priming goals brings motivational benefits without employees' daily schedules skipping a beat.

Second, according to a recent survey, 45% of executives reported time constraints as the number one obstacle to their involvement in daily workplace happenings (Hanratty & Sahl, 2015). Priming goals offers an alternative for impacting employee performance for time-constrained executives. This possibility is magnified in organizations with geographically dispersed workforces and work teams. Because goals can be primed by embedding words in daily workplace communications, as found by Stajković et al. (2018), managers can ostensibly incorporate prime words into emails, news blasts, intranet posts, and training manuals, as well as inserting inscriptions in computer screensavers and backgrounds. Three field studies in the organizational behavior literature likewise found photos to effectively prime goals in work settings. We review this research next to highlight how photos could be used in organizations to enhance employee performance.

Itzchakov and Latham (2018) embedded a prime photo in the background of employee computers. The employees' job was to respond to calls about company products. After each call, the customer rated their satisfaction. The authors measured customer satisfaction for each employee before the photo was inserted as a desktop background. After collecting the pre-experiment data, the authors changed half of the desktop photos to a customer service agent and the other half to a photo of a tree. Employees primed with the customer service goal via the photo performed better compared with their shift before they were primed. This photo prime was effective and had virtually no associated cost to the firm.

Shantz and Latham (2009) conducted a field experiment to test the effects of primed achievement goals in a university call center. At the beginning of the work shift, all employees were given an identical information packet. The packet informed employees they would be soliciting donations for faculty awards, a new athletic center, and a jazz club on campus. Employees randomly assigned to the primed goal group received the packet with a faint background photo of a runner. The other half received the packet without the photo backdrop.

The amount of donations received during the three-hour shift was greater in the primed achievement goal group of employees compared to the neutral group. Two years later, Shantz and Latham (2011) conducted another study in another call center and the results were replicated.

Latham and Piccolo (2012) conducted a conceptual replication, but they added a third experimental condition to the runner and control with a customer service photo backdrop.

Employees who received the customer service photo raised more money than those who were shown the runner photo. Yet, employees in the runner photo group continued to solicit more donations than those

in the control group. This demonstrates that when a prime is more task-specific, a more specific subconscious goal is primed and better results ensue, consistent with goal-setting theory.

Kay, Wheeler, Bargh, and Ross (2004) examined whether business-related photos and objects influence goal striving. To prime a competition goal, the authors showed participants pictures. Participants were tasked with matching the photo with its item description. Participants randomly assigned to the prime goal group were shown pictures of business attire, boardroom tables, and executive pens, similar to the following images:

Participants in the neutral group were shown goal-neutral objects, e.g., a kite, stapler, whale, and toothbrush. After the photo matching task, the authors asked participants to complete the following words from the provided segments: _ in; _ ower; wa _; _ ake; _ ight; c_ _ p _ _ _ tive; en _ _ _; ar _ _ _; bea_. Try completing these words on your own.

Were your completed words influenced by the photographs above? For example, did you write *Tin* or *Win? Lower* or *power? Wax* or *war? Lake* or *take? Light* or *fight? Cooperative* or **competitive?** *Enact* or *enemy? Ardor* or *argue? Beam* or *beat?* Kay et al. (2004) found that people exposed to the business photos compared with the neutral photos used significantly more competition words. In their next study, the same primes were used but were followed by a short vignette describing an ambiguous social exchange. Participants assessed on a nine-point scale the motives of the characters as they related to competition or cooperation. Participants shown the business photos compared with the neutral photos rated the motives to be significantly less about cooperation.

In their third study, Kay et al. (2004) asked participants to engage in an ultimatum game. The game forced a choice; one participant proposed a money split, and the second participant either accepted or rejected. This compelled a strategic decision between profit maximization and social maximization. Out of 11 participants in the neutral group, 10 (91%) proposed an even split of the money. Markedly, only four participants (33%) who were primed by the business objects proposed an even split. When asked if the photos influenced their decision, none reported any connection between the photos and the game.

In their fourth study, the authors swapped out the photos for real objects. Participants in the priming group entered the experimental room and were seated at a boardroom table. Across the table were a briefcase and an executive black-leather portfolio. Directly in front of them was an executive-style pen. When the experimenter entered, s/he removed the survey from a briefcase and instructed participants to place their completed surveys in the portfolio. In the neutral group, the briefcase was replaced with a black backpack, the executive portfolio was replaced with a cardboard box, and the executive pen was replaced with a generic pencil. How did these objects influence the ultimatum game? In the neutral group, 100% of participants proposed a fair split. In contrast, only 50% of participants in the priming group proposed an even split. Thus, common business objects in an office setting can cause people to pursue automatically competition goals.

How Do We Know We Primed a Goal?

We will answer this question by comparing priming traits with priming goals. A portion of human knowledge is organized in traits (Förster, Liberman, & Friedman, 2009). Traits are dispositional variables. They do not dictate the same behavior in every circumstance. Instead, they predict the frequency with which behaviors unfold consistent with a trait. Thus, priming traits (e.g., conscientiousness) triggers behaviors in line with it (e.g., being organized). Research on priming traits has shown that individuals make trait-stimuli-congruent reactions (Robinson, 2007), e.g., extroverts gain more pleasure from positive stimuli and neurotics experience more strain from negative cues.

Traits reinforce the behavior consistent with the trait, but they do not instigate new behavior. In contrast, the hallmark of goals is to guide new behaviors toward a desired end. These ends could be identical to prior pursuits, but often they represent new explorations. Because goals are mental representations of a desired end, the effects of primed goals are enduring during the goal pursuit but are no longer effective after the goal is reached. People need new goals for new pursuits. Conversely, if traits are primed, the duration of the effect will last longer than if goals are primed. This is consequential to recognize in organizations. Because goal priming is characterized by a motivation drop after goal pursuit is completed, a new round of goal priming is needed for new effects.

Can Priming One Goal Lead to Behaviors Unrelated to That Goal?

Yes, unfortunately. Because knowledge is organized in conceptual networks, associations form within the given network (e.g., hospital–nurse; teacher–school; police–safety). Occasionally, a subconscious goal may be associated with unwanted constructs in the conceptual network. For example, in an intriguing study by Bargh, Chen and Burrows (1996), participants who unscrambled sentences containing words related to *old age* walked *more slowly* afterward without being aware of the prime words. Pushing this reasoning further, for example, if a manager primed a goal of being *wise*, employees might work slower because wisdom is also associated with old age in some conceptual networks.

How Can We Prime Goal Interactions at Work?

As described in earlier chapters, an employee may have an assigned goal to finish a task by a tight deadline. Yet, s/he also knows "in the back of his/her mind" that accuracy is the backbone of his/her profession. Incongruence between a conscious goal to "finish fast" and a primed goal to "be accurate" can negatively affect each other; the two goals not only compete for cognitive resources, but they also "pull" behavior in different directions.

A possibility to preempt the development of incongruent goals is by pairing congruent primes with conscious goals, where one goal reinforces the other. For example, to boost speed of performance (e.g., mail delivery), primed speed goals can be added to assigned speed goals. Such an intervention could sprinkle speed words/photos in a memo for employees to read before starting work (e.g., perhaps under the guise of route guidance). Likewise, firms can develop training sessions in which managers and employees work together to identify and discuss potential conflict between conscious and primed goals. To reverse the correlates, employees might harbor dysfunctional subconscious goals discoverable by certain patterns of behavior, such as "protect my group at all costs." The unproductive effects of such primed goals could be mitigated if organizations assign conscious goals that stress cooperation, followed by assessments of cooperative behavior. Finally, there could be cases where employees have unethical conscious goals (e.g., selling with dishonesty to exceed a sales quota). Deliberately priming a goal to be honest might promote ethical behavior, which, in the long run, should facilitate sales, as well.

Ecological and Ethical Considerations in Priming Goals

More often than not, the word "goal" is perceived positively; society applauds people who set challenging goals and stick to them. Research on escalation of commitment shows that those who stick to their tough goals are perceived as "heroes" even if they ultimately fail. In contrast, those who "pull the plug" to get out of the "quick sand" are labeled quitters, even though they made a rational economic decision. Our approach to goals as a tool for cognitive automation does not presuppose a positive or negative view of goals. When we say our view is goal-value-agnostic, we are not saying we endorse unethical goal priming. Rather, we acknowledge that the underlying principles guiding the priming of positively valenced goals would probably work for priming negatively valenced goals too (e.g., maybe we want to use it in a war to confuse enemies without their awareness at little cost).

From a science perspective, it is hard to examine the effects of priming negatively valenced goals in experiments because of ethical considerations. All the studies reviewed in this book comprised positively valenced goals, one way or the other. In studies that used incongruent conscious-primed goals, the conflict pertained to task dimensions, not to ethical clashes. University studies have to be approved by Institutional Review Boards (IRB), and in our field studies, the research design was also approved by firm managers and their HR departments. We thoroughly debriefed participants following the studies.

There are two consequential ecological differences in non-research-based priming in organizations. One is that priming occurs naturally at work, e.g., via tacit influences of organizational culture (Schein, 2009). The other is that priming goals can be a deliberate activity by managers. If managers are engaged in priming, and employees have no choice but to participate, pertinent ethical considerations need to be addressed.

Are we priming (manipulating) employees to do something for the company, and is that unethical because it occurs without their awareness? The answer to the first part is yes, but priming has been around the business world for decades. For example, priming has been applied in advertising and marketing of products and services (Cheskin & Ward, 1948; Hine, 1995), medical practice to increase follow-up compliance (Reilly, Evans, Schaider, & Wang, 2002), jury selections (Rice, 2000), facets of gambling industry (Damasio, 1994), and in education to affect the quality of teaching evaluations (Ambady & Rosenthal, 1993).

Similarly, organizations have long used personality inventories in job interviews and promotions whereby applicants are seldom told what is being measured and how it affects their prospects. Nudges were used by policymakers, employers, insurance companies, and health care providers—to name a few—to alter behaviors in ways companies perceived to be more desirable. For example, Texas officials changed their slogan to "Don't Mess with Texas" to nudge a reduction in littering; countries have flipped the organ donor default from "No" to "Yes" to increase the number of donors; regulating agencies have moved signature lines from the bottom to the top of forms to increase ethical behavior; and, unfortunately, several grocery stores stock junk food on lower shelves to foster sales to children (see Thaler & Sunstein, 2009). Did the people affected by these nudges consent?

Taken together, the content being primed is of concern, but the priming technique *per se* is not as problematic. The gray-area issues are in between, e.g., if priming a goal conflates the positive and negative aspects of an activity, e.g., be more productive but do not request a pay increase. Although not all answers that can help effective practice are ironed out yet, we believe that understanding is advanced by the scientific consideration of priming goals, even if the ultimate practical answers still rest in the eye of the beholder.

References

Ambady, N., & Rosenthal, R. (1993). Half a minute: Predicting teacher evaluations from thin slices of nonverbal behavior and physical attractiveness. *Journal of Personality and Social Psychology, 64*, 431–441.

Bargh, J., Chen, M., & Burrows, L. (1996). Automaticity of social behavior: Direct effects of trait construct and stereotype activation on action. *Journal of Personality and Social Psychology, 71*, 230–244.

Cheskin, L., & Ward, L. B. (1948). Indirect approach to market reactions. *Harvard Business Review, 26*(5), 572–580.

Damasio, A. (1994). *Descartes' error: Emotion, reason, and the human brain.* NY: Harper.

Itzchakov, G., & Latham, G. P. (2018). The moderating effect of performance feedback and the mediating effect of self-set goals on the primed goal-performance relationship. *Applied Psychology, 0*(0), 1–36.

Forster, J., Liberman, N., & Friedman, R. S. (2009). What do we prime? On distinguishing between semantic priming, procedural priming, and goal priming. In E. Morsella, J. A. Bargh, & P. M. Gollwitzer (Eds.), *Oxford handbook of human action* (pp. 173–196). New York, NY: Oxford University Press.

Greenwald, A. G., Klinger, M. R., & Schuh, E. S. (1995). Activation by marginally perceptible ("subliminal") stimuli: Dissociation of unconscious from conscious cognition. *Journal of Experimental Psychology: General, 124*(1), 22–42.

Hanratty, & Sahl. (2015). 45% of executives cite time constraints as number-one problem in achieving professional goals, says new Economist Intelligence Unit report. *The Economist: Intelligence Unit.* Retrieved from www.eiuper spectives.econom ist.com/technology-innovation/45-executives-cite-time-con straints-number-one-problem-achieving-professional-goals-says-new

Higgins, E. T., & Bargh, J. A. (1987). Social cognition and social perception. *Annual Review of Psychology, 38*(1), 369–425.

Hine, T. (1995). *The total package: The secret history of hidden meanings of boxes, bottles, cans, and other persuasive containers.* New York, NY: Little Brown Publishers.

Kay, A. C., Wheeler, S. C., Bargh, J. A., & Ross, L. (2004). Material priming: The influence of mundane physical objects on situational construal and competitive behavioral choice. *Organizational Behavior and Human Decision Processes, 95*(1), 83–96.

Latham, G. P., & Piccolo, R. F. (2012). The effect of context-specific versus nonspecific subconscious goals on employee performance. *Human Resource Management, 51*, 511–523.

Loftus, E. F., & Klinger, M. R. (1992). Is the unconscious smart or dumb? *American Psychologist, 47*(6), 761–765.

Natemeyer, W. E., & Hersey, P. (2011). *Classics of organizational behavior.* Long Grove, IL: Waveland Press.

Nisbett, R. E., & Wilson, T. D. (1977). Telling more than we can know: Verbal reports on mental processes. *Psychological Review, 84*(3), 231–259.

Reilly, B. M., Evans, A. T., Schaider, J. J., & Wang, Y. (2002). Triage of patients with chest pain in the emergency department: A comparative study of physicians' decisions. *The American Journal of Medicine, 112*(2), 95–103.

Rice, B. (2000). How plaintiffs' lawyers pick their targets. *Medical Economics.* April 24, 2000. Retrieved from https://www.medicaleconomics.com/health-law-policy/how-plaintiffs-lawyers-pick-their-targets

Robinson, M. D. (2007). Personality, affective processing, and self-regulation: Toward process-based views of extraversion, neuroticism, and agreeableness. *Social and Personality Psychology Compass, 1,* 223–235.

Schein, E. H. (2009). *The corporate culture survival guide.* San Francisco, CA: Jossey-Bass.

Shantz, A., & Latham, G. P. (2009). An exploratory field experiment of the effect of subconscious and conscious goals on employee performance. *Organizational Behavior and Human Decision Processes, 109,* 9–17.

Shantz, A., & Latham, G. P. (2011). The effect of primed goals on employee performance: Implications for human resource management. *Human Resource Management, 50*(2), 289–299.

Stajković, A. D., Latham, G. P., Sergent, K., & Peterson, S. J. (2018). Prime and performance: Can a CEO motivate employees without their awareness? *Journal of Business and Psychology,* 1–12.

Thaler, R. H., & Sunstein, C. R. (2009). *Nudge: Improving decisions about health, wealth, and happiness.* London: Penguin Books.

Wilson, T. D., & Brekke, N. (1994). Mental contamination and mental correction: Unwanted influences on judgments and evaluations. *Psychological Bulletin, 116*(1), 117–142.

Zedeck, S. (2010). *APA handbook of IO psychology.* Washington, DC: American Psychological Association.

The Past Is Prologue

The future of fruitful organizing—the idea behind forming an organization—is in more cognitive automation, not less. If we failed to make this point, it was not for lack of trying. Cognitive automation will take hold, sooner or later. This is because its aim is akin to technological innovation, which has existed and progressed since the onset of humans.

The shared purpose of cognitive and technological automation is to help people automate aspects of their functioning. The key difference between the two types of automations is in the buy-in. People readily admit to being "just human," and rely on technological assistance. We know we were not designed to move faster than we can run; thus, we travel by car. We know we were not meant to fly; thus, we travel by plane. Yet, how many of us will instantly admit to "illusory" influences guiding our cognitive processing? Pushback against cognitive automation will be more palpable than it was for techno automation.

Our goal was to highlight cognitive overload as a burning problem in the workplace and offer cognitive automation as one potential solution. We presented evidence and examples to show how the complexity of work today has dramatically increased compared with a few decades ago. However, we do not assert causality from work to attentional depletion nor from attentional depletion to work. Data only suggest that the two issues coalesce, e.g., of Americans suffering from moderate-to-severe psychological distress (NCHS, 2013), 90% self-report a connection to work-related issues (Pratt & Brody, 2014).

Verifying this causal dependence will require converging evidence from diverse sources and methods. The sooner we embrace this quest the better, for it will highlight the cause(s) of attentional depletion. Maybe employees come to work already depleted and pressures from work push them over the edge. Maybe it is the other way around. Maybe the first few stressors during the day are insufficient to provoke distress, but they summate over the day to "break the camel's back." For either of these alternatives, theoretical gruel is needed to elucidate this complex chain of causality and guide empirical investigations.

Current literature muddles this causal chain by presenting misleading distinctions. It is little more than a mirage to propagate without qualifying boundaries that humans are better off now than ever before, e.g., railings in houses, fancy kitchens, and beds that tilt. This reinforces false reassurances that things are hunky-dory. Data remind us that advances in bare materialism, though certainly welcome, have an unclear bearing on the more complex and less visible issue of attentional resources being depleted at an alarming rate, coupled with serious health consequences (Hassard et al., 2014).

Research has empirically connected psychological distress with increased absenteeism and turnover, decreased productivity, and poor performance (Hardy, Woods, & Wall, 2003; Prins, Bates, Keyes, & Muntaner, 2015). In the U.S., nearly $200 billion dollars per year are spent on treating psychological distress. This is a five-fold increase over the last 30 years (SAMHSA, 2016). Being able to "turn off the lights" by clapping your hands is not all that helpful when it comes to issues of deeper relevance to cognitive adaptive functioning.

We call for multivariate research on the reciprocal causal chain among life–attentional depletion–work–attentional depletion–life that is not marred by simple misrepresentations of alternative theories, sketchy reviews of the extant literature, and conceptual vagaries leading to misleading claims. Arguably, telling people they are "better off now than ever before" could be contributing to the problem when reports of distress are steadily rising.

There are simpler alternatives to guard against inclemency of cognitive overload, but they are unconvincing. The most obvious one is to reduce employee cognitive load, but that is unlikely given the ever-growing demands on both individuals and businesses to stay competitive. Another is to medicate more people with more pills, but evidence indicates that despite an increase in antidepressant prescriptions, suicide rates continue to climb (Curtin, Warner, & Hedegaard, 2016). Many have tried self-help simplifications of cognitive processing, but an instinctive reaction to these remedies is a shrug. Self-help alternatives are often cleverly advertised but are data-poor; most amount to no more than strong statements with inadequate evidence. Next, we can hope for a sudden growth in human attentional capacity, but the odds of that growth happening anytime soon are not in our favor. Finally, AI-brain fusion could be a bridge to another dimension of thought, but consider the *Science* article in January of 2019 about a Chinese scientist who used CRISPR technology to edit the genomes of twin babies in a heritable way (Normile, 2019). Even though he received both scientific and legal condemnation worldwide, he still said in an interview, paraphrasing, "It was worth it to get a worldwide fame fast."

What about free will? If we just let people be, will they figure out ways to fix their lives? Free will is predicated on freedom as default. We agree in abstract, but this view can be short on actionable information. Here are some free will facts and fiction, as we it.

Conscious processing is not always equivalent to free will. The former can focus on fastidious contemplation of efficient behavior to support goal pursuit. This cognitive process is helpful to human adaptive self-regulation and methodical progress; the problem is that the capacity of this attentional deliberation runs out of steam fast. Cognitive automation mitigates this problem by persisting while maintaining the factual components of conscious deliberation. Sometimes this switch occurs automatically. To automate a goal-behavior association and prime it on purpose, you need to know what works first. This requires training or repeated practice to sniff out the "best practices" for a given goal.

The meaning of free will is in its phrase. It sounds emancipating and easily defendable. Free will is a formidable opponent in a debate because any arguments against it are easily labeled as attempts to turn the social clock back. In the business world, though, we question the practical meaning of free will in professions where wiggle room between disaster and success is narrow. We used examples from the airline industry throughout this book because there is little free-willing allowed in this profession. What about medical surgery? Mental health care of special needs children? Managing a nuclear reactor? Deployment of missiles or navigating aircraft carriers? If free will means or entails ignoring the rules and free-willing regardless of contingent consequences, then evolution would have eliminated this maladaptive mechanism. Maybe free will is God's gift to importance-yearning humans as a metacognitive epiphenomenon to make us feel better by thinking we can act as we please, when we really cannot, at least in many domains of functioning, as illustrated above.

In the final analysis, perhaps the French philosopher Voltaire was correct. Just because we move forward in time does not necessarily mean we are better off. As shown by many available data indicators, psychological distress is at its highest levels today, with grave health and financial consequences. The particular peril of the cognitive overload crisis is its nature as a psychological process; load is invisible and not readily discernable, it unfolds gradually, so terse revelations are not apparent, and it accumulates over time. Some view psychological distress as a personal weakness and keep it bottled inside until it is too late.

Before we run out of runway in this book, we invite you to complete the seven-question survey shown in Figure BM.1 to assess if you are conscious of your subconscious. With some humor, the "test" results can be used as a segue into a polemic with your colleagues.

If your score is 18, you are of this earth. If it is between 17 and 1, you are subconscious of your conscious, but we do not know what to make out of it. If it is zero or negative, then we ran out of tools

Questions:	Please check one box for each sub/question	
	Yes	**No**

1a. Humans need to survive? ☐ ☐

b. For that, they need nearly-perfect deployment of bodily functions? ☐ ☐

c. All of them are currently automated? ☐ ☐

d. God got this automation correct? ☐ ☐

e. Evolution got this automation correct? ☐ ☐

f. Humans cannot be trusted with free will over bodily functions (e.g., ah, c'mon liver give me more love on drinking nights, oops forgot to tell the kidneys to plug away). ☐ ☐

2a. Moses brought down 10 suggestions? ☐ ☐

b. Moses brought down 10 *command*ments? ☐ ☐

c. I personally understand the difference? ☐ ☐

d. After God saw what was happening on the ground due to free will, it would have been easier for him to concur and write on the tablets "… sure, free will everyone, see how that works for you? Good luck!" ☐ ☐

3a. Do Philosophy, religion, and science, at their best moments, search for the truth? ☐ ☐

a. Learning and education: Good, automate? ☐ ☐

b. "We do not need no education," just free will? ☐ ☐

4a. Should you follow some established practices to for socializing children before kindergarten? ☐ ☐

b. If you do not, and let them free will socialize without supervision, they might turn into little monsters? ☐ ☐

c. In the latter case, they will face a lot of angry faces from other children and fake smiles from parents? ☐ ☐

5a. Death to healthy eating rules: Long live junk food? ☐ ☐

b. I have bad cholesterol numbers. Doctor advised me to follow the regiment of healthy eating: Good, automate? ☐ ☐

c. Bad health cannot encroach on me, I have free will? ☐ ☐

6a. Cowboys had no stop lights: It is unclear if some
arbitrary red/yellow/green lights should trump
free will today?

b. Follow traffic rules: Good, automate?

c. Nah, just free-will it?

7a. I shower every day?

b. Good rule, automate?

c. Showering is an imposition on personal liberties?

Scoring: There are 25 questions. Assign one point to each question if you answered it with yes. Except:
If you answered, question #2a with yes, please deduct two points.
If you answered, question #3b with yes, please deduct three points.
If you answered, question #5a, and 5c with yes, please deduct four points for each question
If you answered, question #6a, and 6c with yes, please deduct five points for each question
If you answered, question #7c with yes, you are disqualified from this survey.

to convince you. We close with parting thoughts of political economist John Stuart Mill (1861, p. 63), in *Utilitarianism*, as the philosophical pantheon of our work in this book: necessity (e.g., cognitive automation) is different from choice (e.g., free will). [C]ertain social utilities are vastly more important, and therefore more absolute and imperative . . . and which, therefore, ought to be, as well as naturally are, guarded by the sentiment, not only different in degree, but also in kind, distinguished from the milder feeling which attaches to the mere idea of promoting human pleasure or convenience at once by the more definitive nature of its commands and by the sterner character of its sanctions.

References

Curtin, S. C., Warner, M., & Hedegaard, H. (2016). Increase in suicide in the United States, 1999–2014. *NCHS Data Brief*, 241, 1–8.

Hardy, G. E., Woods, E., & Wall, T. D. (2003). The impact of psychological distress on absence from work. *Journal of Applied Psychology*, 88, 306–314.

Hassard, J., Teoh, K., Cox, T., Dewe, P., Cosmar, M., Grundler, R., . . ., Van den Broek, K. (2014). *Calculating the cost of work-related stress and psychosocial risks*. Luxembourg: Publications Office of the European Union.

Mill, J. S. (1861). *Utilitarianism*. London, UK: Longmans, Green, and Co.

NCHS, National Center for Health Statistics. (2013). National Ambulatory Medical Care Survey.

Normile, D. (2019, January 21). Scientist behind CRISPR twins sharply criticized n government probe, loses job. *Science*. Retrieved from www.sciencemag.org/news/2019/01/scientist-behind-crispr-twins-sharply-criticized-government-probe-loses-job

Pratt, L. A., & Brody, D. J. (2014). Depression in the U.S. household population, 2009–2012. *NCHS Data in Brief, 172*, 1–8.

Prins, S. J., Bates, L. M., Keyes, K. M., & Muntaner, C. (2015). Anxious? Depressed? You might be suffering from capitalism: Contradictory class locations and the prevalence of depression and anxiety in the USA. *Sociology of Health & Illness, 37*, 1352–1372.

SAMHSA, Substance Abuse and Mental Health Services Administration. (2016). Behavioral health and spending use accounts. Substance abuse and mental health services administration. Behavioral health spending and use accounts, 1986–2014. HHS, SMA-16–4975. Rockville, MD: U.S. Department of Health and Human Services Substance Abuse and Mental Health Services Administration.

Authors' Biographies

Alexander D. Stajković is the M. Keith Weikel Distinguished Chair in Leadership and Professor of Organizational Behavior at the University of Wisconsin-Madison. Alexander earned both his Masters and Ph.D. in Organizational Behavior from the University of Nebraska-Lincoln. Alexander's research has been featured in the *New York Times*, *Elle Magazine*, and *BizEd*, as well as in premier journals both in Psychology and Organizational Behavior, such as *Psychological Bulletin*, *Journal of Applied Psychology*, *Academy of Management Journal*, *Organizational Behavior and Human Decision Processes*, *Personnel Psychology*, and *Journal of Management*. He has taught Organizational Behavior in the executive and evening MBA programs, as well as in the doctoral program, at the Wisconsin School of Business for 20 years. Alexander has given over 100 presentations, invited talks, and has consulted globally. For more information, see his website: www.stajkovic.biz

Kayla Sergent is Assistant Professor of Management at Edgewood College. Kayla earned her Ph.D. in Organizational Behavior from the University of Wisconsin-Madison. Kayla's research has been published in *Journal of Business and Psychology*, *Applied Psychology: An International Review*, *Personality and Individual Differences*, and *Journal of Occupational and Organizational Psychology*. She teaches Organizational Behavior in the evening MBA and undergraduate programs at Edgewood College. Kayla has consulted on transformational leadership, creativity, and organizational culture. For more information see her website: www.sergent.biz

Index

Note: numbers in **bold** indicate a table. Numbers in *italics* indicate a figure.

For Product Safety Concerns and Information please contact our EU
representative GPSR@taylorandfrancis.com
Taylor & Francis Verlag GmbH, Kaufingerstraße 24, 80331 München, Germany

www.ingramcontent.com/pod-product-compliance
Ingram Content Group UK Ltd.
Pitfield, Milton Keynes, MK11 3LW, UK
UKHW020941180425
457613UK00019B/495